# Coasting in the Countertransference

*Psychoanalysis in a New Key Book Series*
*Volume 7*

## Psychoanalysis in a New Key Book Series
DONNEL STERN, PH.D., SERIES EDITOR

Volume 1
*Clinical Values:*
*Emotions That Guide Psychoanalytic Treatment*
Sandra Buechler

Volume 2
*What Do Mothers Want?*
*Contemporary Perspectives in Psychoanalysis and Related Disciplines*
Sheila Brown

Volume 3
*The Fallacy of Understanding / The Ambiguity of Change*
Edgar A. Levenson

Volume 4
*Prelogical Experience:*
*An Inquiry into Dreams & Other Creative Processes*
Edward S. Tauber and Maurice R. Green

Volume 5
*Prologue to Violence:*
*Child Abuse, Dissociation, and Crime*
Abby Stein

Volume 6
*Wounded by Reality:*
*Understanding and Treating Adult Onset Trauma*
Ghislaine Boulanger

Volume 7
*Coasting in the Countertransference:*
*Conflicts of Self Interest between Analyst and Patient*
Irwin Hirsch

# Coasting in the Countertransference

## Conflicts of Self Interest between Analyst and Patient

# Irwin Hirsch

The Analytic Press
Taylor & Francis Group

New York  London

Cover: © David Newman, *Countertransference Collage #3*, 1998. 14″ x 17″, cut paper collage.

The Analytic Press
Taylor & Francis Group
270 Madison Avenue
New York, NY 10016

The Analytic Press
Taylor & Francis Group
27 Church Road
Hove, East Sussex BN3 2FA

© 2008 by Taylor & Francis Group, LLC

Printed in the United States of America on acid-free paper
10 9 8 7 6 5 4 3 2 1

International Standard Book Number-13: 978-0-88163-480-8 (Softcover) 978-0-88163-455-6 (0)

**Visit the Taylor & Francis Web site at**
**http://www.taylorandfrancis.com**

**and The Analytic Press Web site at**
**http://www.analyticpress.com**

*In memory of my parents; for my wife—my love and my life partner; and to my children and their children, present and future—my joy and my inspiration.*

# Contents

# Acknowledgments

My parents, people of great integrity, uneducated and unworldly, always made me feel loved and were proud of anything I did (or did not do). I had lots of latitude and little expectancy or judgment from them, and from preadolescence onward I always felt the freedom to do as I wished. From this period forward, I had the good fortune to develop what became enduring friendships, and these boys/men, originally in the beloved Brooklyn of my youth, both broadened my horizons and challenged me to be as smart and accomplished as they were. With the generous help of the City College of New York's tuition-free education policy, I encountered some inspiring teachers and interesting new friends of both sexes, and I became both more intellectually alive and more ambitious. I disliked the behaviorally oriented (Skinnerian) graduate school that accepted me, but I was lucky to find some excellent psychoanalytically oriented colleagues and mentors in the Veterans Administration's psychology trainee program. I also had a very kind and supportive dissertation supervisor to help lead me through this alien graduate program.

Once back in New York City my route to psychoanalysis began in earnest, first as a postdoctoral fellow at Albert Einstein College of Medicine, and then at New York University's Postdoctoral Program in Psychotherapy and Psychoanalysis. My teachers and supervisors in both these venues were, by and large, outstanding. My personal analysis was both illuminating and most helpful. As well, I learned an enormous amount from my peers at these two institutions, and to this day I deeply value these connections. During this period I was first exposed to analytic thinking and writing that had strong resonance, that excited me, and that ultimately inspired me to begin writing myself. Prominent among these influential authors are Harold Searles, Edgar Levenson, and, somewhat later, Merton Gill. The psychoanalytic supervisors whose clinical thinking had the most significant impact are Erwin Singer and Benjamin Wolstein. Of course, I continue to become more educated by the writing and thinking of my peers, and of my juniors as well. There are too many to specify (though one can get an idea by examining my references section), and they come from a range of theoretical traditions. I am fortunate to have teaching and/or supervisory appointments at five different psychoanalytic training programs (The Manhattan Institute for Psychoanalysis; William Alanson White Institute; Adelphi Postgraduate Program in Psychotherapy and Psychoanalysis; New York University Postdoctoral Program, my alma mater; and National Training Program of the National Institute for the Psychotherapies), and this has provided me with multiple homes, and the opportunity to meet and to get to know a long list of deeply valued students and peers. Of these affiliations, the Manhattan Institute, the White Institute, and Adelphi have been very special to me, and the teaching I have done at these institutions in particular has had great influence in the development of my thinking and my writing.

I have deep gratitude to my patients, past and current. Though it troubles me profoundly that I have not always been helpful to them, I have grown immeasurably as a person from my extended contact with so many of them. Being a psychoanalyst is a marvelous way for a relatively reserved person to meet interesting people and to develop many more mutually affectionate bonds than one otherwise might. I feel powerful attachments to many people who under normal social circumstances I might never have had the privilege of encountering, or even would be inclined to avoid. I have become a much more tolerant person in the context of meeting individuals toward whom I feel an initial distaste, getting to know them beyond their character armor and developing strong feelings of affection. I have grown as a person from recognizing and accepting some of the personal shortcomings that became apparent in my relatedness to my patients. I wish I could be friends, outside of our professional context, with many of the people I now see or have in the past worked with as patients. On an especially selfish note, my patients obviously have been instrumental in the formulation of the ideas about which I write, and albeit with much disguise I use them to help me publish articles (and this book) so that I can fulfill some of my desires for recognition and status.

My wife, Willa Cobert, also a psychoanalyst, merits special mention and expressions of gratitude. We met as colleagues at Hillside

Hospital in Queens, New York, and a part of our initial connection was based on how thoroughly compatible our clinical thinking and theorizing were. This area of convergence maintains to the present. She is the best clinician I know, and there is no one from whom I have learned more with respect to clinical and conceptual matters. When I first began to write, she thoroughly critiqued everything and totally corrected my very wanting grammatical constructions. Then and now she tolerates long hours of isolation and of enforced silence, as I try to create pristine conditions for this trying and tension-producing avocation of writing for publication. Though I did not write much when my children were little and wanted me around all of the time, I began to write more as a way of filling the emotional gap left by their expanding their lives to friendships, to outside interests, and now to families of their own. My children made me more alive than I had ever been, and it is this vitality that proved instrumental in fueling my ambitions, and writing has been significantly among these ambitions. I have wanted to match their curiosity and their passion for life with some of my own, and I have wanted to make them proud of me.

On both a professional and a friendship dimension, Donnel Stern also merits special recognition. Not satisfied with being the initiator and force behind my honorary appointments to the White Institute, he repeatedly pushed and cajoled me to do this book. He listened to years' worth of fears and anxieties about undertaking this project, and time after time he reassured me that he would make it as easy as possible to publish this thing under his book series label at the Analytic Press. Indeed, he fulfilled this promise, devoting enormous time and concern, in the context of a very busy family and professional life, with very careful editing, feedback, and anxiety-reducing conversations. This book would not have happened without his efforts, and I am very grateful to him.

My editors at the Analytic Press have treated me with respect and courtesy, and have been patient with a range of my foibles. They have conspired to make this book a better product, and I thank them for making this first effort less stressful than it might have been. Similarly, I wish to thank my extraordinarily helpful computer instructor and technical consultant, who also added talented editorial input.

Some of what I have said here may sound more like autobiography than "acknowledgment." Perhaps it is fitting that a book that focuses on my own and others' countertransference self-absorption has this tone. However, I consciously chose to write this section as I did because I wish to make it clear that many people were pivotal in contributing to my development both as a person and as a psycho-analyst. Though there are far too many to mention by name (and I certainly cannot mention my patients by name) they deserve my notation and my gratitude. My writing of this book, and its content, is an end product of both purely personal relationships and deeply personal professional relationships.

# Foreword

With a depth and authenticity I have rarely encountered, Irwin Hirsch feels a thoroughly unsentimental gratitude, appreciation, and affection toward his patients. You will encounter that attitude throughout this book, beginning with the Acknowledgments. I know that he means what he says in this regard; it is one of the things you feel about Irwin as soon as he starts to talk about the people he works with. (I hasten to add that feeling this way hardly stops him from being as open as anyone I know to his irritation, dislike, hatred, envy, and all the other less warm and fuzzy feelings. That also will be obvious in these pages.) Along with all of this good and bad feeling, I believe that Irwin also harbors a certain melancholy about his work. We all feel our failures; but I think Irwin feels them with a particular keenness, despite the fact that I suspect he has fewer of them than most of us do. His failures lie at the heart of his book.

One of the best pieces of clinical advice I ever got was from Irwin. He described to me his phone calls, long after the fact, to a handful of his ex-patients with whom things had ended unsatisfactorily. Irwin had started thinking about the ways in which he had failed these people. He was distressed about these incidents and these treatments, as we are all distressed by such events and treatments, and he decided that he wanted to see how it was for these people he had worked with. He said little to me about what was said in the phone calls, and I didn't ask. But he made it clear that he was very glad he had called them.

What he told me wasn't advice, actually, because Irwin didn't suggest that I do the same thing. But after thinking about it for a while, I did do the same thing, and as far as I can see it was enormously reparative for all concerned. My former patients, against all my expectations, were relieved, even delighted to hear from me. We talked about what had happened between us. I learned a lot that they hadn't been able to tell me at the time. They were very glad to find out that it had all really mattered to me, and that it still did. These contacts were reparative for me, as they were for Irwin. I think that this book is, among other things, a further reparative effort for Irwin.

For Irwin and those few others who have thought about the everyday problem of the analyst's self-interest (Sandra Buechler [2002, 2004] and Joyce Slochower [2003, 2006] come to mind, and citations of their papers on the subject appear in Irwin's references), the reality is that, much more frequently than we like to think, we all act on self-interest during our clinical work, self-interest that, even as we are carrying it out, we know is not in our patients' best interests. Irwin is not talking about unconscious countertransference here, but behavior we actually have some awareness that we are engaging in. He is certainly not claiming that our willingness to satisfy ourselves this way has nothing to do with the countertransference. In fact, he claims just the opposite: Our willingness to sacrifice the patient's interests for our own comfort and equilibrium has *everything* to do with the particular clinical relatedness with a particular patient. It *needs* to be analyzed. It is precisely because we so often do *not* analyze it, while being aware that it is going on, that such behavior represents "coasting" in the countertransference. The fact that we may not know the unconscious roots of our self-interested behavior, in other words, has little to do (for instance) with our willingness to make a shopping list or scan the internet (Slochower, 2003, 2006) during a phone session.

I think it is fair to say that however clear-eyed we psychoanalysts may be in many respects, and no matter how devoted we believe we are to the ideal of looking truth in the face, we do commonly allow ourselves an idealization of the degree to which we check our self-interest at the office door. Irwin's hope is to contribute to the puncturing of this idealization. But he doesn't want to condemn us. It's not so simple. He doesn't want to make us feel badly, or at least not only badly. In fact, I know he would be unhappy if he thought that were the primary impact of these chapters. His message, instead, is about facing all of what we are and what we do with our patients. In the process, we might have to bear feeling badly about what we conclude we need to face about our conduct. But guilt and shame aren't the point of what Irwin has to say; our awareness of ourselves is. Irwin doesn't tell you what to do, any more than he told me what to do when he told me about calling those ex-patients. But in the course of telling us about his disappointments in himself, he awakens our awareness of our own behavior, and of our similar disappointments in ourselves. If we allow ourselves to see what he sees, we open ourselves to the possibility of a fuller and more satisfying experience — for our patients, yes, but also for ourselves, because managing not to think about our tolerance of self-interest comes at a cost. In the end, I hope this book encourages not only closer and more honest self-observation among psychoanalysts and other psychotherapists but also, through its revelation of the ordinariness of coasting in the countertransference, a greater acceptance of our personal shortcomings and frailties, even if we do not excuse them.

We are always in conflict over what is best for our patients and what is most comfortable for us. For better or worse, in any two-person psychology the analyst as a particular person, right along with the patient, is at the heart of the therapeutic process. Indeed, often an interactive equilibrium, typical of the patient's life and/or the analyst's, is established in lieu of a much less comfortable and more disruptive progression toward new forms of relatedness. This is Irwin's primary theme. But Irwin also shows us in these pages that, if we really do accept two-person psychology, we must also accept that our personalities, our flaws, and our own selfish interests must always and inevitably be taken into account as an intrinsic part of what makes up therapeutic relatedness.

**Donnel Stern**

# 1

# Coasting in the Countertransference
*Analysts' Pursuit of Self-Interest*

I have had, over the years, many informal conversations with psychoanalytic colleagues who are also close friends that focus on some of the selfish motivations both for our work with patients and in our broader professional pursuits. These conversations are often in a humorous vein, sarcastically tweaking both our own self-serving interactions and the myth that those of us in the helping professions are possessed by especially altruistic spirits. In the candor of friendship we have teased one another about a variety of familiar themes; for example, the joys of being the object of sexual desire, especially in the eyes of patients toward whom we are physically attracted; the pleasures of being admired in a myriad of ways, in contrast with being the target of hurtful criticism or scathing anger, even though it is clear to all in the field that anger in the transference is an essential part of any depth analysis; the high that comes from the affirmation of receiving new referrals, having most of our available hours filled, and earning a satisfactory living; and the ever present specter of boredom, and the frequent temptation to not listen carefully to patients. I recall one specific moment of shared laughter and recognition when a colleague quipped to a small group of us that, by far, his favorite form of transference was idealization.

Though conventional wisdom dictates that self-interest is a significant, though not exclusive, motivation for much of what all living creatures do (Slavin & Kriegman, 1992, 1998), psychoanalytic literature has, for the most part, avoided addressing the degree to which this impacts analytic therapy in ways that are sometimes helpful but sometimes harmful to patients. Analysts' pursuit of money, or, put more colloquially, the need to earn a living, has received more attention in the literature than other dimensions of analysts' selfish pursuits (see, e.g., Aron & Hirsch, 1992; Josephs, 2004; Lasky, 1984; Liss-Levinson, 1990; Whitson, n.d.), and I intend to address this important question again in chapters 7 and 8. Recently, Maroda (2005) has emphasized the importance that analysts recognize that, inevitably, they seek gratifications from patients, and that this should be seen as normal and inherently human (Slavin & Kriegman, 1992, 1998). Maroda referred, for example, to desires to be important and effective as virtually standard features of all interpersonal engagement, though she was aware that pursuit of these "normal" gratifications can become overly narcissistic, excessive, and ultimately harmful to patients. In an earlier generation, iconoclastic analytic writers like Singer (1965a, 1965b, 1968, 1971, 1977) and Searles (1960, 1965, 1979) both suggested the ubiquity of analysts' self-interest, and the need to be aware of it, so that the analytic process is neither a sham (i.e., analysts' portrayal of themselves as selfless and as caring only about what is best for patients) nor a vehicle for unrestrained pursuit of this self-interest. Singer implied what is essentially a capitalist ideal—the pursuit of financial compensation and professional recognition is best served by being an optimally competent analyst for patients. Searles suggested that vigorous enjoyment of one's interaction with patients is likely to lead to more authentic and passionate engagement with them. Needless to say, past a certain, difficult-to-determine point, an emphasis on self-interest usually involves at least a measure of disregard for the other.

In this volume I write about the kind of analyst self-interest that is not an aspect of the analyst's character alone, nor simply an expression of a wish to be successful in one's work. My interest lies in pursuits of self-interest that emerge as potentially useful data from the transference–countertransference matrix, though are not necessarily used to further the analytic work. Instead, the analyst can be said to coast in the countertransference, choosing comfort or equilibrium over creating useful destabilization (Mendelsohn, 2002; Slavin & Kriegman, 1992). In this chapter and in what follows, I plan to address a variety of ways that, with at least some consciousness, analysts commonly pursue their own interests at some cost to patients. The first issue I address in this chapter reflects momentary indulgences, the countertransference implications of which the analyst does not use to deepen the analytic process. Lapses in attention and daydreaming are quotidian examples. The second theme in this chapter refers to the way analysts structure their practice, including the length of the workday, spacing between analytic sessions, and competing professional activities. In subsequent chapters (chapters 2, 3, and 4), my attention focuses upon analysts' unique personalities and the situational factors in analysts' lives. These enduring and/or transient states generally lead analysts, usually unwittingly at the start, to shape the analytic relationship to conform, more or less, to their most comfortable and preferred relational states. At some point these interactions inevitably become conscious to the analyst, and the choice presents itself whether to create a disquieting disequilibrium by using these interactional data to productively address the transference–countertransference theme, or, conversely, whether to coast with the status quo and maintain what might be a mutually comfortable equilibrium between patient and analyst. I am suggesting that it is more common than one would suspect from the psychoanalytic literature for analysts to consciously choose to maintain personal and/or mutual states of equilibrium with patients over the promotion of therapeutically useful mutual destabilization. Perhaps the most common example of this can be seen in many long analyses, where a dependent patient wishes to remain eternally, and an analyst, gratified by both a sense of importance and an economic annuity, chooses not to address the mutually gratifying nature of the transference–countertransference relationship (Renik, 1995, 2006). Along the same lines, a situational factor of analysts' loneliness (Buechler, 2004; Fromm-Reichmann, 1959) may readily lead to efforts, unconscious at first, to facilitate patients' excessive dependency and to discourage separation and autonomy.

In chapter 5, I address the often powerful role that any analyst's cherished psychoanalytic theory may have in both structuring and understanding the therapeutic dyad. Analysts' respective theoretical heritages provide comfortable and familiar homes for them, and patients are commonly shoehorned into a conceptual space that is designed to reinforce analysts' sense of stability. In chapter 6, I discuss the rarely addressed issue of male analysts' and/or patients' baldness, and the enormous anxiety that either state may create within the analytic dyad. I argue that analysts' avoidance of dealing with this issue is more characteristic than otherwise, for it may readily create in both parties what could be experienced as a premature confrontation with mortality. In my final two chapters (7 and 8), I emphasize the degree to which analysts' economic needs may influence every aspect of the analytic relationship. I underscore that the impact of therapists' economic concerns reflects the single biggest dilemma in any of the helping professions.

Slochower (2003, 2006), referring to what she called everyday "crimes and misdemeanors," wrote with unusual candor of the inherent conflict that may exist at any moment of analytic work between attention to patients' and analysts' wishes and/or interests. Though it seems so obvious after it is noted, Slochower highlighted what has rarely been acknowledged in the literature—the difficulty of suspending attention to one's interests and listening carefully to others for even one analytic session, much less all day long. The joke that ends in the analyst's shrug of his shoulders and his question "Who's listening?" is a reflection of how well most analysts know privately that they do not always listen to patients, choosing instead, at any given moment or for much longer, to attend to themselves in priority. Slochower argued that pursuit of self-interest of any kind is most harmful when analysts fail to acknowledge this phenomenon as a powerful force in any given analytic experience. Needless to say, analysts who face themselves and embrace their deficiencies with a good measure of honesty are less likely to *persistently* pursue selfish interests to the severe detriment of patients. For instance, because most lapses in attention by the analyst have something to do with the patient or with the analytic interaction, each instance of this becomes an opportunity for analytic inquiry. Few of us use productively *each* such instance. However, though no analyst can operate with this degree of presence all of the time, some approach this ideal more consistently and, of course, with some patients more than with others.

Self-awareness, however, is not a guarantee that any given analyst will change the way he or she is relating to a particular patient, either at specific moments or over extended time periods. The power of the quest for personal comfort and equilibrium, with each unique individual patient, is always potent. In the dyadic work of analysis, it is quite common that analysts' self-interest and patients' comfort levels dovetail, and persisting in perhaps stagnant but relatively anxiety-free enactments or mutual configurations is compelling for both parties (Feldman, 1997). For instance, think of the schizoid patient who is quite comfortable with the analyst's withdrawal, the overdependent patient who relishes the analyst's infantilization, the sexually provocative patient who enjoys the analyst's flirtations, or the masochistic patient who expects to be ignored. Analysts' awareness of such engagements or enactments has the potential to lead to

a useful deconstruction of them, but because they can be so mutually gratifying, this is often not the case. On a conceptual level, most
contemporary analysts agree that the analysis of a mutually constructed configuration is the sine qua non of the process and that
such interactions are hard to meaningfully address unless they have
been enacted within the transference–countertransference matrix
(Black, 2003; Bromberg, 1998, 2006; Gabbard, 1995, 1996; Greenberg, 1991, 2001; Hirsch, 1996, 1998a; Jacobs, 1986; Levenson, 1972,
1981, 1992; McLaughlin, 1991; Mitchell, 1988, 1993; Poland, 1992;
Renik, 1993; Sandler, 1976; Stern, 2003, 2004; Varga, 2005; Wachtel,
1980). The issues addressed here, however, focus on analysts' conscious disinclination to assert the effort to put these interactions
(unwitting enactments) into words, choosing instead to remain in a
comfortable moment, or in a long-standing equilibrium of what may
perhaps be either free of anxiety for the analyst singularly or a familiar and therefore comfortable mutual enactment for both analytic
participants. Implicit in this exegesis are the ideas that analysts often
fail to use countertransference productively and that the thoroughgoing embrace of countertransference experience in much of contemporary two-person psychology theorizing may not be sufficiently
thought out. A more genuine two-person relational psychology
cannot assume optimistically that each unique analyst will engage
countertransference experience to good end. Analysts' idiosyncrasies dictate that each individual analyst will at times indulge his or
her countertransference, and that patients will be the worse for this.
If the examination of the experience and participation of both parties in the dyad is to be as thorough as interpersonal and relational
writers suggest it should be, there will have to be added a focus on
how often patients' progress is limited by analysts' failures to trans-
late what they know about their countertransference experience
into helpful shifts in analytic relatedness. That is, the inclination to
pursue self-interest must be included as a feature in any conception
of a mutually subjective (Aron, 1991, 1996; Benjamin, 1995; Hirsch,
1990; Levenson, 1972, 1981, 1992; Renik, 1993, 1995; Singer, 1977;
Stern, 1997; Wolstein, 1954, 1977, 1997), two-person psychology of
psychoanalysis. Though I do believe that analysts' unwitting participation is inevitable and virtually always potentially productive, I also
believe that analysts too often are willing to coast with comfortable
modes of participation after they become witting. What Buechler
(2002, 2004) has called "effort fullness" reflects her recognition of

how counterintuitive it is for anyone to choose discomfort and dis-equilibrium in preference to their opposite states (Slavin & Krieg-man, 1992, 1998). Theories of therapeutic action are based on ideals and on analysts behaving ideally, though each individual analyst is, indeed, a flawed human being who operates selfishly and falls short of analytic ideals very often.

In what follows throughout this volume, I will address a variety of ways and contexts that reflect analysts' at least somewhat conscious choices to maintain self-interest, or to coast, and to make less than optimum effort to use immediate experience to help patients prog-ress to satisfactory termination (Renik, 2006). Though, as noted, I will try to separate these pursuits of self-interest and personal equilibrium into discrete categories, inevitably there is much over-lap between categories, and they are not at all independent of one another. In the remainder of this chapter I address the particular theme of analysts' lapses of involvement and attention, and the often selfish way analysts structure their workday and integrate their range of professional commitments. Implicit throughout all chapters is the concept that analysts need to tolerate disequilibrium and to person-ally change in relation to patients, if patients themselves are expected to change (Buechler, 2002; Mendelsohn, 2002; Slavin & Kriegman, 1992, 1998; Wolstein, 1954, 1959).

## The Analysts' Lapses

It is worth restating Slochower's (2003, 2006) obvious but rarely addressed acknowledgment of how difficult it is to suspend atten-tion to one's own concerns, and intently listen to another person for 45 or 50 minutes, much less do this repeatedly over the course of an entire workday. Indeed, this seems to me quite impossible, and I believe every analyst has lapses in attention for some fractions of time in every session. When these periods of inattentiveness occur, of course, are crucial data, because analysts' boredom or affective withdrawal is usually related to the patients' participation and to ele-ments of the analytic interaction. As well, the content of analysts' ideation during periods of inattentiveness may be highly informa-tive about patients and about the analytic interaction. Ogden (1994) and Wilner (2000), from very different analytic perspectives, both suggested that *all* of analysts' fantasies or reveries are related to the analytic interaction not only in form, but in content as well. In a sense, they imply that analysts never really withdraw from patients, because every withdrawal and how it is spent are actually just other forms of being involved with patients.

Though I agree that this often is the case, this conception seems to me somewhat idealistic, and a denial of the flawed humanity of all of us who practice analysis. It suggests that analysts never retreat into privacy and self-involvement for reasons that are largely narcissistic and selfish, and that are more often than acknowledged independent of patients' participation. I do believe that every act, when with another person, indeed does have *some* interpersonal meaning. However, this meaning could be far secondary, for instance, to an analyst's communication of the wish for privacy or respite, or a statement, for example, of analysts' fatigue, preoccupation, worry, or looking forward to what lies ahead in the day or evening. Most analysts will acknowledge privately that boredom is an occupational hazard, and that this experience is not *always* primarily related to a particular interaction with a given patient. I will say more about this later in this chapter, but boredom is often related to how many patients are seen in a day, how they are spaced, the time of the day, and competing activities. I suggest that although analysts are, of course, more likely to withdraw into boredom and self-involvement with some patients more than with others (and that this is always of informational value), the reverie involved in these withdrawals sometimes reflects exclusively analysts' narcissistic concerns (Bach, 1995; Blechner, 2005b; Fiscalini & Grey, 1993; Hirsch, 1993), and may not at all be of informational value in understanding patients.

Although some analysts are better able than others at suspending attention to their own concerns during sessions, and most analysts can do this best when not especially busy or fatigued, or when their personal lives are relatively smooth, I do not believe that anyone does not use his or her workday, in some degree, to retreat into privacy. Indeed, the structure of the analytic situation lends itself to this. Psychoanalysts are expected to be quiet and reflective, and patients quickly learn not to expect very much verbal interaction. When patients lie on the couch, they face away from the analyst, and the analyst probably speaks less often, so that both visual and auditory cues about the analyst's experience are less available to patients than when they sit up. I am not sure, though, that patients on the couch know as little about the analyst's ongoing experience as analysts often seem to think. I have always believed that patients *are* able to read our sentiments, attitudes, and levels of engagement despite even lengthy silence and/or not seeing us. However, because analysts' roles, even in current times, are defined by at least reserved or infrequent verbal and nonverbal expressiveness, it is difficult for patients to entirely trust their perceptions about analysts' momentary, or sometimes even long-term, disengagements. Indeed, analysts often do not encourage patients to challenge them about their withdrawals, preferring instead to remain in such states, often protected by patients' unwillingness to be overly critical and to lose analysts' affections. Because analysts' work is defined more by listening than by speaking (we are supposed to be "good" listeners), we can usually get away with brief or even extended periods of listening to ourselves more than to our patients. Obviously, this is more likely with patients who do not expect and/or demand a great deal from us, or from relationships in general. Independent of particular transference–countertransference interactions, I believe that the use of the analytic couch lends itself to analysts' taking selfish leave from patients. Designed to minimize analytic influence on patients and to provide analysts optimal freedom to use creative reverie in the service of helping patients, this freedom, unfortunately, extends to greater latitude to be absent without detection—to be self-involved, and "missing in action." Slochower (2003, 2006), with some self-effacing humor, cited a variety of ways that she and/or her colleagues have taken leave from patients, aided by the absence of visual cues afforded by the couch or, even more extremely, in the context of telephone sessions. Indeed, this latter phenomenon has become more common in recent years (Richards, 1999). Slochower's examples include making shopping lists and schedules, paying bills, scanning the Internet, and looking at personal photographs. The humor involved in noting such unabashedly selfish pursuits is the humor of recognition—each analyst feeling some personal exposure to what Slochower called analytic "crimes and misdemeanors." In face-to-face analyses, one must learn to be more subtle, to scan the Internet of our mind, so to speak. Paying attention to oneself and not to patients will never be eliminated by any of us—it will only at best be controlled when analysts fully acknowledge this to themselves and encourage patients to make us uncomfortable by expressing, not containing, their transference-related perceptions of us (Aron, 1991, 1999; Blechner, 1992; Fiscalini, 1988; Gill, 1982, 1983, 1984, 1994;

Goldstein, n.d.; Greenberg, 1986; Hirsch, 1998a; Hoffman, 1983, 1987; Singer, 1968; Stern, 1987; Wachtel, 1982).

Later in this chapter I refer to circumstances that make analytic disengagement more likely, independent of particular transference–countertransference configurations. Nonetheless, as noted earlier, analysts' boredom, retreat into privacy, and the like are usually related to the person of the patient, and to the nature of the interaction at any given moment. I want to emphasize that I do not consider experiences like boredom, lapses in attentive listening, and affective retreat and isolation as unmediated expressions of the analyst's character or personality, and therefore as countertransference in the one-person sense described by writers such as Reich (1951). Instead, I view such states as intrinsic to any interpersonal situation that endures for even a modest period of time. What is problematic (albeit universal), and reflects my emphasis throughout, is analysts consciously choosing to remain in these states because this represents the most comfortable place to be situated at any given moment for the analyst, and often for the patient as well. Analysts' failures to make the effort to return from lapses in attention and pursuit of personal reverie, and/or to use these retreats for therapeutic ends in order to expose mutual enactments, comprise the countertransference theme most unaddressed in our literature. Here is a brief illustration.

Hillary* has been in analysis for some time, and has made only modest gains in her original presentation of herself as depressed in a "low-grade" (her words) way and passionless in both her marriage and career pursuits. She reports "the blahs" and, indeed, relates to me with a flatness and absence of verve or of urgency, virtually regardless of the seeming importance of the issue she brings to me. This was so when she told me of uncovering her husband's sexual infidelity, as it was true of her recent report of the acute mental collapse of her elderly mother. Our interaction follows a pattern. I usually tell her that she is speaking in a flat and disinterested tone about something I know that she has strong feelings about. She takes note, though continues in the same vein. I begin to become bored and retreat into my own private world, and then mobilize, and convey to Hillary that she still sounds like she's deadening her feelings. Hillary agrees, yet continues true to form. I resort to interpretive comments, reminding

---

* In this and other clinical examples used throughout the book, names and other identifiers have been changed to protect confidentiality.

her of the origins of her retreat. In capsule, the origins to which I
refer are largely the loss, in her early teens, of her romantic fantasies
with, and strong sense of being special to, both her father and her
brother, a loss brought on by her mother's success in "stealing back"
her father, and the beginning of her brother's relationship with a girl
who eventually became his wife. Until her acquiescent father withdrew profoundly, Hillary describes herself as having felt special to
him and, as well, felt vivacious and excited about life. Subsequent to
this period, she usually chose safety, including a marriage to a man
she knew she was not in love with, but whom she perceived as steady
and potentially a good provider economically. This combination of
safety and dependency has characterized our relationship, and in an
effort to emerge from an incipient boredom and retreat that I know
will soon intensify, I interpret to Hillary that she is playing it safe
with me and, as well, isolating what she might be feeling about her
mother's deterioration. My patient agrees, genuinely I believe, but
very soon again returns to pattern. In this context, my retreats and
my private reverie become longer. Depending on the day, my reverie
could be about anything from phone calls I must make, to what I
am doing that evening, to worries about one of my adult children, or
even to all of the above and more in the course of one session. What
I wish to emphasize is that, with Hillary (and others), for periods of
time I desist from making the effort to return to the key issue of her
emotional retreat and its impact on me, and I just coast with this
impact. During these periods I am pursuing my own self-interest,
soothing myself and ignoring my patient, as I feel she is ignoring me.
Though I am not these days usually conscious of feeling hurt, angry,
or retaliatory, indeed I have often used this obvious instance of projective identification, in the form of an interpretation to Hillary, as
an additional way of combating my withdrawal. Earlier in our work
together I had made much of her passive-aggressive withdrawal as
a reflection of her transference and her usual retaliatory anger, and
conceptualized my own affective retreats from her as reflections of
my anger in relation to Hillary's deprivation of me. These interventions were seemingly accepted and understood, but I found that they
did not advance our situation. Indeed, were I to have been making a consistent and persistent effort to be optimally present, there
would have been much process and content to address with Hillary. Unfortunately, she evokes my withdrawal by her flatness and

absence of excitement about me, and then is content to let me stay there, leaving herself with the considerable safety of emotional distance in a context where she feels certain that I will not abandon her entirely. Part of Hillary wishes to remain this way with me forever, dissociated from her emotional dependency on me, though part of her also wishes to risk being more vulnerable and alive. I depend on my initial comments and transference observations and interpretations to energize me, and when she rejects them by returning to her withdrawn pattern, I may disappear, in part hoping that Hillary will bring me back. We are, however, in a state of mutual equilibrium. My patient almost never challenges my withdrawals. I know that it is solely my responsibility to make the requisite continuous effort to emerge from the safety and comfort I often feel when I coast in my own self- absorbed and self-enclosed rumination or reverie.

Related to the theme of effort is the question of analysts' memories about patients' life history, significant details of current life, and dreams. Bion (1967), in his well-known directive, recommended that analysts do best when free of memory or desire. He suggested that this position allows patients to be uninfluenced by analysts' wishes, and enables them to address only what is of most urgency to themselves at any given moment. In addition, analysts' knowledge of history or of previous dreams readily leads to interpretive bias on analysts' part. That is, there is risk that immediate experience is seen less as something fresh, and to be examined with naïve curiosity, than as something that fits into a schema that is based on past knowledge. In Bion's eyes, analysts' attention to immediate experience reflects the heart of the process.* Indeed, analysts' attempts to not make the effort to recall data about patients, for the reasons Bion advised, seem to me like one reasonable view of ideal analytic process. This corresponds to a traditional classical Freudian perspective, in which meticulous care is exerted to avoid influencing patients with analysts' subjectivity. Though central to the relational turn in

---

* Though it is not my intention to discuss Bion's significant contributions beyond the one segment that is relevant directly to the issue of analysts' memory, it is worth noting that Bion has developed an intricate theory of therapy. In contradiction to his care to avoid analysts' influence on patients, looking at analytic process through his theoretical lens creates a distinctive perceptual set of biases (Hirsch, 2003a).

psychoanalysis* is the argument that analysts' subjectivity is irreducible (Renik, 1993) and must be examined in the analytic process, it is the rare analyst who advocates purposeful attempts to influence patients, or influence the material that patients present. That is, analysts' subjectivity is viewed as unwitting, and not consciously designed to bias either the analytic data or the patients' choices. In fact, analysts' unwitting influence on patients ideally is to be carefully analyzed, in a verbal forum (Aron, 1991, 1996; Blechner, 1992; Friedman, 1988; Gabbard, 1995; Gill, 1982, 1983, 1984; Greenberg, 1995; Hirsch, 1987, 1996, 1998a; Hoffman, 1983, 1987; Levenson, 1991, 1992; Mitchell, 1988; Sandler, 1976; Stern, 1987, 1996a), in part as a means of trying to neutralize analytic influence and the power of the analyst as a person.

Returning to the question of analysts' memory, I suggest that although some analysts may try to not remember material in order to keep the analysis optimally pure, most forgetfulness exists for less noble reasons. Indeed, depending on how many patients a given analyst sees, it is often very difficult to recall, in particular, many details of life history. I believe that the majority of analysts value remembering as much as possible about each patient, though there is much individual difference in how much effort is expended in remembering. The most vigilant analysts may keep detailed notes of history and of each session, and review the former periodically and the latter prior to each session. This, of course, is very time-consuming, and dramatically so when one sees many patients. Nonetheless, this does seem like the most responsible approach if an analyst is to maintain an optimal presence in the effort to know a patient as thoroughly as possible. It reflects a commitment to patients at the considerable expense of analysts' time—a choice of interest in the other in priority to self-interest. Though I believe this last statement to be true, I do not routinely review patients' life historical data, nor do I keep

---

* For example, Thompson (1950), Sullivan (1953), Wolstein (1959), Schachtel (1959), Tauber and Green (1959), Fromm (1964), Searles (1965, 1979), Singer (1965a), Levenson (1972), Barnett (1980), Wachtel (1982), Hirsch (1987), Mitchell (1988, 1993, 1997, 2000), Greenberg (1991), Davies (1994), Benjamin (1995), Josephs (1995), Aron (1996), Slochower (1996), Stern (1997), Rucker and Lombardi (1997), Bromberg (1998), Hoffman (1998), Layton (1998), Frankel (1998), Pizer (1998), Cooper (2000a, 2000b), Grand (2000), Knoblauch (2000), Bass (2001), Berman (2001), Fonagy (2001), Crastnopol (2002), Beebe and Lachmann (2002), Dimen (2003), Fosshage (2003), Safran (2003), Seligman (2003), Bonovitz (2005), Harris (2005), and Skolnick (2006).

detailed notes of sessions in order to review them prior to any given appointment. I believe that in this regard I am in the majority, especially among analysts who have at least a reasonably large practice.

It is difficult to rationalize the many lapses in memory that I think exist in most analyses. Clearly, some analysts listen more carefully than others, are more passionately involved, and are likely to keep in mind a considerable amount of data about their patients. It is equally apparent that some patients' lives are more compelling, and/or their presentation more demanding, making their analysts' memory for details about them better than it is with other patients. And, when patients are seen multiple times per week and/or over a number of years, analysts tend to remember more historical detail as time goes by. Though these features are all highly relevant transference–countertransference data to explore with patients, the fact remains that I and most of my colleagues, especially those with large practices, do not always make the maximum effort to know our patients in full by having life historical details at hand to use in any given session.

Murray has a very spare personal life, and spends much time in fantasy and in intellectualized ideation. He speaks to me in a manner that is stilted and impersonal, barely above a whisper, and maintaining attention to him takes much work. This is, of course, is a key transference–countertransference theme, and Murray has a long history of being relatively ignored. He has developed a marked passive-aggressive character in response to this, and has become a master of ignoring and thwarting others. Despite how little he gives me on a manifest level, I am sure Murray is both attached to me and dependent on me. He has opened up with me more than he has ever done with anyone, and I am his most intimate contact except for his dog. I try to stay alert by challenging him about his passive-aggressive retreats, but all too often I withdraw into my own ideation. Murray never challenges me, and I feel that I could get away with entire sessions of not listening to him, or literally not even hearing him. He demands nothing from me. Murray comes from a large family in a small town, where grandparents, aunts and uncles, pastors, neighbors, storekeepers, and others played important roles in his own and his siblings' development. Though Murray's interest in history (his own as well as American history) is among the most interesting things about him, I have an awful time remembering which brother is which, and which grandparent was warm and caring, and which was neglectful and harsh. I have a very good sense of the doings in his current life, and about the way he relates to me and to others, but there is much in his life history that he has told me, and that is clearly significant, that I do not hold on to. I never take a detailed history when I begin with patients, and I learn about history as the work proceeds. I do take notes early in the analysis, but as treatment proceeds my notes become perfunctory, more for legal requirements than for information. I can consult my notes and study Murray's history, but I usually do not. I ignore aspects of him, passive-aggressively, as he can ignore me. I rationalize that if I help him come alive in the here and now of our exchange, I will naturally recall his history in more detail. I tell myself that transference and attention to the immediacy of process are far more central than historical detail per se, and though I do believe this to be true, my failure to remember is *part* of a transference–countertransference enactment, and I do not make the full effort to pull myself out of it. As I write this, I resolve to examine my notes and get Murray's life history straight, prior to each session if need be. This will take time and effort, and perhaps interfere with the number of patients I can see in each day, for Murray is not the only person whose historical data elude me. This would represent a financial sacrifice. Murray wants to emerge from his state of withdrawal, and he wants to be loved and attended to. He is, however, too comfortable and too familiar with both receiving and giving less than full attention. We both can live with our situation the way it is, but it is my place to make the effort and the sacrifice, and to create a situation of greater discomfort and disequilibrium for both of us.

Rory is young, exceptionally handsome, athletic, and successful; he is charismatic and charming and seductive. He has many close friends, and was always very popular and a leader throughout school. He feels special and central to both his parents. Though his divorced parents are both very troubled people, Rory has never doubted their love and commitment to him. Rory initiates analysis because *he* cannot commit. He has so many career opportunities and is so heavily recruited that he does not know what to pursue. Similarly, he is involved with a young woman who is desperate to marry him, but other women are constantly falling into his lap. He fears that he is similar to his father—never able to love anyone but his son. Though I have seen Rory for a much briefer time than Murray, I remember everything Rory tells me. I am always on my toes and never tempted to wander. Though I do not think he would tolerate my lack of attention or absence of memory, my near perfect recall of Rory's history and our previous sessions is effortless. It is not so much that he is particularly involved with me—he commands my total attention without reciprocating. Rory's narcissism and absolute sense of entitlement comprise our central transference–countertransference theme, yet I have been reluctant to address it in the extratransference, much less in the transference. The issue of forgetting or remembering details of patients' lives merges at this juncture with a theme to be discussed next—analysts' inclination to avoid uncomfortable transference themes (Gill, 1982; Goldstein, n.d.). This latter factor is yet another way that analysts may maintain a mutually constructed equilibrium and fail to make the effort to promote potentially productive discomfort.

Whereas I am quick to challenge and confront Murray about almost anything (when I am not withdrawn from him), I am very careful with Rory. Not only am I on my best behavior with regard to an almost photographic memory about his life and life history, but also I am never inattentive even when he obsesses endlessly about which job offer to consider. Rory is often late for sessions and in paying his bills, and on a few occasions he has forgotten to come altogether. He is very well bred and is always apologetic, though he has little awareness of his degree of self-centeredness. His looks, charm, and considerable intelligence have always given him much latitude with others, and I find myself reluctant to address his palpable narcissism in the transference. In contrast with Murray, I feel lucky to have him as a patient, and I, along with everyone else he knows, offer him my royal treatment. To the extent that I recognize a highly significant transference–countertransference enactment and do not address it, of course he actually receives very poor treatment from me. Rory is comfortable with being special, and even though I am not comfortable with my role in this mutual configuration, I avoid the greater discomfort of raising his ire and his disapproval. Rory reports that he has a short fuse, and is quick to walk away from situations that get what he calls "too sticky." I know what I must do in this situation, and I trust that I will be more courageous at some near point, and risk losing him.

I wish to highlight that it is quite common for analysts to withdraw in this way. Though this is a very different sort of withdrawal than retreat into boredom, or forgetfulness, it is also similar. Conscious avoidance of a palpable and key transference theme (Aron, 1991, 1996; Friedman, 1988; Gabbard, 1995, 1996; Gill, 1982, 1983;

Greenberg, 1995; Hirsch, 1996, 1998a; Hoffman, 1983; Jacobs, 1986, 1991; Mitchell, 1988; Renik, 1993) reflects being less than present in a social context, and suggests an analyst's preference for the maintenance of mutual equilibrium and minimal anxiety. Freud (1912/2000) long ago observed that transference is both the heart of analysis and the hardest part of analysis. Gill (1982, 1983, 1984, 1994) supported analysis of transference as the sine qua non of the process, while noting that examination of transference is commonly avoided by many or most analysts who adhere to this principle in theory (see also Goldstein, n.d.; Hirsch, 1987; Hoffman, 1983, 1987; Stern, 1987, 1997). As reflected in my work with Rory, transference is often consciously avoided when it creates anxiety in the analyst. Addressing transference themes in the context of extratransference content shifts the focus to a you–me, here-and-now engagement, a level of interaction far more intense than most other analytic data or content. The intimacy involved in dealing with immediate interpersonal experience, regardless of the feelings involved, is in and of itself potentially difficult to endure with some patients more than others, and/or with multiple patients per day. As well, different analysts are more or less comfortable with different affective states, and it is quite common for analysts to consciously avoid some and encourage others. Among the feeling states commonly avoided in the transference are disrespect, disappointment, disinterest, anger, sexual interest or disinterest, and dependency (often reflected and enacted in overly long analyses). In my work with Rory, I fear his disrespect, and I fear direct confrontation with his disinterest. For Rory, being angry usually means walking away—there are plenty of others who want him. In listening to his extratransference content and not taking him up on his narcissistic entitlements and his forgetfulness, I am consciously retreating from him and depriving him of proper psychoanalysis. I suggest here, with Gill (1982, 1983, 1994), that analysts generally are comfortable (though often bored) listening to excessive extratransference reporting, in which patients may express affect about parents, lovers, colleagues, and so on. When we are relatively at ease with the affects expressed, we are more likely to introduce transference implications and/or parallels. As reflected in my work with Rory, analysts are often quite conscious of transferential themes they are not addressing, although they often rationalize this by claiming that the patient is not ready to hear something (Coen, 2002; Fromm, 1964; Hirsch, 1987, 1998a; Mitchell, 1988;

Searles, 1979; Singer, 1965b, 1968, 1977; Thompson, 1950; Wolstein, 1954, 1959). Though I believe that addressing uncomfortable transference themes often raises anxiety in patients, this often evokes even greater anxiety in analysts. My most frequent intervention, when I supervise others, is to point out reluctances to address transferences. It is relatively easy and anxiety-free, if sometimes tedious, to listen to patients' reports of their extratransference interactions, though the power of the analytic process, and the part of the work that is much harder for analysts, lies in making use of the ways in which what the patient says and feels shapes the experience and interaction of analyst and patient. I always encourage supervisees to allow themselves to become uncomfortable and to deconstruct mutual equilibrium (Levenson, 1972, 1983, 1988, 1991), whereas I, in full consciousness, may choose a path of self-interest and self-preservation with Rory, and with all too many others with whom I am anxious. Analysis of transference is usually in direct opposition to coasting in the countertransference, and forcing oneself to use countertransference experience to address destabilizing mutual patterning is, I believe, the best analytic hedge against a comfortable status quo. Excessive focus on extratransference material reflects a very common lapse, one that is invariably fueled by avoidance of anxiety related to expected transference affect.

## The Structure of the Analytic Setting

Our psychoanalytic literature, with some exceptions (e.g., Abend, 1982; Basescu, 1977; Blechner, 1993, 2005a, 2005b; Boulanger, 2007; Buechler, 2004; Cole, 2002; Crastnopol, 1999, 2001; Drescher, 2002; Frawley-O'Dea & Goldner, 2007; Frommer, 1994, 2006; Gartner, 1999; B. Gerson, 1996; Goldman, 1993; Hoffman, 2004; Hopkins, 1998, 2006; Kantrowitz, 1992, 1993; Lasky, 1993; Leary, 1997; Nachmani, n.d.; Newman, 2006; Pizer, 1997; Richman, 2002, 2006; Singer, 1971, 1977; White, 2002), has not attended to the myriad of personal and professional variables that impact the way analysts work with patients during any given hour or day, or over extended periods of time. Prominent among these unaddressed professional variables is the way analysts structure their working day. The personal and professional are inseparable. For example, if one is worried about personal health issues or a breakup of a love relationship, does this lead to throwing oneself into work, or being unable to concentrate on work? In either case, if there are preoccupying factors in an analyst's personal life, does this lead to being intensely consumed with patients as a way of casting worry aside, or to considerable distraction from patients?

Though most professionals are aware of this and would not deny it, I believe it is fair to say that self-interest is the first consideration in choosing the length of sessions, which hours to hold sessions, how many hours to work each day or week, the spacing between analytic sessions, and what other professional activities compete with commitment to one's patients. If patients' interest was analysts' primary concern, we would conduct longer rather than shorter sessions, work during hours most convenient to patients, work only a modest number of hours each week in order to maintain optimal involvement with each patient, space our sessions sufficiently far apart so as to be able to reflect on each patient hour and prepare for the next, and orchestrate our workday and schedule in a manner that maximizes what physicians like to refer to as *patient care*. Though I do not think of psychoanalysis or psychotherapy as at all part of a medical model, and the term *care* in this context has always struck me as cloying and insincere, I do think a concept of *optimal patient involvement* is relevant for analysts to reflect upon.

I will rather quickly refer to the matter of length of sessions and the time of day they are scheduled—I think that there is only a little bit to say about this. Analytic sessions used to be 50 minutes, with a 10-minute break built in, in order to add up to a legitimate "hour." Currently for me and most colleagues, the "hour" lasts 45 minutes, usually without a break scheduled between any given sessions. One thing that happened to the 50-minute hour was that the break in between disappeared, and sessions were commonly scheduled in succession. Given this purely economic-based practicality, 50 minutes became an odd and arbitrary number, and scheduling times emerged at awkward and difficult-to-remember times (e.g., 2:50 p.m.). Thus, with the loss of the between-session break, the more sensible number of minutes to be with patients was rounded *down* to 45 minutes, which is easier to keep track of. It could have been rounded up to 60 minutes, a true "hour," and even easier to remember. Though I know a number of analysts who still meet for the traditional 50 minutes, I know of no one who holds full-hour sessions, and hardly anyone who *tries to* schedule a 10- or a 15-minute break between sessions. I am not here challenging the importance of maintaining boundaries and structure with patients—of choosing a set amount of time and working strictly within this. I do think, however, that it is impossible to avoid the conclusion that seeing patients back-to-back, *and* reducing analytic time by 5 minutes, works strictly for analysts' benefit in priority to patient interest. Who would argue that for the same fee, 50 minutes would not be more beneficial to patients, or that rounding up to 60 minutes would not have been more of a patient-oriented choice for our analytic culture to have adopted?

The time of the day analysts choose to work is a complex variable, because it combines analysts' preference with the question of when patients are available, as well as how busy any given analyst may be. There is little to say about this except that it is usually ruled by the capitalist law of supply and demand. Those analysts who are in sufficient demand can work whatever hours they choose, and need not take into account what is convenient for patients. Most patients with full-time jobs prefer to come either before or after work hours, though analysts who are in great demand often prefer not to work during the evening. Analysts who are more "accommodating," for example to patients' wishes for evening hours, usually do so because their preferred daytime hours are not sufficiently filled up. In order to earn a reasonable livelihood, most analysts feel they have no choice but to work at times they would prefer to be at leisure. Indeed, much analytic work is conducted in the evening, a time of day when one's concentration may be less than optimal and one's wish to be working at low ebb. I recall many years ago a colleague who was in analytic training, which required him to be in analysis four times per week with one of a number of training analysts, all of whom practiced in Manhattan. My colleague lived in Manhattan but worked in a nearby suburb, and commuted back and forth from his place of work for each session, in the middle of the day. I remember thinking he was either crazy or masochistic, and that this senior analyst must be an absolute monster to not even see him *once* each week in the early morning or in the evening, when my colleague was already in Manhattan. Now, in my own more senior status, I think I would do my best to move such a patient into an early morning or late afternoon hour, or 2:00 or 3:00 p.m. if they became available. But maybe I would not, and in that case I would be as selfish as this sadistic analyst of yore. My colleague *was* an accommodating (masochistic?) man, and he was willing to take analytic hours totally convenient to his analyst. Am I sure

I would give up a harder-to-fill, middle-of-the-day hour and transfer him to a more precious time, given his willingness to come at my behest? What if I did this and someone interesting came along who *claimed* he could come only early or late in my day, and I now had no such available time? In such an instance, *I* would probably have been the masochist. If this new patient were Rory, would I do everything possible to accommodate him—perhaps start my day earlier, or end later? I know that I would more likely do this for Rory than for Murray. In any of these situations, would I use the scheduling issue to deepen the analysis? Would I address with my masochistic colleague (were he my patient), or with Murray, his pathological compliance and his passivity, thereby placing my comfortable schedule in jeopardy? Would I address in any way with Rory how desirable he was to me, and how much I accommodate him? In these situations I speculate about, I think that many analysts would be likely to continue engaging in ways that are both practically and emotionally comfortable, choosing consciously not to address themes that would be too disruptive to the respective psyches and/or selfish conveniences of perhaps either coparticipant, and to the enactments that evolve from these configurations.

In the realm of the structure of the analytic setting, perhaps the purest illustration of analysts' self-interest can be seen in the choice of how many patients (and/or supervisees) are seen on any given day, and how these sessions are spaced. Given the choice, for economic purposes I believe most analysts will see as many people as possible, short of mental exhaustion. If referrals are plentiful, it is likely that many of these sessions will be conducted back-to-back, perhaps in clusters of 3, 4, 5, or more hours in succession. Speaking personally, when I have the choice my ideal day consists of seeing 11 people, starting at 7:15 a.m. and ending at 6:30 p.m., recently with a one-half day on Friday. There are days when I will see 12 individuals, sometimes even 13, though I prefer not to do this. Again, when I can choose, I will see individuals in clusters of three to a maximum of six sessions with no break (I prefer no more than four consecutive sessions), though I have seen as many as eight people in succession. I am taking the liberty of assuming* that, with regard to scheduling, most analysts place economic concerns in higher priority to patient

---

* This is not simply an assumption, for I have both observed and spoken with many colleagues about these matters.

concerns. That is, as a group we are quite conscious that seeing fewer patients, and not seeing them back-to-back, generally allows us to devote more affective and cognitive energy to each individual. There is no benefit to our patients to be one of many, or to walk in and sit or lie down in a warm chair or couch just vacated by a "sibling." Of course, this issue is ripe for analytic exploration and should be used to this advantage, but analysts' motivation is clearly to maximize income. Though I have developed the ability over the years of quickly shifting attention from one person to another, and of keeping in mind who each of my patients is, can there be any doubt that my concentration would be more acute if I saw fewer people and took a break between each one? If I had 10 or 15 minutes between patients, I *could* look back to the last session to refresh myself about an important dream, or I could look at my notes and try to get straight some details about siblings or grandparents. A near ideal commitment and passion to patients cannot exist under the conditions I describe as my own, and those of virtually every colleague I know who has the same opportunity or luxury.

The impact of analysts' busy schedules and selfish use of time will invariably affect interaction with different patients in different ways. Rory will get my attention no matter how busy I am and regardless of when in the day or in a sequence of patients I see him. I will remember his siblings and his recent dreams without checking notes. When I am tired or in the midst of a demanding day, Murray's interests are not well served by my relative inattentiveness. Murray is comfortable in his schizoid isolation, and will allow me to relax, to be less intent on his every word or gesture—actually, even to ignore his nonverbal *and* his verbal communications. When I see patients back-to-back, or if I see Murray at a time of day when I seem most sleepy (early afternoons, around 1:30–2:30, just before my lunch/gym break of 2 hours), I will often take a respite from listening and escape into daydreams, reverie, and the like. When a patient who asks for little follows someone who is demanding, or where the former session has been particularly affectively intense, the second patient is likely to be *used*, at least to some degree, as a vacation—a respite. I now schedule Murray early in my workday, when I am most alert, and his analysis has benefited from this timing.

However, I do see Jack three times per week in the early afternoon, and this is far from ideal for him. Jack is not employed, lives off of a trust fund, and can come at any time of the day. He is very dependent on me, for I am one of the few people who populate his life. I am his primary human contact, and if I permit this, I will be able to see him interminably and use him as a financial annuity.* Jack is most ambivalent about restarting his career ever since he lost his high-tech job during the recession. Similarly, he refuses to risk loss of any kind in his personal life, and allows no sexual or personal intimates. His personal contacts are restricted to the bar where he hangs out each night (reminding me of the television series *Cheers*), and the musicians he sometimes jams with. He spends much time with pornography, and is quite used to taking care of himself and living a life of solitude. One might think that Jack is psychotic, or near this, by the way he lives, but I know that he is not. He is very lucid and clear thinking and articulate, and is by now conscious of many of his motives. Jack is clear that he wants to play it safe in life, and he sees the historical antecedents that have brought him there. He also sees that he rejects anyone who comes too near to him, doing to them what his caretakers did with him. Jack has let me into his life and does not want to lose me. He will come to see me whenever I wish, for as long as I allow him. Where I place him in my daily schedule takes advantage of his dependence on me, and his compliance toward me. If I am fatigued, or if I had a trying session prior to his, he will allow me to coast, to listen to him with one-half an ear. He teases me when I forget things, but his anger does not intimidate me, and there is no threat of losing him. I do, of course, address his dependence and his wish to be with me forever. However, at least one of his sessions should be at a time of the day when my alertness is optimal, and I have not facilitated this, nor have I addressed *this* element of his compliant dependency with him. I reserve my early morning times for those patients who cannot come during their workday, and I do not risk Jack demanding that I give this up for his benefit. It might benefit both patients if I attempted to trade Jack's time slot with Rory's. However, at the point of this writing my self-interest and my mutual equilibrium with each of these patients stand in place.

Analysts' self-interest and the practice of less than optimal analytic treatment can also be seen in the way patients' lateness and/or

---

* I will address this issue in more detail in two ensuing chapters. I will at this point only note that long analyses are very often driven by analysts' economic needs (Aron & Hirsch, 1992; Renik, 2006).

absence may be handled. It goes without saying that both lateness and absence invariably reflect transference feelings of some sort, and *always* should be examined, with an eye to minimize this form of acting out a particular affective expression. However, in the context of a busy schedule, especially when seeing patients in succession, I sometimes find myself wishing that my next patient will either be late or not show up at all. Because analysts are not penalized economically by lateness or by last-minute cancellations, there, indeed, is something to be desired about being paid for taking a break and relaxing in the midst of a demanding workday. It is difficult to avoid wishing for free time, even though lateness and absence might reflect some problem in the analysis. Given this selfish desire, it is quite likely that we sometimes communicate encouragement to our patients who are anyway inclined toward lateness or absence. The most likely way to encourage patients in this way is to avoid *diligent* exploration of each late minute and absence. When analysts too readily accept excuses that are, on the surface, quite reasonable, this is likely to convey to patients that lateness or absence represents a comfortable state for both parties, albeit perhaps for very different reasons. Although the patient, for example, may be characterologically conflicted about engaging with emotional intensity, the analyst may be conflicted more situationally, based on the analyst's heavily loaded schedule. Of course, it is quite possible that either the analyst or the late or absent patient is conflicted about consistent and intimate relatedness.

Terence drives from the suburbs to see me in Manhattan at 9:30 a.m. The traffic is awful and not entirely predictable. It is clear that to make this trip is effortful for him, and that it reflects a strong commitment to analytic work. He is not someone who finds such emotional commitments easy, and he tends to live more in his head than in a world of emotional mutuality. I find him quite interesting to be with, yet I am often relieved if he is 5 to 10 minutes late, for he is the fourth person I see in succession, and I can use a break by the time he arrives. Terence always seems troubled and apologetic when late, and he seems to believe that his tardiness is all traffic related. I, of course, have challenged this, suggesting that leaving earlier would provide a hedge against unpredictable traffic, and that his lateness has personal more than practical meaning. He groans that he knows this, but already wakes up so early to see me. I let Terence off relatively lightly, and I do not press the issue for meaning nearly as much as I could. I know that there must be a subtle communication that this equilibrium suits both of us, if not on a deep emotional level (for me), then at least on a practical one.

Dorian is a banker, earns a great deal of money, and works very long hours. He has always been a very high achiever and a thorough, if not compulsive, worker. He has great emotional investment in his career, and in the considerable stature this brings him. Dorian has never been comfortable within the confines of intimate personal relationships, and he began analysis at his wife's behest for this reason. I have been pleasantly surprised at how well he has taken to analysis, and the degree to which he has been willing to examine himself. He appears fond of me and attached to me, though often he is called on to address some important business deal with very little notice, and he cancels far more sessions than most other patients. I have worked with a number of individuals in his field, and I know that many such absences are unavoidable. Dorian, however, has more than his share of last-minute cancellations, and I often cannot discern what is necessary and what is avoidable. He is unusually compulsive about his work, and he is probably unusually prone, even for someone in his field, to give work priority over other activities. We have discussed this theme often and in great detail, and Dorian acknowledges how much easier work is for him than the "personal stuff" we do. Besides, he argues, the way he goes about his career has worked for him, and he loves his success and the financial rewards and prestige it brings to him and to his family. Despite how much we have focused on this issue, and on the cancelled sessions that are so emblematic of it, as with Terence I sometimes find myself anticipating with relief Dorian's last-minute call to tell me that he cannot get out of a meeting. The reason for my relief is not that I find Dorian difficult to be with. Actually, I feel quite the contrary. My relief is based on the free time his cancellation affords me, again somewhere in the midst of a number of successive sessions. My patient's cancellations represent crucial data about who he is as a person, yet my anticipation of these cancellations must communicate to him conflicting messages. On the one hand, I convey to him that I wish his intimate presence, yet on the other, I tell him that I am all too comfortable with his emotional disconnection. The latter state represents what has come to be a comfortable equilibrium for both of us.

## Summary

I have used examples from my own clinical work to illustrate some fundamental ways that self-interest influences the quotidian elements of my engagement with patients. Some of the particular ways that self-interest enters and impedes my work are unique to me, and reflect my particular character structure. These factors will be more dramatically illustrated in subsequent chapters. Other forms of the pursuit of self-interest, like the way I structure my workday, seem less idiosyncratic. Were these clinical illustrations simply confessionals, it would be safe to say that the sole purpose of this volume would be geared to some expiation of my crimes. Though I believe that I may be more narcissistically engaged than many of my analytic colleagues, I do believe that largely unspoken conscious pursuit of self-interest exists in different ways, and to different degrees, for everyone who practices this work. All of us analysts coast with our countertransference experience to some degree or another, and we do this in ways that reflect who we are as unique individuals, the situational factors that may be dominating our lives, and how these intersect with each idiosyncratic patient we see. At this juncture I feel compelled to say, albeit defensively, that though I am concerned that the interactions I have delineated in this section (and will in subsequent chapters) may reflect egregious behavior to some, if one were to secretly videotape a large sample of practicing analysts, I believe the findings would suggest that situations parallel to those I have described and illustrated might be closer to the norm than the exception.

# 2

# The Influence of Situational Factors, in Analysts' Lives and Analysts' Preferred Relational States, on Analytic Participation

It now seems only obvious that, in this analytic era characterized by the relational turn, who the analyst is as a person will have a significant impact on each unique patient. Though the concept of transference still refers to the internal world of the patient that is brought into each human interaction, it is now widely agreed that the person of the analyst has an impact on how and when different elements of transference are expressed (Crastnopol, 1999, 2001; Dimen, 2001; Gill, 1982, 1983, 1984; Hirsch, 1993, 1994; I. Hoffman, 1983, 1991; M. Hoffman, 2004; Kantrowitz, 1992, 1993; Maroda, 1981; Mitchell, 1988, 2000; White, 2002). Most contemporary analysts will no longer speak of transference in isolation from countertransference (Blechner, 1992; Coen, 2002; Davies & Frawley, 1994; Friedman, 2006; Hirsch, 1995; Jacobs, 2001; Wachtel, 1982), the analysts' participation in what is often called the *transference-countertransference matrix* (Mitchell, 1988, 1993, 1997). The concept of mutual enactment* has taken center stage in characterizing the analytic situation, taking into account how transference experience is played out somewhat differently with each unique analyst as coparticipant (Fiscalini, 2004; Guarton, 1999; Wilner, 2000; Wolstein, 1977, 1983). Later in this chapter I will discuss the potential impact of analysts' personalities on analytic work, and how analysts' maintenance of stable personality features can obscure

---

* Levenson (1972, 1983), Sandler (1976), Jacobs (1986), Friedman (1988), Greenberg (1991), McLaughlin (1991), Poland (1992), Renik (1993), Gabbard (1995), Aron (1996, 2005), Hirsch (1993, 1996, 1998a), Bromberg (1998, 2006), Stern (2003, 2004), Black (2003), and Varga (2005).

the emergence of certain features of patients. In this section I hope to highlight that analysts' life circumstances also may have considerable effects on what patients express or fail to express, and also significantly color the quality of the interaction. Indeed, either situational or enduring aspects of analysts' lives could be a prime source in shaping the heart of the analytic relationship.* These factors are often either not considered or, if they are considered, not addressed or explored in the context of the transference–countertransference matrix. Consider, for example, the sexually deprived analyst who is more than usually stimulated by his physically attractive patient; the elderly analyst who wishes his young patient were sexually attracted to him; the gay analyst who, especially in years past, feels that he must hide his sexual orientation from patients and/or colleagues; the lonely analyst who cherishes time spent with patients, for this may represent the most intimate exchange in the analyst's life; the analyst who has young babies, and can barely keep his eyes open during sessions; the analyst who is ill, and preoccupied with this; the analyst who has a sparse practice and can ill afford to lose patients; the analyst who is so booked up that a patient's departure might be welcomed; and the analyst who is so involved with and/or excited by a given professional situation (e.g., writing an article or book; developing a conference presentation; or preparing for a new course, an institutional appointment, a promotion, or an institutional setback) that involvement with patients becomes of secondary importance. As in every other patient–analyst dyad addressed to this point, factors like those just noted will play out differently with each unique patient. For instance, the fatigued or the preoccupied analyst will be more alert with some patients than with others—Rory may still get near full attentiveness, whereas Hillary and Murray will facilitate their analyst's withdrawal into private concerns. Analysts' self-interest will prevail in either case, because the issue of Rory's entitlement and my wish to keep him as a patient may very well be enacted without being analyzed, and Hillary's and Murray's schizoid retreats may be reciprocated instead of being challenged.

---

* Singer (1971), Basescu (1977), Abend (1982), Prince (1985), Hirsch (1993), Frommer (1994), Leary (1997), Crastnopol (2001), B. Gerson (1996), Pizer (1997), Gartner (1999), Grand (2000), Dimen (2001, 2003), Cole (2002), Drescher (2002), White (2002), Cohen (2003), Blechner (2005a, 2005b), D'Ercole and Drescher (2004), Frank (2005), Newman (2006), Richman (2006), Boulanger (2007), Frawley-O'Dea and Goldner (2007), and Szymanski (n.d.).

I will devote chapters 7 and 8 to addressing the impact of analysts' financial needs on analytic work. Short of extreme crises (Boulanger, 2007; Richman, 2002, 2006) and/or acute illness in the analyst or in an analyst's family (Pizer, 1997), I believe financial needs have more impact on shaping the way analysts work with patients than any other single variable. In my next chapter I give an extended illustration of a patient (Peter) who made it very easy for me to withdraw during a period in my life when I was both sleep deprived by and preoccupied with my two young babies. I knew I was often barely paying attention to my patient, yet I allowed this situation to proceed without sufficiently addressing it with him. He was willing, in an unspoken way, to give me the respite I so wanted. I coasted with his masochistic compliance, and his low expectancies for interest in him, without challenging this and risking losing what was a mutually comfortable equilibrium for both of us, and certainly a very familiar one for Peter. Fatigue related to babies and being preoccupied with loving them reflects something wonderful in analysts' lives, albeit not necessarily something ideal for their involvement with patients. Family illness, or the analyst's illness, is quite a different sort of preoccupation. Though there is significant literature on what analysts should tell patients about illness (e.g., Abend, 1982; Cole, 2002; B. Gerson, 1996; Lasky, 1993; Nachmani, n.d.; Pizer, 1997; Singer, 1971), there has been less said about how health concerns may affect the analyst's presence and level of engagement during the ongoing analytic process.

A couple of years ago I had a bad MRI result, and I thought I might need back surgery. This possibility terrified me, and for the 3 or so weeks when my symptoms were acute, I became highly preoccupied and ruminatively depressed. When with family, friends, and patients alike, I was markedly lifeless, self-absorbed, and disengaged. Of course, my patients wished to be heard, but I barely heard anything beyond my own worried voice. I did not tell any of my patients what was going on, planning to say something only if surgery was required (it ultimately was not). Most of my patients said nothing about any changes in my demeanor they may have noticed (or not noticed). Those who remarked on my manner asked if something was troubling me, or if I was unusually tired. I acknowledged that something troubling was on my mind, but not of life-or-death proportion. I believe that my patients were very generous with me, for no one became angry, or pushed me too hard to speak about what I was clearly reluctant to discuss. Sally, a banker in her late 30s, whom I had been seeing for less than one year, had focused almost exclusively on her mercurial and fundamentally unsatisfying life history with men. I had been, in the transference, the quintessential unavailable man whom she pursued. She had recently begun to date a man who she found interesting, though there were indications that he too was still involved with another woman. She feared that her passion for his exclusive interest would drive him away. This also had been a long-standing pattern in her romantic miseries. My patient desperately wanted from me some useful observations about this question, though I failed to see that this relationship reflected an all too familiar pattern. Fundamentally, I was dysphorically involved with my own worries, and my gaze was inward and not toward my patient. I basically had no idea of how to respond to Sally and her crisis—I was not seeing her very clearly. In my pressure to respond in some meaningful way to her urgent demand for feedback, and conceal my withdrawal from her, I told Sally that it was my impression that she was approaching this romantic relationship as anyone in the early stages of love would, and that this engagement probably did not reflect her characteristic neurotic pattern. My *guess* was dead wrong: The romance crashed, and my patient was justifiably furious at me for failing her. She saw that I missed badly, but was herself too self-absorbed to perceive the factors within me that led me to be as off the mark as I was. Had I been willing to be appropriately exposed to her, I would have questioned why she had not noticed my recent demeanor as exacerbating my place in her life as the quintessential unavailable man. I would have told her that I had no idea about this relationship because I had not recently been attuned to her, and then invited her to respond to this disclosure. I was very conscious that my far greater than normal anxieties and dysphoric preoccupations removed me from Sally in a way that was familiar to her. An opportunity to address this urgent enactment was lost largely due to my choice to perpetuate a selfish comfort in hiding and in efforts to soothe myself.

My sometimes inclination toward hypomanic denial was touched upon in a clinical paper addressing the aftermath of the September 11, 2001, tragedy (Hirsch, 2003b). As noted, after an initial period (3 months or so) of acutely sharing the fears of many of my patients, I stopped thinking about this national and local trauma, and I stopped worrying about subsequent terrorist attacks on my city. A number of my male patients, particularly those who were driven in their careers, also seemed to feel no anxiety. Rather than challenge them about this, I shared in their denial and reinforced their insensitivity and their hypomanic ways. Unfortunately as well, I ignored to a great extent the near surface fears and anxieties of other of my patients. With these patients I professed an unrealistic optimism about our future, uncharacteristically adopting a reassuring stance, and implying that their anxieties were overblown and neurotic. Some of these individuals never had the chance to fully articulate and to explore their fear-laden experience. I had some awareness that I impeded their expressiveness, and did not allow their anxieties to affect me. I was particularly vulnerable to fear with regard to my adult children, who regularly used New York City subways, and I knew that I wanted to disconnect from this as much as possible. With hindsight, I think that I believed that I could not function in my work in the context of consciously experienced fears that related to my concern for loved ones. This state was opposite to the depressive self-absorption I described when my worries centered on damage to my own body. My manic denial about present and future terrorist risks created a comfortable equilibrium with a few male patients who shared this reaction. I did not help them face their anxieties, nor did I help my anxious patients face their fears, because I myself was so intent on making light of them. My failure to see that some individuals who did not lose loved ones were, nonetheless, consciously or unconsciously traumatized by the events of September 11 reflected a lost opportunity for a number of my patients to address significant themes (Boulanger, 2007; Cohen, 2003; Frawley-O'Dea & Goldner, 2007; Gartner, 1999; Grand, 2000; Prince, 1985; Richman, 2006).

Addressing analysts' personal life issues, like the need for income, depression or physical illness, and acute crises, is a delicate matter. As noted earlier, there still exist the remnants in analytic lore that such matters will not make much difference in the analytic work and that patients' transferences will play out in the same way in any "standardly conducted" analysis. I have argued throughout that analyses are never conducted in a standard way, though explication of analysts' selfish interests and other personal qualities that help make each analysis unique is generally underaddressed in psychoanalytic literature (Fiscalini, 1994, 2004; Guarton, 1999; Hirsch, 1993; Wilner, 2000; Wolstein, 1954, 1959, 1975, 1977, 1983, 1997). For example, given the same patient, how can working with an analyst who is lonely and has a spare personal life be the same experience as working with an analyst who is either happily and/or with relative exhaustion dealing with an intensely populated personal life? Similarly, if a patient is one of very few whom an analyst sees each week, and this analyst desperately needs both patient contact and income, this cannot possibly be the same experience as being with an analyst whose clinical schedule is overloaded, who feels overworked, and who has minimal financial worries. In my next chapter I report an extended example about an analytic situation where the analyst feels strong personal commitments that serve to pull him away from patients, especially those patients who are comfortable within the configuration of emotional isolation and being ignored. On the other hand, analysts who are lonely and/or have few intimates in life may readily rely exclusively on patients to satisfy desires for love and attachment. I think of colleagues who have no significant other (and who want one), or have never had children, or whose children are grown and not in intimate touch. Some who are currently alone and lonely may have had a history of strong adult attachments, but their love might be deceased or otherwise gone. It stands to reason that those analysts who have had the least intimate contact, or have gone the longest without it, might provide more loving attentiveness to patients and/or place greater emotional demands on them. Of course, it is possible that analysts in this situation are so conflicted about intimate relatedness that no such issue exists, and actually, the absence of life attachments may parallel a relatively detached analytic demeanor. Clearly, there is no standard formula, though I have observed among some colleagues a tendency to substitute intimacy with patients for loneliness (see Buechler, 2004; Fromm-Reichmann, 1959) in life. Blechner (2005a), on a somewhat different vein, using the publicly hidden homosexuality of Harry Stack Sullivan as a dramatic illustration, has described poignantly the loneliness inherent in analytic work when there is a felt need to conceal fundamental sexual preferences from colleagues and/or patients (see also Blechner, 1993, 2005b; Cole, 2002; D'Ercole and Drescher, 2004; Drescher, 2002; Frommer, 1994, 2006).

I recall the loneliest time in my own adult life. I was in my late 20s, absent a significant romantic relationship, tired of serial dating, and worried that I would never love a woman enough to marry and have children. I worked in the day hospital section of a psychiatric hospital. The patients were mostly young and middle class, and had usually recently been inpatients, based on having had acute psychotic episodes or having made suicide attempts. Sending them home each late afternoon created an atmosphere of general anxiety among the staff, especially the new professional staff like me. One of my earliest patients, Daniel, was a very bright and educated young man who had dropped out of an excellent school and retreated to his family home. His seemingly solid and concerned parents were bewildered by his obsessive ruminations and hard-to-articulate fears. He had regressed and ceased to function in the world in some way that was difficult to diagnose, though he was entirely lucid, was interesting to engage, and functioned very well in the day hospital community. When there, it was hard to distinguish him from the young professional staff, and, indeed, the two of us shared many interests. I felt that in other circumstances we could have been friends, or played basketball together. After 4 or 5 months in day treatment, discharge was being planned, with the hope that Daniel would return to college and finish up the little bit he needed to graduate. In my eyes, at this point he seemed to function at least as well as many of my own friends and colleagues, and I was feeling full of myself for the work I had done with him. It might not surprise the reader that Daniel soon began to regress into an obsessional paralysis, characterized by irrational fears and suicidal threats. He did not wish to leave his family home, his therapist, or the hospital setting. Indeed, he had been so gratifying a patient to me that I was conflicted about his discharge. I felt I was losing a friend at a time when most of my old friends were with their significant others and were less close with me than in our younger years. I believe that I indirectly communicated these feelings to him, and what I was experiencing fit neatly into Daniel's regressive dependency and his reluctance to separate. It had seemed clear that his initial "break" was related to a family configuration where separation was subtly discouraged. Because of his regression, the staff decided to extend his stay. This more regressed version of Daniel was more clingy and infantile than he had been. On weekends and some evenings, he would routinely telephone the hospital's emergency line, and speak of his unbearably acute and free-floating anxiety. I gave him my home telephone to call instead—at the time, my home telephone number and my nascent private office number were the same. I am embarrassed to say that I often welcomed his phone calls, especially on weekends when I found myself at home, alone and lonely. Daniel was regressively dependent, and I desired someone who desperately needed me. I unwittingly encouraged Daniel's phone calls despite *knowing* I should not, and despite this exchange being antagonistic to day hospital policy. I was not yet in analytic training, though the atmosphere in the day hospital was distinctly psychoanalytic, and I myself had recently begun personal analysis. These were the days prior to the existence of terms like *enactment*, though my understanding of the term *countertransference* informed me that Daniel and I were engaged in a way that reflected both my own self-interest and his preferred equilibrium. I *was* conscious of my self-interest, yet rationalized that *he* needed my emergency-based contact.

I suggest that many long analyses,* as well as therapeutic emergencies, are based on a mutual configuration of dependency, and wish for human contact. I have a couple of colleagues whose personal telephone conversations commonly are interrupted by emergency telephone calls from patients. Their patients always seem to have a crisis that must be addressed immediately, whereas this now occurs only rarely with my patients, and with patients of other colleagues with whom I have spoken about this issue. It is possible that the patient populations are different, though I believe that my interaction with Daniel comes closer to capturing the meaning of most of the crises. Two of the colleagues I am referring to are women who wanted families but never married or had children. I want to be clear that I am not suggesting that women analysts without children as a group tend to infantilize their patients, and relate to them as the children they never had. I do observe, however, that in aggregate, the absence of children is often experienced with more sadness by the women I know personally than by men in that same situation. However, I am suggesting that analysts' loneliness, regardless of its source or the gender of the analyst, makes for a greater vulnerability to co-create dependent and crisis-oriented patients, and to blur some of the traditional analytic boundaries. This configuration may be more marked when a particularly lonely analyst also does not have a large practice, and every patient becomes an especially precious object of attachment.

A few years ago I supervised Caren, an analyst in her early 50s who had neither a significant long-term love relationship nor children. Caren had many interests and some close female friends, and I found

---

* I believe that the strongest motive for long analyses on analysts' part is financial need or greed, and this issue will be the exclusive focus of chapters 7 and 8.

her to be warm, personable, of considerable intellect, and strongly connected to psychoanalysis as both a profession and a culture. She not only read seriously but also attended a prodigious number of colloquia, conferences, and workshops; had hired private supervisors for a number of years post training; and was a very active participant not only in institutional committee work but also in a variety of Internet study groups, discussion groups, and listservs. Caren's practice was modest in size, though she did not appear to be strongly motivated by money, or under financial stress. Despite her broad professional base, she did not seem to get very many new referrals, and those patients whom she initially presented to me all had been with her for some time. Caren knew that I worked differently from her, and she professed to want to learn more about working in the immediacy of transference experience, believing that an excess of what transpired with her patients, as an aggregate, focused around external crises and the difficulty in finding romantic partners. Caren stated that she found it difficult to link up her patients' unfulfilled lives with the way they were with her in the analytic playground. Further, she tended to feel accusatory when she pointed to anything that her patients were doing in the transference that was other than expressing pain, hurt, longing, or sadness. Her patients were not asked to examine their overdependence, anger, or conflict about love relationships (see Coen, 1992, 2002). Caren was so empathic with her patients' injured or victimized self states that they rarely were asked to address their unconscious motives for repeating internalized past injuries in their contemporary lives (Greenberg, 1986, 1995; Hirsch, 2003b; Mitchell, 1988, 1997; Singer, 1965a; Thompson, 1950). And, as noted in my report of my ill-fated work with Daniel, Caren was the recipient of many urgent phone calls and requests for extra sessions.

It was not too long into our supervisory work that I suggested to Caren that she may be overly identified with her lonely patients and, indeed, might be providing both them and herself with the mutual nurturing contact otherwise lacking in their respective adult lives. I emphasized that failure to address this as an enactment could be self-serving on her part, and a denial of her patients of the opportunity to find more complex and mature relationships beyond the cloistered analytic dyad. I urged her to examine with her patients how they were conflicted about engaging in the very romantic relationships they believed they simply longed for. I added that such a focus might more readily create separation from Caren and from parental introjects, and begin to provide her patients more of a sense of agency (Frie, 2002; Fromm, 1941, 1964; Hoffman, 1987, 1998; Mitchell, 1988; Singer, 1965a, 1965b) with respect to the repetitive patterns that they orchestrated unconsciously. I shared my story about Daniel, and the potentially insidious impact of co-creating crises and emergencies. I argued that these patients could conceivably be hers for her professional lifetime, and that ultimately she may feel like she had hurt them more than helped them, as I felt with Daniel.

Caren never challenged my observations or disagreed with them, and continued to claim that she wanted to add to her repertoire a way of working with patients similar to my own. The closest she came to disagreement was in her speculation that I may see a very different population of people, perhaps one less damaged and needy than her patients. Indeed, she did see my point about how her loneliness may be a factor in understanding the consistent sort of relationships she found herself engaged in with her patients. I believe that she disagreed with me far more than she acknowledged, and her lack of candor about this was parallel to how avoidant she was in dealing with the angry, stubborn, and willful aspects of her patients. Perhaps Caren *did* wish to work in a different way, but she was certainly persistent in continuing to do what she had done throughout her career. I believe I helped her become somewhat more conscious about the impact she had on her patients, but this way of being with them was so familiar and so comfortable for both her and her patients that nothing really changed as a result of our yearlong supervision. In retrospect, I am sure Caren and I enacted something of what Benjamin (1995) has labeled the "doer and done to" configuration of polarities, and that my polite but critical attitude reinforced for her the idea that loneliness and victimhood occur in tandem.

This example readily leads into the next section of this chapter, one that addresses the impact of analysts' personality and preferred or most comfortable relational states. It is arbitrary to separate situational factors in analysts' lives from the more ongoing features of analysts' personality. Though being embroiled in a young family, illness, exposure to terrorism, and loneliness are all situational, the way each individual negotiates these states is reflective of larger personality issues. Not everyone who needs surgery becomes depressed, withdrawn, and preoccupied, and not everyone who has young children becomes emotionally unavailable to patients. And, of course, all lonely analysts do not use their patients to replace the loved ones who never materialized. However, although each analyst's distinct life situations and personality play out in ways that reflect his or her unique individuality (Wolstein, 1977), analysts' conflicts between self-interest and patient interest are always present.

## Analysts' Personality: Preferred Relational States

The research of Kantrowitz (1992, 1993) suggests that although there is no single analytic personality that can be demonstrated to be better for all patients, or even for patients with particular problem constellations, the analyst's personality nonetheless has impact on the process. Analyses evolve *differently* with different patient–analyst pairings, even if one cannot demonstrate distinctions in the ultimate quality and utility in the process that is based on these matches (Hirsch, 2003a; Slochower, 2003). Crastnopol (1999, 2001) addressed this theme in the context of discussing the esteemed analyst Harry Guntrip's reports of his analyses with Fairbairn and then Winnicott (Guntrip, 1975). In very brief summary, Guntrip claimed to have achieved much insight and self-awareness, including learning how to conduct an analysis himself, from Fairbairn, but was able to resolve a crippling trauma that had led to chronic depression only in his work with Winnicott. Guntrip, elaborated by Crastnopol, pointed to the contrast in temperament and personality between Fairbairn and Winnicott: Fairbairn was austere and intellectualized, and Winnicott warm and nurturing. Guntrip seemed clearly to conclude that one analysis was superior to the other, though even if one were to dispute this, there is little question but that they were as different as were the personalities of his two discrete analysts. Hopkins (1998, 2006) and Goldman (1993) each addressed Winnicott's clinical work in the context of Winnicott the person. Both writers demonstrated repeatedly the difficulties Winnicott experienced with his patients' anger, sadism, and destructiveness. Hopkins and Goldman both indicated that patients whose psyches were characterized by these features (e.g., the well-known psychoanalyst Masud Khan) tended not to be helped to resolve them under Winnicott's therapeutic regimen. The fact that three very prominent analysts—Guntrip, Khan, and Margaret Little (1990) too—have had so much written about their work with Winnicott the analyst and the person presents a rarely opened window into the intersection of analysts' and patients' personalities.

Their reports all clearly seem to indicate Winnicott's preference for engaging in nurturing relationships in priority to challenging and limit-setting ones, though it is difficult to assume that this personality feature, in isolation, was responsible for better or worse analytic outcomes. Indeed, the substantial amount of interpersonal subtlety in each unique dyad cannot be ignored during the effort to understand the ultimate outcome of an analysis. That is, I suspect that many different elements of Guntrip's self states in interaction with those of his two analysts accounted for much of the variance in the respective outcomes. I do not think that one can account for the difference by pointing *only* to Fairbairn's austerity and Winnicott's warmth. I argue that these qualities must have contributed to a very different qualitative experience for Guntrip, but these qualities alone cannot stand as an explanation for relative success or failure in a relationship as complex and multifaceted as an intense analysis. As well, though, Fairbairn's austerity may have intersected with Guntrip's need for nurture in ways that were not helpful; the former's reserve may have been quite helpful to a different needy patient. Because each analytic dyad is so unique, we stand on firmer ground when we identify analysts' preferred and more comfortable relational states than when we draw conclusions or make general statements about what is better or worse in any aggregate way. And, considerably more important even than each analyst's comfortable and most characteristic relational states is the key question of analysts' willingness to abandon equilibrium when this is creating a stagnant analytic process. One way to think about mutative action is in terms of analysts' willingness, when ultimately aware of mutual enactments, to abandon preferred relational states that have created comfortable mutual equilibrium (Buechler, 2002; Feldman, 1997; Levenson, 1972; Mendelsohn, 2002; Slavin & Kriegman, 1992, 1998; Slochower, 2003; Wolstein, 1959), and to expose themselves to being with others in ways that may be both unfamiliar and disquieting.

Indeed, one can say something similar about the distinctly different and competing analytic theories in our field. On one hand, it is often tempting to think that a particular patient will do better with an analyst who subscribes to one or another theory of therapeutic action. That is, one can speculate, for instance, that a patient suffering from early trauma or from deprivation might do best with an analyst representing a Winnicottian (e.g., Winnicott, 1958) or a Kohutian (e.g., Kohut, 1984) point of view, a rigid and repressed but high-achieving individual might particularly flourish with an ego-psychologist (e.g., Lasky, 1993), or an angry and withdrawn patient is likely to respond well to the challenging tendencies of an analyst influenced by the interpersonal tradition (e.g., Singer, 1965a, 1965b). Though there is a certain amount of professional security in being able to make such predictions, I believe that the variable of the unique analyst in interaction with each new patient (Fiscalini, 1994, 2004; Wolstein, 1975, 1977) renders such forecasts irrelevant. Particular theories, like particular personality configurations, lend themselves to particular relational configurations, though analytic benefit can be derived from very different configurations. There is no Freudian or Winnicottian patient—only the unique integration of the range of qualities possessed by each unique analyst and patient, along with the situational variables influencing the analysis, will ultimately tell a successful or a disappointing story about the process. Individual analysts will always resonate to both theoretical positions and personal configurations that are most comfortable and equilibrium creating. How these intersect with each patient, and what is done with these individual or mutual states of equilibrium, will determine the relative success of the analytic enterprise. The analyst who fears anger *can* help a sadistic patient if that analyst is willing to live with the disequilibrium and discomfort of fear, and of embracing his own sadistic self states (Bromberg, 1998, 2006; Davies, 1994, 2004; Stern, 1996b). The lonely analyst who wants patients as children *can* help patients become autonomous, if that analyst is willing to live with even greater loneliness (Buechler, 2004). Analysts' levels of comfortable self-interest always operate in some tension with the best interest of patients, and this conflict exists regardless of any given analyst's personality or preferred theoretical allegiance.

I earlier spoke of Caren, an analyst whose loneliness and whose spare practice made it difficult for her to facilitate her patients' independence and separation, especially with patients who were themselves overly dependent. I also referred to a period of my professional life when I, too, wanted my patient's presence to an extent that I stretched preferred analytic boundaries and helped create malignant regressive experience for him. In this section I emphasize enduring aspects of analysts' personality features, and the inclination to create relational configurations with patients that reflect an attempt to fit comfortably with analysts' preferred self states (Bromberg, 1998, 2006; Davies, 1994, 2004). As already noted, although all analytic process usually begins with patterned unwitting interaction, I suggest that analysts' self-interest may lead to maintaining comfortable and familiar self–other integrations long after consciousness exists. There are many possible examples: Some analysts are comfortable with intense mutual affective involvement—others prefer emotional reserve and distance; some like people to be dependent on them—others feel burdened or trapped by dependency; some enjoy idealization—others are made uneasy when elevated; some feel energized by angry confrontation—others fear patients' and/or their own anger, and prefer to avoid this when possible; and some derive pleasure from sexual flirtation and/or being the object of sexual desire—others are uneasy with their own and/or their patients' sexuality in the analytic space. Additionally, analysts' choice of the variety of possible theoretical perspectives with which to identify is often related to aspects of analysts' personality (Hirsch, 2003a). Two especially stark prototypes of difference, both in terms of which data are most closely examined and in relational style, exist between classical Freudian analysts and colleagues identified with self psychology and with the middle school of object relations theory. Freudian analysts have always emphasized sexuality and rivalry in the transference, view patients' conflictual desires as driving personality, and engage with patients with relative reserve, encouraging, in particular, patients' affective states of sexual desire and aggression. Self psychologists have as their core concept empathic immersion with patients and, like middle school object relationalists, are inclined toward a nurturing stance and toward an emphasis on patients' presexual and baby self states that have been insufficiently gratified (Hirsch, 1987, 1994). The emotional texture and the interpretive schema both are quite at variance between these two prototypes and their respective patients, though it is impossible to say whether allegiance to either is a function of analysts' personality, or related more to situational factors, like where one trained and who was available as a training analyst (Hirsch, 2003a). I suspect, however, when analysts' personality features are in too strong harmony with the biased predispositions of each theory (Feldman, 1997), there is risk that patients could have a limited experience. Identification with one theory or another should not, for instance, lead to avoidance of sexual material, any more than it should lead to excessive analytic coldness or an absence of kindness. However, if a particular analyst is anxious about sexuality *and* prefers a theory that emphasizes the wounds of the deprived infant, there is risk that the emotional equilibrium of the analyst will coast along without concern for the erotic material that is excluded from the transference–countertransference mix. I wish to be very clear that I do not believe that analysts' personalities and/or preferred theories are inherently limiting. In the best of all worlds, analysts become aware of their personal and theoretical zones of comfort, and strive to minimize these as factors of influence on patients. The problem I underscore throughout relates not to limitations of any particular type of personality or theory, but to analysts' conscious choice to perpetuate a comfortable equilibrium and thereby to choose, with some consciousness, self-interest in priority to a more mutually destabilizing patient interest.

Anna had been the most attractive patient I had seen—a combination of physical beauty, comfort with her body and her sexuality, elegance, and a strong wit and intelligence made her exceptionally compelling to me (Hirsch, 1994). Indeed, men found her irresistible, and there was never a shortage of them in pursuit of her. Anna claimed interest in a long-term love relationship, but she was enjoying a very active sex life with a range of very interesting and high-powered men. Everywhere she went, she seemed to find someone. In one instance she had minor surgery, and while in the recovery room she and the chief resident had a torrid sexual encounter. The theme of doctor–patient sex did not escape me, particularly in the context of her vivid and steamy accounts of her invariably quite passionate sexual experiences. There were moments when Anna reported sexual attraction to me, but for the most part I was viewed more like a safe container than an object of desire. I felt like a eunuch in this context, envious and competitive with the charismatic-sounding men who so excited her. I wanted her to feel more sexual toward me, though I tried to affect the position of the neutral, concerned, and benign professional. Along the way Anna met a man who seemed more stable and less dominant and exciting than her other lovers. He was reserved, was not consumed by sexuality, and had a rather nurturing demeanor toward her. I assumed that this relationship had some transference meaning, and my patient confirmed that he reminded her of me in some ways. When she became bored with him and sought out more transient and exciting sex, my interpretive schema emphasized flight from intimacy, tenderness, stability, and the like. Though these interpretations had good basis, my subtext was a preference for the man who was my stand-in, and some relief that I was less in the loser position to her train of charismatic and powerful men. Anna's attraction to this quieter and more passive man reflected her attraction to me, indeed, a choice of me in preference to those toward whom I felt inadequate. This new configuration dovetailed with the part of Anna who recognized some of the problems inherent in the way she had been living, and with her wish, albeit conflicted, of wanting stability and a family of her own after years of "screwing around." Though this could be considered a healthy choice in terms of generic psychoanalytic aims, I did not question her rather abrupt shift in emphasis nearly to the extent I should have. I knew that I felt better about myself in the context of Anna's new relational configuration. Further, I felt important—I had had an impact on her choice to settle down and build a family, a result that had the appearance of psychoanalytic "cure." Although I now felt far more potent than I had earlier in our relationship, I knew at the time that my potency played too large a role in the direction of my patient's life choices. I did rationalize that I was helping Anna with the gift of stability and potential family, and this was also what she wanted to some degree, and I coasted with this expression of self-interest.

Writing of other analysts' expressions of self-interest is less secure, for I cannot possibly know how much consciousness exists in anyone's choices but my own, or perhaps those whom I supervise. Remaining with the theme of patients' sexual interest (or lack thereof) in analysts, I feel comfortable in asserting that most of us would prefer to be the object of desire than otherwise, particularly with patients we ourselves find attractive. To the extent that this is generally true, it becomes difficult to know how much patients' sexual transferences to us are stimulated by our efforts to develop these desires, as was the situation between Anna and myself. There are different ways to try to build sexual desire in patients, though the two most common relate to the power inherent in being the wise, stable, and strong male other, in the context of another person opening up and telling all, and the sometimes profoundly sexual interpretive schema we use in interpreting patients' transferences. In the more statistically normative heterosexual configuration, the older male analyst and the younger or peer female patient illustrate this situation most vividly. In being the strong, silent, and benign male, analysts create a prototype of either what was a loving father–daughter Oedipal situation or what was wished for by a girl who lacked such an ideal relationship. Our flaws and weaknesses are reasonably well concealed behind paternal stoicism, and male analysts become easy and likely objects for heterosexual female patients to adore and to idealize. Individual differences among male analysts notwithstanding, this configuration tends to feel quite good most of the time. I would guess that the more the particular analyst lacks being the object of desire in his personal life, the better it feels to be sexually loved by patients. I think older male analysts can be especially vulnerable here, because advancing age is often correlated with being less sexually attractive. How an analyst tries to make himself the increased object of desire can be hard to pinpoint, for it is so built into a system characterized by one person's strength, concern, and attentiveness, and another's overt dependency and vulnerability. Because of this, it is extremely difficult to determine which patients' feelings emerge naturally from the process, and which from analysts' unconscious *and* conscious efforts to stimulate patients' longings. One can only make inferences from examining the text of other analysts' work, and one can only *know* from the examination of one's own body of analyses. With regard to Anna and me, I knew that I wished for her desire—there was consciousness in this process.

One clue to determining the presence of analysts' efforts to construct patients' sexual desire is to examine the interpretive schema in the text of the analysis. This is, of course, quite complicated, because Oedipal sexuality is central in the theoretical belief system of a major theoretical perspective. How does one determine whether the interpretation of Oedipal sexuality is "accurate," based on the execution of a profoundly old and well-respected psychoanalytic theory, or based on the older male analysts' sometimes desperate wish to be desired by often young and attractive female patients? Patients' acceptance of analysts' interpretations is a poor criterion, because integral to the psychoanalytic configuration is the potential for patients' suggestibility and idealization, possibly the very fabric of the mutual creation of sexual desire as well. In examining text, one can only make a subjective judgment about analysts' intentions, and then not at all be sure if these intentions are unconscious or conscious. Dewald's (1972) report of the text of almost an entire analysis of an attractive young woman reflects an excellent example of this dilemma (Hirsch, 1992; Levenson, 1982). Dewald wrote this volume as an example of how a successful classical analysis plays out, and he was critically acclaimed for this, especially among his theoretically compatible colleagues. In every traditional sense, his patient did well—allegedly resolving internal conflict as it ought to be resolved, settling down and marrying, having children, and so on. Dewald's patient expressed deep gratitude for what he had done for her, just as she had expressed perennial sexual excitement in his presence over the course of their time together. I do not know any heterosexual male who would not have delighted in the graphically described fantasies of adoring fellatio that this beautiful woman conveyed to her aging analyst, very frequently over the course of a number of years. I have quipped among my colleagues that the combination of Oedipal theory and our ability to use this theory to our advantage has prolonged the well-being of generations of older male analysts, no longer desired sexually by anyone except for their idealizing and compliant patients. Indeed, I am cynical about Dewald's motives, and I can only suggest that one read this text to make an independent judgment. However, only Dewald knows whether he was following his theory and had no conscious intention of creating a comfortable and self-interested mutual configuration, or whether he was aware of how much he delighted in the figurative fellatio consistently provided by this attractive young woman. By exposing almost the entire transcript of a complete analysis he performs a service, and makes himself vulnerable in a way that few analysts are willing to do, subjecting himself to the darker interpretations of his work, and his other than purely benign therapeutic motives. However, I argue that close scrutiny of the transcripts of *every* analyst's work will uncover areas of conscious self-interest taking priority over patient interest.

As much as conventional wisdom confirms the logic of one's enjoyment in being the object of sexual desire, or being adored in any way for that matter, it makes comparable sense that being the recipient of anger, contempt, disrespect, and disappointment can be most unappealing. Just because every analyst learns that we must allow for patients' transferential anger to emerge does not mitigate that this is often relatively neglected (Coen, 1992, 2002; Singer, 1965a). Further, I believe analysts quite commonly behave with patients in ways that actively discourage the latter's anger, and both avoidance of addressing anger and preempting this are sometimes engaged with analysts' consciousness. In using the terms *contempt, disrespect,* and *disappointment,* I am identifying particular expressions that I believe are often even more difficult for analysts to absorb than, for example, a state of rage or a burst of criticism. It seems easier to attribute these latter moments either as irrational or as transferential displacements that have little to do with the actual participation of the analyst. Of course, in more contemporary times, characterized by psychoanalysis' relational turn,* it has become more difficult for analysts to ignore their role in the transference, and believe for a moment that patients' anger has *only* to do with projections from the past, and *nothing* to do with the quality of analysts' engagement. Because it is now more difficult to hide behind theories that once characterized analysts as either nonparticipatory blank screens or empty containers for patients' projections, I believe patients' anger, especially in the forms of disrespect, contempt, and disappointment, is more discouraged than at earlier psychoanalytic eras. To the extent that analysts believed that they played no role in patients' negative transferences, such feelings were less likely to touch the person of the analyst, and more likely to be encouraged. Though these very unpleasant feelings were directed toward the analyst, and often quite difficult to tolerate with equanimity, we could always take a step back and reassure ourselves that these are simply patients' projections of introjected bad mothers and fathers. Though this position characteristically avoided analysts' examination of the interactional factors in the here and now encounter, and blurred the examination of the all-important mutual enactments taking place, there was often more space for patients to display ugliness and sadism.

The person of the analyst creates a dilemma for analysis regardless of the theoretical position one chooses. On one hand, at the cost of not examining the transference–countertransference matrix and mutual enactments, analysts are more free to encourage patients to express their more ferociously rageful and hurtful selves to them. On the other hand, when analysts acknowledge to themselves their witting and unwitting participation with patients, there is no way to escape patients' criticism as a more personal expression. It is largely because of this significant theoretical shift that contemporary analysts have

---

* For example, Wolstein (1959), Searles (1965), Singer (1965a, 1977), Levenson (1972), Wachtel (1982), Gill (1982), Greenberg and Mitchell (1983), Hoffman (1983, 1998), Hirsch (1987, 1994), Mitchell (1988, 1993, 1997, 2000), Dimen (1991, 2003), Greenberg (1991, 1995), Davies (1994, 2004), Aron (1991, 1996, 1999), Slochower (1996), Leary (1997), Stern (1997), Bromberg (1998, 2006), Layton (1998, 2004), Pizer (1998), Maroda (1999), Frankel (1998), Frank (1999), Grand (2000), Bass (2001), Berman (2001), Knoblauch (2000), Crastnopol (2002), Cooper (2000a), Fosshage (2003), Seligman (1999, 2003), Safran (2003), Bonovitz (2005), Harris (2005), and Skolnick (2006).

become more likely to attempt to prevent anger, or to fail to address it when it is expressed subtextually. I believe that both these situations exist often with analysts' considerable consciousness, and reflect a choice of self-protection over what is in patients' best interest.

Everything that analysts do in a professional context has both theoretical-conceptual significance and personal significance. In the era of extreme analytic reserve and the hegemony of the blank screen model, analysts' protection of their personal selves was both theoretically sensible and personally protective. The belief that the person of the analyst could almost totally be concealed was integral to practicing analysis in a way that was believed to be most profound and ultimately fulfilling to patients. Analysts were cautioned about being too verbally active, too gratifying, and too expressive of their warmth, lest patients were made to temporarily feel good, instead of engaging in the more profound process of internal conflict resolution. Within this theoretical context, however, personal differences among analysts inevitably emerged. Indeed, some traditional Freudian analysts spoke more than others, and there was a wide range of subtle expression on the warm–cold continuum. This, of course, depended on both individual differences among analysts and each unique analytic dyad. An analyst whose personality was characterized by remoteness and coldness was able to justify this way of being by embrace of a theory that could be understood as compatible with extreme reserve and emotional isolation. If patients were angry because they felt deprived, this could readily be seen as ideal—the way the process is supposed to work. In a sense, it was difficult to conceptualize patients' anger as related to anything but patients' internal states, because analysts were simply operating according to proper technique. As well, analysts were able to avoid self-examination because it was so easy to hide behind proscribed technique, for example, "I'm not cold; I am just conducting an analysis according to standard technique."

The relational turn in psychoanalysis corresponds to the waning of a standard technique.* Though there has been no change in

---

* Thompson (1950, 1952), Sullivan (1953, 1954, 1956), Fromm (1955), Wolstein (1959), Winnicott (1958), Searles (1960, 1965, 1979), Singer (1965a), Levenson (1972, 1983), Maroda (1981), Greenberg and Mitchell (1983), Kohut (1984), Hirsch (1987), Fiscalini (1988), Mitchell (1988, 1993, 1997), Blechner (1992), Ehrenberg (1992), Renik (1993), Greenberg (1995, 2001), Josephs (1995), Satran (1995), Aron (1996), M. Gerson (1996), Stern (1997), Hoffman (1998), Kwawer (1998), Langan (1999), Imber (2000), Wilner (2000), Bass (2001), Fosshage (2003), Seligman (2003), Fiscalini (2004), Ianuzzi (2005), Kuriloff (2005), and Bromberg (2006).

the value of maintaining the basic analytic boundary, analysts are given considerably more leeway in the way patients are engaged, as compared with an earlier era (Hoffman, 1991, 1998). Though there is not a new book of rules, this new analytic culture is, nonetheless, transmitted subtly, through the normal channels of teaching, supervision, and personal analysis (Berman, 2001, 2004; Eisold, 1994, 2000). What is appropriate and inappropriate is viewed relativistically, and notions of clear technique of any sort are eschewed as positivistic and rigid. Though there are certain rules that remain, spontaneity and "throwing the book away" are recommended in dialectical tension with traditional analytic ritual (Hoffman, 1991, 1998). Specifically, there is now great variation in use of the couch versus a face-to-face physical arrangement, and more importantly, analysts are given a wider berth with regard to both the quantity and quality of verbal participation. Whereas analysts of another era were advised to restrict their verbal participation to questions and interpretations, contemporary analysts may be likely to make subjective observations about patients, disclose something about their own personal life, and express their heretofore private feeling states (Bromberg, 2006; Hirsch, 1984, 1995; Tansey & Burke, 1989). Though deliberate self-disclosure of information and of feeling states remains the most controversial dimension of analytic procedure, there is now a wide literature that finds value in its selective use (e.g., Davies, 1994, 2004; Ehrenberg, 1992; Epstein, 1984, 1999; Epstein & Feiner, 1979; Hirsch, 1995; Hoffman, 1998; Maroda, 1999, 2005; Renik, 2006; Searles, 1979).

Just as a particular analyst's remoteness or coldness could be rationalized by the cloak of the blank screen model, the personal desire for engagement and the wish to be loved can be embedded in the adoption of some contemporary interpersonal or relational models. We can be warm, outgoing, and engaging because this is humane and is compatible with current analytic theories of therapeutic action, or we can be this way because we are uncomfortable with patients' anger, dislike, and disappointment. Similarly, analysts can disclose personal information and/or affective states because this is believed to be therapeutically useful at a given moment, or because we fear a patient's reaction to our more withholding stance (Aron, 1996; Gill, 1982; Hirsch, 2003a, 2003b; Hoffman, 1983; Mitchell, 1997). It is safe to say that most things we do may have elements of our own self-interest—doing what is comfortable for ourselves, and what we hope might be useful to patients. Nonetheless, there are many occasions where analysts' self-interest is more heavily weighted, and I believe that efforts to avoid patients' anger, contempt, disrespect, and disappointment reflect common illustrations of this. As well, I believe that a fair percentage of deliberate self-disclosures of both personal data and affective states are motivated by the wish to be seen by patients as warm and/or open, and to garner affection and admiration from them (Aron, 1996).

Walter is a wealthy banker who has overcome a humble background to make a rich and luxurious life for himself and his family. His children go to the best schools, and he has beautiful homes in the city and the country, travels extensively, eats in wonderful restaurants, has excellent seats at major New York sporting events, plays golf at an excellent country club, and more. These aspects of his life are truly rewarding, and he genuinely enjoys them—they are not for show primarily. Walter is very smart and sharply perceptive, and uses this to very good end in business. Unfortunately, he also uses his incisive intelligence sadistically toward his wife and his son. I am afraid of Walter, because I know that he can probably see my every flaw and weakness. I know that he feels far superior to me economically, and that he disrespects the amount of money he pays me, and his calculation of what this and my other fees add up to for me on an annual basis (see Josephs, 2004; Liss-Levinson, 1990; Myers, 2008; Whitson, n.d.). He knows that I'd love to frequent the restaurants he does so regularly, that I'd relish his incredible seats at Madison Square Garden basketball games, and that I envy how much time he takes for both business and vacation travel. However, when I ask him whether his contempt and disrespect for his wife and for some associates generalize to me, Walter demurs. He is likely to tell me how much he respects my choice to use my intellect in pursuit of a profession that is geared to helping people, but a smile crosses his face as he lies to me. When I point to his smile, Walter acknowledges that he knows I must envy his wealth and what it affords him, but that I must have other gratifications from my work that he does not have. He tries hard to not unleash his sadism to me, fearing that it might destroy the entire enterprise. I, too, try to limit his opportunity for anger and contempt. I find that I challenge him less than others, and I am quicker than I normally am to be empathic, or to be easy on him when he reports some dispute with his wife, his son, or a colleague. As well, I am more likely than normal to answer questions he might pose to me, instead of wondering why he is asking, or what *his* fantasy might be. I attempt to gather courage to be more questioning and challenging, believing that he would likely have greater respect for me if I were, and as well that this ultimately would be more analytically useful for him. Despite this awareness, I know that I am prone to be submissive with him and consciously choose to be on his side, and to maintain a degree of sadomasochistic integration. This is not normally my area of comfort, though in this relationship the submissive side of me emerges. In some respects I am reminded of the efforts I made in high school to be the object of interest of my most popular classmates.

I am more likely with Walter than with most other patients to disclose aspects of my personal life. He will ask me if I saw a particular New York Knicks game he had attended, if I had ever eaten in a particular restaurant he just dined at, where I went on vacation, where my kids went to school (we live in the same neighborhood), and, if I have one, where my country home is located. I know that embedded in these questions is Walter's wish for dominance and his competitiveness, though he will admit only to curiosity and to being friendly. Indeed, on the surface he is very cordial and congenial. When I have not answered Walter's queries and instead asked about his motives, he has gently mocked my "standard" analytic attitude, exposing my concealment as more likely either a rigid adherence to technique or personal defensiveness. He reiterates that I am probably self-conscious about all that he is able to do with his wealth, but I need not be, because he knows that my being in this helping profession comes with other satisfactions. I feel silly and exposed at such moments, and am often disinclined to challenge his questions, and I too often take the more comfortable route and answer his questions. If he is going to disrespect me, it might as well be for tangible things like watching basketball on television instead of being there in one of the courtside seats. There is an additional element to my personal disclosures—in some dimensions that he asks about, I do feel superior. Indeed, my kids went to a better private school than his do; I actually know far more about sports than he does, even though I view my games on television; and my country home is far less expensive than his, but it is in an area that is less glitzy and currently is beginning to have even more cultural cachet than where he resides.

Whether I avoid Walter's disrespect, contempt, and disappointment by being less challenging than I should, or by being more self-disclosing and less inquiring, I am often aware that I am choosing to maintain an equilibrium with my patient that is more comfortable than the alternatives that I foresee. This competitive and sadomasochistic relationship is familiar and comfortable for Walter, and though I do not at all like my positioning here, it seems less painful than the upgraded version of what it could be. I am not implying that most attempts at empathy, or the majority of self-disclosures, are motivated by either the wish to be loved and/or a bribe to avoid decimation. I *am* suggesting, however, that analysts' avoidance of patients' anger is a very serious and a ubiquitous current problem in our field. Just because the more overtly engaged and vulnerable contemporary relational or interpersonal analyst is less rule-bound does not make us less prone to rationalize the pursuit of self-interest as expressions of humane and creative technique. Being manifestly warm, giving, caring, and openly disclosing are multidetermined behaviors. Self-interest may play as large a role in such engagement as it did when analysts protectively hid from patients behind an alleged blank screen, because they were advised by their elders to be detached and aloof. I believe that a thoroughgoing psychoanalysis is not possible without patients' examination and transferential expression of hurtful, angry, contemptuous, and disappointed aspects of self-experience (Coen, 1992, 2002; Epstein, 1984, 1999). Because analysts find it more difficult to deny that such expressions are directed to the analyst as coparticipant (Fiscalini, 2004), and not *only* as the patient's internal object, unless the analyst is a masochist, such expressions invariably feel unpleasantly painful. Some contemporary theories of therapy make it easier for analysts to rationalize coasting in mutually giving and generous engagement, while ignoring the darker and uglier side of immediate, here-and-now experience (Coen, 1992, 2002). Those analysts who have the most trouble in dealing with their own and their patients' destructiveness are more prone to adopting legitimate analytic technique in the service of perpetuating comfortable self states in interactions with patients.

## Summary

The conflict between analysts' listening to patients and being influenced by them, and listening to and being motivated by our own private desires, is ubiquitous. The pursuit of self-interest can be compatible with pursuit of patients' interest, but these are often in conflict as well. Analysts' consciousness is the potential solution to such conflicts, though it is naïvely idealistic to expect that consciousness will always be used for the benefit of one's patients. Many conscious choices that analysts make are to the end of maintaining a mutually comfortable and familiar status quo with patients, and though countertransference awareness always offers the potential for productively destabilizing interventions, analysts instead frequently coast with this awareness. In a psychoanalysis enlightened by the two-person, interpersonal, mutually participating analyst of the relational turn, there is no way to take the person of the analyst and the situational features of the analyst's life out of the dyadic equation. It is simply more human than otherwise (Conci, in press; Sullivan, 1953), for the inherently flawed analyst, to both unconsciously and consciously strive for interpersonal comfort and equilibrium. The fact that such conscious strivings are often not in the best interests of our patients does not always deter analysts' selfish engagement. Acute recognition of the extent that pursuit of personal equilibrium guides our invariably flawed personal and professional interactions offers the only hope for analysts to at some point shift toward more uncomfortable ways of relatedness, in order to be more useful to patients.

# 3

# Analysts' Character Structure and the Wish for Emotional Equilibrium

In the late 1970s I vowed to myself to someday write up my confessions related to a few long-term analyses that essentially went nowhere. I knew back then that these analyses failed largely because of my own personal limitations, and how these qualities intersected with the personality structures of three affectively restricted and emotionally isolated male patients in particular. In this chapter I will present one of these experiences in some detail. I sensed at the time that it was not my personality features alone that accounted for my patients' not sufficiently benefiting. More than anything else, it was my lack of resolve to push or stretch myself to get beyond my limitations and to be a better analyst for these men, in the context of external life circumstances that were pulling me away from requisite devotion to my work (Buechler, 2002; Mendelsohn, 2002, 2004; Slavin & Kriegman, 1992, 1998; Slochower, 2003, 2006). As well, the patients I refer to were all too comfortable in relationships that were both affectively stilted and depriving. Fundamentally, I coasted with my countertransferences, and regrettably I was at least partially conscious of this at the time.* As will be illustrated in my description of my work with Peter, this experience played out as it did as a function of my patients' and my own lack of resolve to push beyond a shared personal comfort and equilibrium, in the context of a life situation that made coasting more compelling to me than it otherwise might

---

* I do not imply that I have nothing to confess in my current practice. I am the same person and have the same personal shortcomings, and, needless to say, these qualities and my failure to push beyond them still influence my work. I believe, however, that I now appreciate or embrace more who I am, for better and for worse, and I am currently less likely to engage the way I did back then for quite the duration of an analysis.

have. Only recently, as discussed in chapter 1, have I thought of a meaningful frame within which to place these unfortunate moments and their contemporary corollaries, so that I am not simply "confessing," or implying simply that some of my own personality features are inherently disadvantageous in conducting analytic work.

This frame emerged from my observations of my own and my colleagues' dramatically disparate personal responses to the tragedy of September 11, 2001 (Hirsch, 2003b), referred to in chapter 2, and from Buechler's (2002) discussion of analysts, in sometimes full consciousness, maintaining emotional comfort in priority to being usefully and productively disruptive to stagnant transference–countertransference equilibrium. Though I will focus on particular aspects of my own personality that have dented my analytic work, I do not suggest that there is an ideal personality constellation that optimizes one's potential to be a competent psychoanalyst. I ponder that there might be such a cluster of "good" analyst traits, because some of my own personal qualities appear so counter to what psychoanalysts ought to be like. I conclude, however, in agreement with Kantrowitz (1992, 1993), Crastnopol (1999, 2002), Berman (2001), Buechler (2002, 2004), Mendelsohn (2002), and Slochower (2003, 2006), that fully facing one's shortcomings and willfully struggling to push oneself beyond zones of comfort are more crucial a matter than any particular personal temperament per se. The main locus of this chapter concentrates on the clinical impact of some of my own qualities, summarized very imperfectly with somewhat technical terms such as *emotionally isolated, obsessional,* and *narcissistically self-absorbed.* I address what happens when I and other analysts, with some degree of consciousness, indulge tendencies such as these, and possible consequences that ensue when these qualities intersect with patients who may share these qualities and/or are comfortable living in relationships characterized by mutual disengagement.

As already noted, on September 11 and in the immediate couple of months thereafter, I was as deeply shaken and frightened as most colleagues with whom I talk about such matters. Almost every session with almost all patients had some reference to this event and its aftermath, and I was far more symmetrical than normal for me in my interactions with patients in expressing fear, anxiety, and sadness, as well as opinions about the state of the world. After 2 or so months, I returned to my normal selfish preoccupations and worries, and my sessions with patients contained sparse references to

9/11. Some of my colleagues continued to remain at a high level of anxiety and shared with me that feelings related to 9/11 continued to take up considerable space with their patients in sessions. This difference was highlighted dramatically on the first anniversary of the trauma, when I had nary a thought about this, and my patients as well made hardly any reference to fears or to the significance of the day. In stark contrast, a female colleague shared with me how many feelings and fears the anniversary stimulated in her, and how virtually all of her patients were similarly very expressive in their respective analytic hours. In my paper (Hirsch, 2003b), I questioned whether my colleague saw such different patients, or whether my own inclination toward emotional isolation, compartmentalization, and narcissistic self-absorption led me to not recognize certain feelings in my patients and/or inhibit them from displaying such feelings to me. Of course concluding the latter, I reflected upon whether these characteristics of mine and my relative comfort with them did not run counter to what we analysts are supposed to do: help people feel all of their feelings, be attuned to all our own affective states, be open to receiving patients' split-off feelings, and empathically immerse ourselves in both gross and subtle expressions of patients' affects. I recalled the analytic failures I have referred to already and other more contemporary situations of a similar kind. It became quite clear to me that I have not always tried hard enough to push beyond these same traits (e.g., compartmentalization, emotional isolation, and self-absorption), and that my reluctance to do so has intersected with somewhat similar qualities in some patients. My tolerance for this kind of interaction, I saw, has been instrumental in current and past analytic impasses and/or failures, though at times when I chose disequilibrium and pushed beyond personal comfort, my awareness of such characteristics and the relationships structured by them has proven beneficial to my patients. As counterintuitive as it may appear, I believe that any personal quality in the analyst has the potential to be either fruitful or harmful to analytic work. This depends largely on whether this quality is indulged, or efforts are made to stretch oneself to areas of discomfort, thereby serving to potentially expand the analytic relationship.

Buechler (2002) wrote of analysts' schizoid qualities in particular, and how the inclination to emotional retreat is ever present, especially in tandem with patients who are also comfortable with emotional distance. She argued that analysts' comfortable and familiar schizoid retreat can be overcome only by analysts' full awareness and willful resolve.* Again, as noted in the previous chapter, Crastnopol (1999, 2001) contrasted Guntrip's analyses with the emotionally isolated and intellectualized Fairbairn and the nurturing and spontaneous Winnicott. She concluded, as did Guntrip, that the former analysis was less helpful largely because both participants were too comfortable with reserved and obsessional forms of relatedness. Indeed, Fairbairn did not seem to make sufficient effort to be with his patient in ways that were mutually unfamiliar and destabilizing, though there is no evidence that he was conscious of his having held back. Crastnopol noted that although Winnicott proved a good match for Guntrip, he had serious problems with other patients, especially those who were aggressive and emotionally destructive (see also Goldman, 1993; Hopkins, 1998, 2006). Kantrowitz (1992, 1993), Crastnopol (1999, 2001), Berman (2001, 2004), Slochower (2003, 2006), and I (Hirsch, 2003b) all concluded that there is no single ideal analytic personality, though some patient–analyst matches can be more easily facilitating for both parties. Note that although Winnicott found it easy to be sensitive to Guntrip's dependency longings, it was harder for him to be present when confronted with other patients' violent affect. In the latter, in order to be a useful analyst, Winnicott (see Goldman; Hopkins, 1998, 2006) would have needed to make a conscious effort to do what was destabilizing for him (Mendelsohn, 2002; Slavin & Kriegman, 1992, 1998) and for his patients. Invariably, this was more difficult and effort full than what Guntrip seemed to require from him in order to be helped. This issue of match is further complicated by the likelihood that in each analyst, multiple self states exist (Bromberg, 1998, 2006; Davies, 1994, 2004), and, despite dominant personality features, no analyst is simply comprised of a singular and exclusive self (Stern, 1996a, 1996b, 1997). Different patients seem to evoke different dominant self states within each unique analyst. For example, though I tend to be self-absorbed, I am hardly that way at all with some patients. Someone who is overtly angry, challenging, seductive, or otherwise quite engaging may stimulate my rapt attentiveness and engagement over much of the course of the analysis. Whether this intensity of relatedness is entirely productive is a matter that would require extended discussion. I am certain, however, that we can never be in a mutually comfortable analytic relationship

---

* Buechler (2002) used the term "effort fullness."

for an extended period without this indicating that something disquieting and potentially destabilizing is being avoided (Levenson, 1983, 1991). Even in analyses that appear to be going quite well, analysts' effort to deconstruct familiar equilibrium is called for. Such an effort is inevitably in conflict with analysts' self-interest in remaining comfortable in the therapeutic dyad.

The personal qualities that Buechler (2002) addressed in highlighting the significance of analysts creating effort fullness bear some similarity to what I struggle with. I am all too familiar with engaging affectively isolated patients in ways that are safe emotionally and comfortable for both of us. Slochower (2003) suggested that regardless of one's personality, there is inherent conflict between analysts' and patients' self-interest around the issue of attentiveness to self and to other. Maroda (1981, 1999, 2005) argued that analysts invariably pursue self-interest, and that such pursuits have potential to be either helpful or harmful to patients. Analysts with the full range of personality characteristics are continually in conflict between the desire to enact self-interest and the desire to live up to analytic ideals (Slochower, 2006). As noted, it is inherently difficult, throughout an entire day, to listen seriously, be emotionally involved and caring, and suspend personal desires. However, this is obviously harder for some analysts than for others, and with some patients more than others. Indeed, for analysts who tend toward emotional isolation and self-absorption, attenuated and engaged listening to another can be especially conflictual. Some degree of boredom is inevitable in analytic work, though analysts' indulgence of attenuated boredom reflects a failure to address some of the very qualities in patients that they pursue analysis in order to resolve. Though boredom can be painful, it can also lead to analysts' extended comfortable and self-soothing reveries, an essential abandonment of and withdrawal from patients. Most analysts can identify in their clinical experience moments and/or periods of not listening, listening with one-half an ear, or otherwise behaving robotically, affectively engaged more with self than with other. If this particular type of engagement reflects a comfortable fit for a particular patient, or this patient is masochistic enough to expect very little, such coasting can become patterned and develop into the normative way of engaging in any given analytic dyad. That said, analysts with personality configurations characterized by schizoid or narcissistic withdrawal are more prone to fully dive into this sort of mutual enactment.* If, for instance, this same hypothetical patient becomes angry or overtly dissatisfied, or perhaps threatens to quit, it is likely that the analyst's coasting will convert to rapt attentiveness. There is nothing like threat of failure and/or loss of income to break a stagnant enactment or a comfortable long-term equilibrium between patient and analyst (this factor will be addressed in detail in chapters 7 and 8). Ideally, it is the analyst who is willing to take the emotional risk of disturbing mutual equilibrium, though patients' own self-interest often leads to productive disruptions in stagnantly patterned engagements.

I want to underscore that *effort fullness*, or lack thereof, refers to participations of the analyst that are characterized by consciousness. I am *not* addressing mutual enactments per se, though I have written about them elsewhere (Hirsch, 1993, 1996, 1998a). Central to mutual enactments is analysts' unconscious or unwitting participation with patients. What I am writing about here is the situation in which the analyst continues to engage in a mutually comfortable equilibrium even after the nature of an enactment becomes consciously known to the analyst. The following clinical illustration speaks to this theme directly, that is, the indulging of countertransference, in the form of affective isolation and self-absorption, to the considerable detriment of the analytic process. Though this is safely taken from my practice over 25 years ago, as I already noted my interaction with this patient reflects themes with which I still actively struggle.

## Clinical Illustration

I began to see Peter during the period when both of my children were born, and I was both very in love and immersed with them, and tired from sleep deprivation. I was in analytic training, new to full-time practice, and worried about all the money it would take to raise two kids in New York City. He paid my highest fee and came three times weekly, and I felt lucky. Peter, a Caucasian man some 10 years older than me, had been recently pushed out of his investment banking job, where he earned enough money to never need to work again. He

---

* Implicitly, analysts with other characteristics have their own reduced thresholds for readily enacting different transference–countertransference configurations, and as well remaining comfortable within these mutually constructed integrations.

was very alone, had no close friends or family (he was raised in the Midwest), and was looking to change his life in the direction of the arts, which he loved and thought provided opportunity to meet gay men. Peter was closeted, and his only sex was with young African American men whom he would meet in the artistic and fashionable neighborhood where he lived, or at one of a few local jazz bars where he'd spend each night. He would get drunk every night and hope to be loose enough to meet someone, though he hooked up only infrequently. Most of his sex was paid for, and this was not frequent.

Peter was tall, slender, baldish, and very tight, inhibited, and conservative in appearance. I did not find him esthetically, much less sexually, appealing. He spoke in a stilted manner, and though very smart and cultured, he was not colorful. His aim was to come out sexually, loosen up socially, find a real lover, and get involved in some arts-related business venture.

Peter was the youngest of two—his older brother was also smart, but outgoing and athletic. Peter was very close to his mother, realizing in therapy that his father never really liked who Peter was, and his father felt far more affinity for Peter's brother. Father was a successful, athletic, and handsome man who seemed to try, but never was able, to warm up to Peter. Mother was very protective of Peter, and they were very much in synchrony until late high school, when he began to take his distance and become emotionally estranged, as he did eventually to all in his family. He did brilliantly in school and quickly succeeded on Wall Street, despite the absence of male camaraderie usually so integral to functioning in that subculture.

It was obvious from the beginning that Peter was sexually interested in me, even though it was difficult for him to speak about such feelings freely. He was, however, very cooperative as a patient, speaking openly about his barren current life, his life history, and his dream life. Despite his obvious involvement, for some time I could not warm up to him, or really like him—he was stilted and dry, and spoke in a monotone. It took some time to recognize how much my response to him paralleled that of his father. In today's parlance, Peter and I enacted that relationship. I also was somewhat uneasy with his sexual interest in me, not so much that it was homosexual, but that it was paradoxically obvious and very secret or private. Another gay man, with whom I worked at the same time, would be openly provocative, teasing, and flirtatious, and I found this a lot easier. Peter's dreams captured something important—they were long and extremely detailed. I'd record them in writing with rigor, though we rarely got anywhere. It took so much time to relate these dreams that the details took priority while the affective meaning got lost in the ground. In retrospect, his dreams were both a form of compliance and a display of his schizoid character—the content was boring and probably almost irrelevant.

Peter was pleased to be with me—I started off very challenging, and he felt attended to. By the time I lapsed into my more withdrawn self state, aided by baby-stimulated sleep deprivation, he had connected with me as a seemingly interested and exciting other. I was the only consistent person in his life—indeed, the man with whom he believed he had been the most open and close. He asked for very little beyond my physical presence, and did not seem to notice how disengaged I could get, and how often I felt drowsy and/or drifted away. It did not seem to matter, for instance, that we never made much of his dreams. I sometimes looked forward to his presence as a respite from others who demanded more of me—he was to me a pressure-free patient. Peter was comfortable with this—it was familiar from his relationship with his father. At the same time, in his frame of reference, it was intimate. His much disowned dependency was lived out with me, and he enjoyed experiencing some of what he had known with his mother (minus the overt symbiosis), and longed for with his father and brother. The two of us created equilibrium—I was well paid and adored, and he came at the times most convenient to me. He let me take respite from my demanding life and sink into a self-absorption that was familiar to me. I never considered myself a particularly exploitive person, but I knew that I was engaging Peter at about 50% of my capacity. I rationalized that this was all he could integrate, but I knew otherwise—I was not pushing myself to be sufficiently present for him. Further, I fantasized seeing him for many years, and there were moments when I envisioned him as a loving uncle to my children (I had no siblings) and their benefactor in case I died.

We did do some meaningful analytic work. I recognized that my failure to find him appealing lined up well with his father's sentiments, and the impact of his relationship with his father and brother became clear to him. He became quite aware of how his identification with his mother negatively affected his father and brother, and how he needed emotional distance to escape the pain of this, as well as to flee from symbiosis with his mother in order to make his way in the world. It became evident that feeling the press to distance himself on one hand, and not feeling loved on the other, helped teach him to sustain himself in the context of a spare and private life characterized by few felt needs. Peter and I had an equilibrium—I was the best he had in the way of a man, yet was similar enough to his father and brother for me to be familiar to him. He could long for me without getting lost in a maternal symbiosis. And so he stayed with me, lonely but less so.

I had my emotional equilibrium, some economic security, low personal demand, and enough useful input so that I didn't feel compelled to confront fully what I was doing. I worked far too much in the extratransference, for if I did otherwise I would have had to be more affectively present and address the long series of transference–countertransference enactments of his compliance, unfulfilled longing, being insufficiently loved, dependence without mutually felt passion, and schizoid equilibrium. I would have had to risk losing him either by his getting better and finding someone else to love, or by his facing fully the deficiencies in our relationship and his justifiable anger at me for my large part in this. Peter was masochistic and expected very little from relationships with men, and he feared attachment with women. He was able to maintain himself with only the bare minimum of human contact. He had enough money and enough interests, and did not need to force himself out of his self-enclosed world. He was depressed, but used to this. He loved jazz, stayed up all night drinking at jazz bars, and was excited by the unlikely prospect of a sexual encounter. He slept for part of the day, visited me, monitored his investments, and pursued a few potential entrepreneurial opportunities. With my presence in his life, albeit at only a percentage of my capacity for engagement, Peter, by his own criteria, had it pretty good. From his conscious perspective I was interested in him, and my many lapses in engagement were so much a part of his landscape that they did not appear to register. He was comfortable and willing to stay with me while making minimal progress in his personal life and his sex life. Peter was most uneasy with any form of overt affective intensity and dependency, and our manifest tepid connection seemed just the right temperature for the two of us.

After 8 years together, Peter developed a number of interesting businesses, and his life got more rich and busy. I became less important to him, and he began to acknowledge that the "relationship" part of his life had shifted minimally. His ardor for me gradually faded, and he got colder, but never really madder. I was too cowardly to confess to him what I believed had transpired—I even feared he might sue me. My practice was developing reasonably well, and I needed Peter less. Our history seemed too deeply grooved to overcome, and I did not fight to keep him, urging him to accept my referral to a colleague who I told him could likely take him further. He never took my referral, and I never heard from him again—our goodbye was very restrained. I phoned him a few times in the ensuing years, but he never called back. It has been over 20 years since I have seen him, and I do not think that he ever returned to therapy. He would now be in his mid-70s, but based in part on how much he smoked and drank and how alone he was, I doubt that he is still alive.

## Discussion of Clinical Illustration

I think this is about the worst I've done in an extended treatment, though certainly there have been other experiences that approximate this, and even successful clinical outcomes where for periods I engaged (and still do) like I did with Peter. Given my inclination toward emotional withdrawal, compartmentalization, and narcissistic preoccupation, it takes considerable effort to deal with the inherent conflict between attending to my own preoccupations and those of my patients. That effort is made with varying degrees of success, and it is hardest when the equilibrium of affective distance is comfortable for my patients, or if these individuals expect little from human interaction. I firmly believe that everyone who enters therapy wishes to change, even though leaving behind internalized self–other configurations is always powerfully conflictual, inevitably creates disequilibrium, and challenges stable adaptations. People like Peter who are embedded in their profoundly schizoid compromises, and who feel unentitled to be loved, find transference–countertransference enactments like I described above all too easy to endure. It is often so-called difficult or borderline patients, those who demand a great deal or who become readily outraged, who pull me out of my withdrawn proclivity. Sometimes I am too frightened to dare to retreat, and I am able to maintain intense alertness and presence. This is also characteristic of me with patients who, despite certain problems, were deeply loved in their life and, indeed, feel quite entitled to be loved and attended to. They often engage me in ways that are so alive and vital that my self-interested desires for narcissistic withdrawal are barely present. It is actually often more interesting to be with them than with myself. This also can be true with female patients who are flirtatious and toward whom I am attracted. I always intend to address these themes in the transference, and when I do, this only makes these situations more alive, and the time passes very quickly.

I have developed over the years some antidotes with patients whose personalities and internalized configurations resemble Peter's. This has helped me wrestle with my indulgence of boredom that translates into an inclination to self-interested retreat. For one, I totally stopped using the couch sometime during my work with Peter. Without someone looking me in the eyes, the invitation to retreat had been far greater. I avoid telephone sessions as much as possible, for these represent golden invitations for withdrawal. My most valuable antidote to withdrawal is my increased commitment to work in the here and now of the transference–countertransference matrix (Aron, 1996, 2005; Friedman, 1988, 2006; Fromm, 1964; Gabbard, 1995; Gill, 1982, 1983, 1984; Greenberg, 1986, 1995; Hirsch, 1987; Hoffman, 1983, 1987; Jacobs, 1991, 2001; Levenson, 1972; Mitchell, 1988, 1993; Renik, 1993, 1995; Searles, 1965, 1979; Singer, 1965a, 1968, 1977; Stern, 1997, 2004). I had always subscribed to this in theory, but since the days of Peter I have been more committed. One of my principles is to say something about the state of an interaction whenever I feel bored and/or drifting. I push myself to do this, though even this measure is certainly not successful in preventing my withdrawal on many occasions. Aside from the variables of my own and my patients' personality configurations, there are always situational factors (e.g., fatigue, time of day, personal problems and worries, or too demanding a work schedule) that play a role in narcissistic retreat. I am motivated by guilt—guilt in relation to Peter and others who I failed. I make mental lists of the patients from whom I most withdraw, whom, parenthetically, are often making the least progress. I highlight these people in my mind, and I vow to try to come more alive with them by addressing the very issues or adaptations that have led to mutual affective deadness. My success is varied, made easier or more difficult by the large and small slings and arrows of my everyday life.

The concept of "work ego" (Schafer, 1983) is relevant here, though I do not believe it fits every analyst well. Schafer referred to the inescapable conclusion that psychoanalysts as an aggregate have at least as many unresolved conflicts and personal limitations as do the educated population on the whole (Racker, 1968; Searles, 1960, 1965, 1979; Singer, 1965a, 1965b, 1971; Sullivan, 1953, 1954; Thompson, 1950, 1952; Wolstein, 1954, 1959). He suggested, however, that analysts can often give the best of themselves to their work; therefore, the quality of what is affectively given to patients may transcend the limitations of other private, personal attachments. Even though personality displays a great deal of consistency over time, different aspects of our multifaceted selves emerge in different personal contexts (Bromberg, 1998, 2006; Davies, 1994, 2004; Stern, 1996a, 1996b). Therefore, a particular analyst, for instance, who is emotionally withdrawn in his or her personal life may find emotional safety in the structure and in the boundaries of the analytic situation, allowing the emergence of strong affective involvement. Parenthetically, for some analysts who are too intense in their personal lives, the analytic spacing may help create useful affective modulation. In fact, for such analysts, the couch may prove a great advantage in their work. As it is impossible to write, theorize, or work independent of one's own person (Hirsch, 2003a), Schafer himself and others whom he knows personally, indeed, may have professional relationships that far transcend in quality their relations outside of the work space. For myself and for others, however, perhaps many male colleagues in particular, the inherent boundary of the analytic situation makes it easier to withdraw—easier for me than is the case in my family life in particular. Though my affective involvement clearly varies from each unique patient to each unique patient, what I expend emotionally in my immediate family, on balance, leaves *less* for my patients. I believe that the concept of work ego would hold for me were I estranged from my family, or had never remained in a long marriage and had children. For one who has developed personal characteristics that lean toward the inward and affectively reserved end of the continuum, personal demands in any one walk of life usually raise conflict, and expectancy of intense emotional presence in both the love and the work dimensions is never easy.

It may appear paradoxical that one who is quite self-absorbed would pursue a profession where personal presence is so warranted and, once professionally engaged, experience such conflict about what seems so naturally called for. I believe this can be accounted for in two ways. For one, the traditional description of the role of the analyst is one that is close to a detached scientist, initially a "blank screen," though more recently a participant–observer, observing participant, or thoroughly subjective other. Even when exposed to contemporary two-person models, many young analysts-to-be enter the profession believing that their subjectivity will be used only to understand the patient and to illuminate the analytic interaction. Or, on the other hand, others believe that qualities like caring, kindness, and empathy are central, and that indeed they have an abundance of these qualities to give to patients. Fewer individuals enter the field with the anticipation that they will be pulled to engage affectively and *unpredictably* (Stern, 1990, 1996a, 1997)—that is, that they will be drawn into a relationship in ways that they can never anticipate, and that the entire range of their personal qualities will emerge at some time or another in the context of clinical work. Most young analysts do not yet recognize that *technique* accounts for only a percentage of what we do, and that the technical aspects of interpreting, inquiring, empathizing, holding, and containing are background, and the easiest part of analytic work (Levenson, 1983, 1991). One can do technique without being affectively involved (and this is often the case), though the analytic work will likely not bear fruit. A second way to account for emotionally isolated people like myself entering this field is to posit that there exists a hope that being a psychoanalyst will either be helpful in making us less schizoid, or provide us with relationships in lieu of having significant others outside of work. The former motivation emphasizes analysts' striving to fix themselves through engagement with patients (Searles, 1965, 1979; Singer, 1971), and the latter, a way to deal with loneliness (Buechler, 2002, 2004; Fromm-Reichmann, 1959). Any conscious or unconscious motive for doing analytic work can be either harmful or helpful to patients. What is most central is analysts' striving for self-awareness in the context of their work, and the effort to push beyond states of comfortable equilibrium to states of disruption and surprise (Eisold, 2000; Hoffman, 1987; Levenson, 1988, 1991; Stern, 1990, 1997). This is most decidedly what I did not do in my work with Peter.

To summarize, three factors that determine the degree of analysts' engagement or disengagement are the analyst's personality configuration (Crastnopol, 1999, 2002; Kantrowitz, 1992, 1993), situational factors and/or enduring circumstances in the analyst's life,* and the nature of the patient–analyst mix. For a basically moral or ethical analyst to conduct long-term analytic work with the absence of sufficient effort, as I perpetrated with Peter, all three factors are likely to be strongly influencing the process. However, for myself and for many colleagues, the inherent conflict between paying attention to oneself and to others is ubiquitous (Slochower, 2003, 2006), and the press of strong situational factors need not be present in order for us to consciously remain inattentive to patients for brief or perhaps extended moments in the analysis. I will illustrate with more contemporary clinical situations.

Ralph began analysis at the behest of his wife, who threatened to leave him if he continued to be as withdrawn, withholding, and emotionally isolated as he had been for most of their marriage. Ralph acknowledges that his wife's complaints have good basis, and ever since he can remember he has been someone who prefers solitude, and who has eschewed overt displays of dependency. Nonetheless, he claims to love and to value his wife, and fears he will deteriorate into a depressed recluse without her. He makes efforts to engage her, but usually lapses back into his normal privacy. Ralph works as a research scientist in a laboratory and is highly skilled, respected, and accomplished. His work is impeded by the presence of other people, usually students or technicians whom he supervises. He not only dislikes this dimension of his work, but also recognizes that he is an impatient teacher, regularly leaving his charges with only the sparsest counsel and direction. Like his wife, they feel starved by Ralph, who in turn feels grateful that he has no children to cope with. My patient has few friends, and generally puts off those few whom he has, as well as his family members, by notoriously failing to return phone calls and e-mails. Though he has a very active sexual interest, Ralph prefers masturbation and pornography to having sex with his wife. When confronted with her sexual frustration, he claims low libido and/or depression, not telling her about his preference to have sex with himself or with Internet photos. Because Ralph is anxious about being left by his wife, in analysis he tries to reflect on his life as

---

* Singer (1971), Becker (1973), Prince (1985), Hoffman (1987, 1998), Blechner (1993), Hirsch (1993), Frommer (1994), B. Gerson (1996), Pizer (1997), Gartner (1999), Grand (2000), Cole (2002), Drescher (2002), White (2002), Cohen (2003), D'Ercole and Drescher (2004), Newman (2006), Richman (2006), Boulanger (2007), Frawley-O'Dea and Goldner (2007), and Szymanski (n.d.).

part of an effort to change, at least to some extent. He speaks of his father's withdrawn demeanor with his children, in contrast with his celebrity and gregariousness in his work and social life. Ralph refers to his mother's extreme unevenness of mood as a way of explaining how he learned to play it safe and withdraw, rather than try to predict if he will encounter his nurturing mother or his enraged and dominating mother. With some pride, he describes how early he developed self-sufficiency.

Ralph is cordial to me, and speaks openly of how difficult it is to visit me and come up with things to say. He acknowledges that he does not want to tell me everything that is on his mind, speak about sex in particular, or make transference observations about me. He'd rather not come at all, or, if here, he'd prefer to sit quietly and not succumb to the external pressure he feels to talk and to "relate." He speaks at a very low volume, and I often ask him to repeat himself. He agrees that he is profoundly passive-aggressive, having heard this accusation from his wife and from siblings. Although Ralph makes an effort (or doesn't) to be present with me, I am in a constant struggle to pay attention to him. When he is especially quiet or speaking without affect, I tend to become bored and drift off into my own private reverie. Though it is possible to construe that the content of my self-absorbed reverie is informatively related to my patient's unconscious (Ogden, 1994), I do not think that this is often the case. Instead, I believe what links me and Ralph is the *fact* that we both tend to take advantage of opportunities to engage in the context of a withdrawn privacy, and to stay there unless chased out. I often allow what in retrospect usually seems like too much silence, for I am tempted toward passive-aggressive retaliation, while at the same time finding some solace or satisfaction in my private preoccupations—in being left alone. When Ralph is speaking too softly for me to hear everything, I sometimes do not stop him. I might allow him to continue, and not listen to some of what he is saying. Because, metaphorically and literally, he prefers masturbation to sex, Ralph may or may not know that I too am withdrawn, but either way he is largely more comfortable when both of us are at least relatively disengaged. He makes little demand and is easy for me to be with as long as I nourish myself with my own reverie. To break this configuration, I must be "on him" pretty constantly—challenging and confronting his passive-aggression, conscious withholding, and withdrawal. I feel more satisfied when I am doing this, though I do not find it easy to maintain this kind of engagement on a consistent basis. Were I seeing Ralph at the same point in my life that I saw Peter, I am certain that I would be making less effort to engage than I now do. That said, Ralph is so inviting of retreat and retaliation that I too frequently take advantage of his withdrawal by engaging my reciprocal self-absorption. Ralph's schizoid embeddedness makes this so easy for me, and indeed, this equilibrium is the point of maximum comfort between us.

Jill and Alan, both of whom presented with strong and urgent symptoms, were more conflicted about maintaining a mutually isolated equilibrium, and elicit(ed) greater degrees of guilt in me when I withdraw(ew) affectively from them. Jill, my age exactly (early 50s when we began), was a moderately successful artist, married, with two young and troubled adult children. She suffered from insomnia and chronic stomach, head, and joint pain, much of which was medically believed to be a combination of hysteria and psychosomatics. Jill linked all of this to a history of egregious sexual abuse perpetrated by her biological father, between ages 6 and 11. These memories had been dissociated and recovered in the context of a psychotherapy experience a few years earlier. She believed that she needed a more psychoanalytic experience to help her work through these discoveries, and of course to alleviate the symptoms that so impeded her life and her experience of pleasure. Despite this history of the most egregious sexual abuse I had ever encountered personally, Jill reportedly had a reasonably satisfying sex life in the context of a stable marriage, and produced a noirish visual art that did not sell for much money, but was critically well received in her circles.

Jill initially believed I was an ideal analyst for her, for she perceived my reserve as similar to that her authoritarian father, and she reported a strong sexual attraction to me from the time of our first contact. Throughout our work together she noted the prominence of sexual fantasies related to me, though it took her some time to explicitly tell me what they consisted of (they were not violent, and were quite mutual). Both of us recognized quite early in our work that Jill's interest was incestuous, and that she was tempting me to cross the line, while simultaneously hoping I would not. She dressed tastefully, though quite provocatively—all of her skirts and dresses were at least a little too short for her age, and her blouses and sweaters often either tight or low cut. Other than this, her demeanor was shy, reserved, and demure, and her manner did not otherwise feel flirtatious or sexually provocative. Though a reasonably attractive woman by whatever criteria one might apply, I never felt sexual desire for her, nor did I feel sexually stimulated by her short skirts and low-cut blouses. Further, though Jill was very smart and literate, did interesting cultural things, and had a very compelling life story, I did not find her interesting, nor did I especially look forward to our meetings. She spoke very softly and with inhibition, and her affect was usually dissociated from the content of the dialogue. This was especially marked when she recalled her memories of sexual abuse, and her childhood terror and adult rage toward both parents. Often on those occasions, but also when she addressed more quotidian matters, I found myself drowsy and struggling to maintain attention. I came closest to literally falling asleep with Jill more so than with anyone else I was seeing at the time or, for that matter, for quite some time. She sometimes pointed out my lack of presence and/or my looking "out of it," but always in a disappointed though gentle manner. I experienced considerable guilt, and we talked about my sleepiness as a representative facsimile of her dissociation while being sexually assaulted by her father. That is, Jill believed that the dissociative way she coped with years of genital, anal, and oral rape was by mentally disappearing from her situation—not literally sleeping but otherwise being in an altered state. My projectively identifying with this experience made considerable sense to both of us, but my disconnection did not cease despite this mutual awareness. Selfishly, and in an effort to make myself more alive, I encouraged Jill to be more expressive with her anger and more explicit about her sexual fantasies toward me. She found this difficult and had limited success with this, though I do believe she tried.

On one hand, Jill and I had an equilibrium—she felt her incestuous sexuality in the context of someone who was no danger to violate her boundaries, and I felt like the object of powerful sexual desire in the eyes of a woman whose idea of a positive male–female relationship was something akin to "Do no harm" (Jill's husband was quite passive and allowed her to control their personal and sexual lives entirely). I felt that by not sexualizing her, I was being a new and good object, though I also knew that I was seriously abusing Jill by my retreat from her. I was not violent like Jill's father, but I watched her being neglected (by me) like her mother. Sometimes writing off her father as criminally insane, Jill felt more anger toward the mother who let her be raped for years on end. Though these transference–countertransference enactments were

discussed repeatedly and in detail, I never managed to become sufficiently alive and interested while with her. Jill left analysis after 3 years
for this very reason. She felt pleased that she had been able to speak
very explicitly about her profound trauma, to embrace the part of her
that wished that I would repeat the criminal boundary violations of
her childhood, to identify with her father's incestuous sexuality in the
transference, and to experience her hatred for her parents and toward
me for all of her egregious abuse and neglect. However, Jill's hysterical
physical and psychosomatic symptoms did not abate, nor did she feel
that she had had a healing experience with me.

Jill associated an active and passionate involvement with a man
as having no end other than violent incest in deed or in thought.
There was little danger with me, for despite her sexual provocation,
I was never interested. Unfortunately, I never helped her experience
my passionate interest in her in ways other than the sexual dimension either. Though she grew to feel safe with me, she did not feel
enhanced by me. Jill did not evoke in me the interest and passion
of one who has received unselfish love from caretakers. She wanted
more than safety, and I failed to push beyond this equilibrium of
safety, even as I was conscious of not being optimally present for Jill.
I was able to get away with my comfortable state of affective isolation, hoping that my patient would do something to bring me more
to life. As noted, I would even ask her to help me engage with her.
Of course, this was not her place—I was the one responsible for the
requisite effort fullness to engage in ways that proved not natural for
me in this context. At the time I felt that I *could not* get myself to a
state of greater presence, but in retrospect I feel that I *did not* make
sufficient effort. Indeed, I feel considerable guilt about not giving
more to someone who so clearly deserved more, and for taking the
opportunity for affective respite with someone who was used to this,
expected this, and tolerated this. Perhaps my state of respite with Jill
allowed me to give more to other patients I was seeing at the time,
though I find little consolation in this thought at this time. During
the period I was seeing Jill, I could claim none of the conflicting pull
of taking care of young children and relative sleep deprivation that I
experienced with Peter. I had no external reasons to be drowsy, and
the busy clinical and academic schedule I had was of my own choice
and design. I was sleepy because I projectively identified with my
patient's dissociative states (Bion, 1967; Feldman, 1997; Grotstein,
2000; Meltzer, 1994; Racker, 1968), and because I closed my eyes to

her wishes, as did her mother. The former motive proved insightful and useful to Jill, but the latter was all too familiar to her, and the insight only potentially useful if accompanied by a new experience with me. Other patients at this time got more from me, and I was conscious that my affective respites with Jill reflected my pursuit of relative comfortable equilibrium with a woman who wanted and deserved more, but expected only very little.

Alan, a divorced research scientist with one preteen child, was about to perpetrate the dissolution of his career and his financial security. He had done this on two prior occasions, in the context of an obsessive pursuit of expensive prostitutes hired to abuse him in profoundly physically painful and humiliating sadomasochistic ways. Marijuana and other drugs always accompanied this sort of sex, which, along with depleting him economically, left him hung over in the mornings. His pattern was to be late to work, irritable when he arrived there, and careless in his highly technical endeavors. Capable of brilliant work when in post–sex and drug mode, Alan garnered both anger and disrespect from colleagues and bosses. He initiated analysis because he saw himself about to implode his career for a third time, and to once again humiliate himself further by going to his parents for economic help for himself and his child.

I suspected that I would somehow enact a sadomasochistic configuration with Alan, and it happened quickly. I found myself recoiling from and very critical of his extreme sexual practices; of his foolishly giving away his money; of his irresponsible child care; of his, for a very intelligent man, profound lack of insight into himself; and even of the self-detracting way he dressed and carried himself. These sentiments were clear to him both by my attitude and in my words, and Alan seemed fine with this, hoping it would also be accompanied by direct counsel from me about how to stop his compulsive sadomasochism. He was so concrete and unreflective in his thinking that I fairly soon became bored with him and with his most recent horror stories related to his various forms of masochistic expression. My disrespect for Alan congealed into disinterest and affective withdrawal, and I sometimes believed that this was a better alternative than being overtly critical of him. No matter how much I escaped into my own reverie or wanderings and how little I paid attention, Alan would never challenge me. I retreated more and more, saving my energy and commitment for those who commanded my passionate interest and attentiveness.

Of course, I was quite conscious of this expression of my sadism, and of how closely this resembled the position of my patient's passive-aggressive father. Alan's mother was manifestly the family sadist, perennially humiliating her husband and son with her scathingly critical and castrating commentary and her thoroughly controlling ways. He describes her with the pejorative one would use for a "raging borderline." Alan felt great compassion for his humiliated and overtly sweet father, failing to recognize his anger toward his father's failure to both defend his son and provide a model for strength. His father did not respect himself, and Alan began to recognize that he was disrespected, in different ways, by both of his parents. As he became somewhat more insightful, I began to gain more respect for him. I realized that my interest and my respect were what he most wished for, and that he had consistently invited the opposite from me. It also became clear to me that regardless of how much I withdrew from my patient, he would never confront me. He had a dream about our session being interrupted by my taking a phone call from another patient, and not apologizing to him for this. This critical transference dream, and the change in Alan's expectancies reflected in his telling me the dream, helped me gradually emerge from my depriving affective isolation. I became more alert and interested in my patient. I began to ask him more consistently about how he perceives me responding to him, listening to him, and treating him with or without admiration. He became increasingly free to tell me how much my interest and my respect meant to him, and to make note of it when I either was critical of him or failed to pay attention to him. At this juncture in our work, I am far more interested in Alan and respectful in my attitude toward him. When I lapse into comfortable and self-interested retreat, he is far more prone to bring me back than he used to be. Outside of the transference, his interest in other than sadomasochistic relatedness has expanded considerably.

There are times with Alan that I am regretfully reminded of Jill, wishing that I had been able to transcend my sleepy isolation and become more of a generous presence to her as well. It is not entirely clear to me why I was ultimately able to push beyond my affective retreat from Alan, and failed to do this with Jill. I can find no external life circumstances to point to. Both patients presented with acutely painful symptom patterns, and both portrayed tragic and compelling life stories that I felt sympathetic toward. Indeed, Jill's history of incest was the most egregious I had ever encountered in my practice. In both analyses I became aware of entering a mutual enactment characterized by sadomasochistic withholding and neglect, but only in one did I sufficiently abandon my part of this configuration. It is possible, of course, that my affective isolation from Jill was more entrenched by a fear of becoming sexually involved with her, though I experienced no conscious wishes in this direction, nor did I have dreams about her that pointed there. I *was* quite conscious of my sadistically critical feelings toward Alan, and my disinterest in Jill had always been less articulated and more puzzling to me. Her life outside treatment was vital and interesting, yet with me she was so contained that I often felt boredom and drowsiness. Though I have to conclude that there were more unconscious forces operating within me in relation to Jill than there were, perhaps, with Alan, I did have sufficient consciousness about my retreat from her to make more of an effort than I did. I think that I too much liked the image of not exploiting her sexually, that is, I was too satisfied in being sexually benign to feel the urgency of my maternal neglect. I sometimes think, probably with defensiveness, that if Jill had given me more time, I would have been able to come more to life for her. I think that if only she had been more overtly angry *without* terminating, I might have been more responsive. For example, it occurs to me now, as superficial as the following manipulations might seem, that I could have ingested unwanted caffeine prior to seeing Jill; or I might have scheduled, at the sacrifice of my time and finances, a break before her sessions; or I might have given her a coveted early morning hour, the part of the day when I am usually most fresh and alert. Needless to say, such external manipulation does not address unconscious interactional phenomena, but it may very well have reflected a *conscious* effort to be more present, when more subtle and powerful forces were allowing me to remain in a disengaged mutual enactment that was all too familiar to Jill and to me. The effort, in the form of an act, to do something for Jill that was clearly inconvenient to me might have helped erode an equilibrium that maintained until Jill's act of termination. As noted, I believe that in order for analysis to be effective, the analyst as well as the patient must stretch beyond familiar and comfortable states of being (Buechler, 2002, 2004; Levenson, 1972, 1983; Mendelsohn, 2002; Slavin & Kriegman, 1992, 1998; Wolstein, 1954, 1959).

At first glance, it seems hard to think of affective disengagement in any positive way. On further reflection, however, it does seem that the qualities that predispose analysts in this direction may also help them to avoid certain pitfalls. For example, the analytic ideal of strong emotional presence can lead to analysts' inordinate neediness for patients' reciprocal involvement. This in turn may lead to patients' potential guilt, or to their inhibition of uncaring, selfish, and malevolent characteristics, in or out of the transference. The highly emotionally present analyst runs some risk of imposing presence on a patient who does not desire it, and/or holding out this quality as a goal or value about how people and therefore the patient ought to be. The imposition of such analytic ideals can be judgmental and moralistic, and this could stifle patients' expression of the darker sides of unique individuality. Analysts' emotional availability may help create malignant dependence as well as "healthy" dependence, and make it more difficult for patients to find their own idiom distinct from that of their analyst's personalities and values. A strongly caring or nurturing analyst may be more likely to infantilize or pathologize his or her patients, providing insufficient space for patients' expression of agency and will.* I offer two illustrations from my supervision of analytic candidates.

A very capable and deeply engaged analytic candidate (Dr. D) had begun working with her training case (Edward), a man who was dramatically withholding and emotionally cold, especially in relation to women who were interested in him. He had become worried that he would never allow himself to commit to any love relationship. He started analysis to address this issue, in the context of a relationship that seemed worthwhile, in spite of his familiar desires to flee into new and exciting sexual encounters.

Dr. D had a small practice, was very invested in her analytic training and in this particular patient, and had no romance in her life at this time. Though I have no evidence that Dr. D experienced any significant erotic countertransference to her attractive patient, she readily embraced the cause of Edward's girlfriend. Despite my supervisory caution, she actively interpreted Edward's ambivalence toward this girlfriend as part of his long-standing pattern, and made light of the reservations he expressed about this woman and, more importantly, about monogamous relationships in general. In her

---

* Fromm (1941, 1955, 1964), Wolstein (1954, 1959), Schachtel (1959), Tauber and Green (1959), Singer (1965a, 1965b), Becker (1973), Searles (1979), Barnett (1980), Mitchell (1988), Hirsch (1998a), Hoffman (1998), Kwawer (1998), Imber (2000), Coen (2002), and Frie (2002).

identification with Edward's girlfriend, it was difficult for Dr. D to appreciate Edward's growing ambivalence in the transference. She was selling her patient on the virtues of long-term love (for a discussion of this issue, see Blechner, 2005; Dimen, 2003; Hirsch, 2007), yet he wished to address the pitfalls of such commitments. When I pushed my supervisee to listen to her patient's sentiments about the dangers of monogamous love, she reluctantly began to make sense of his conflicts about loving, and how such conflicts had proven adaptive in Edward's life historical context. Nonetheless, Dr. D's eagerness to advocate analytic intimacy, and to promote to her patient the psychic health of intense affective relatedness, dominated both her explicit and implicit communications to Edward. Even with her awareness of enacting the rejected woman, Dr. D continued to usurp her patient's aims, and it became her mission to get Edward as affectively involved with her, in the transference, as she was with him. I stressed addressing conflict, yet Dr. D believed that what she perceived as growing analytic intimacy would generalize to Edward's girlfriend and allow him to make a long-term commitment. Edward agreed superficially, and paid lip service to his analyst, but he was not yet interested in living up to his analyst's standards of human decency, nor her criteria for optimum mental health. Dr. D was uncomfortable with her patient's malevolence, and selectively attended to signs of transference love. Edward did not feel that expressions of destructiveness were welcomed in direct verbal intercourse. She made it hard for Edward to express in words both his unrelatedness and his sadism. In short order, Edward expressed these sentiments in action—he quit precipitously with a rather lame excuse, and refused to come in and discuss this. Ultimately, Edward did not wish to match his analyst's attachment to him, and did not want to adhere to her values. In parallel, Dr. D did not wish to live in her patient's sadomasochistic world, and believed that her overtly benign presence would melt her patient into a state of transference love. As her supervisor, I failed to help Dr. D endure a relationship that was profoundly disruptive and far out of her zone of comfort and familiarity. Though her unconscious conflicts about intimacy and/or her own sadism certainly may account for many of her problems in working with Edward, she was conscious *enough* of her lack of acceptance of her patient's coldness and affective isolation. Dr. D's own personal loneliness undoubtedly made it more difficult to accept Edward's disinterest, though here too she had become aware of how her longings impeded his freedom.

Dr. D did not make sufficient effort to live with Edward's disinterest, and to abandon her more comfortable equilibrium of a woman looking to "warm up" a recalcitrant man.

Another supervisee, Dr. J, had finished her heretofore incomplete undergraduate degree, and achieved a graduate degree, immediately after her children had become young adults and left for university themselves. She had loved being a full-time mother and never had regrets about the long postponement of her academic and professional ambitions. Along the way, Dr. J's husband left her for another, and the impact of this manifested only when her children became more independent of her. Resumption of ambition became a good solution for Dr. J, and this bright and lively woman speeded toward two degrees and analytic training with the same vigor she approached mothering and all its related features.

I supervised Dr. J on her second training case (in her second year), a professional woman (Kitty) in her mid-20s who was struggling to salvage a relatively new marriage. Kitty was naïve, parochial, and profoundly attached to her own mother. Kitty's mother had married right after college, apparently out of a combination of social pressure and fears of being alone. Her husband had been her first boyfriend, and by the time Kitty sought analysis, her mother's marriage had become cold and barren. At the advice of one of her frightened mother's friends, Kitty sought help for a variety of phobic and anxiety symptoms related to the possibility that her own marriage would not last. She had become terrified of being alone in her apartment, or in hotels used for business travel. She experienced panic ("panic attacks") whenever she was asked to do something new at work, or when her husband stayed away from home more than usual. Dr. J, a warm and nurturing presence to begin with, felt a strong empathic connection to the fearful and overdependent sides of her young patient. Despite my counsel to examine the patient's half of the responsibility for her marital estrangement, Dr. J maintained a primary attunement to Kitty's husband's selfishness and emotional abandonment. Though aware that Kitty's primary attachment was to her own mother, and the fact that Kitty had married more out of fear than for love or for attachment, Dr. J argued that her patient was in too fragile of a state to address her own conflicts related to emotional engagement. Though I was convinced that the key to helping Kitty was to deconstruct her symptoms, allowing her to see how they were directly related to crises around dependence, I believe that Dr.

J reinforced her symptoms, enacting a facsimile of Kitty's mother–daughter configuration. Though I objected strenuously, in an effort to soothe her patient's panic, Dr. J became increasingly available to Kitty's emergency telephone calls, sometimes on weekends and late at night. In the context of this interaction Kitty's symptoms worsened, and a variety of anti-anxiety and antidepressant medications were employed.

Perhaps quite belatedly, I began to turn my supervisory focus toward my supervisee's disagreements with my approach to this patient. She and I spoke about our respective backgrounds, and how elements of our respective troubled pasts led us each toward analytic work. This relative mutual openness allowed us to examine how much Dr. J's affinity for mothering, along with her suspicion of men, created what amounted to an iatrogenic situation with her dependent patient. A combination of character style, situational loneliness, and a sparsely populated practice had led Dr. J to enhance her patient's pathology, and Kitty's belief that she was incapable of functioning in even a relatively autonomous manner. Though the emergency phone calls and the moments of panic abated to a reasonable degree, Dr. J was still inclined to help create an overly dependent patient. Dr. J acknowledged how much more comfortable she was in a maternal caretaking mode, and how difficult it was to be as "autonomy-oriented" (her term) as I was. Indeed, she had become aware that she felt quite gratified in this caretaking role, and became aware of the extent to which she missed the everyday presence of her children. Dr. J did not wish to abandon this configuration. She rationalized that there was more than one way to help patients, and hoped that she could help Kitty by being the self she (Dr. J) most identified with. Though I agree that there are multiple ways to do productive analysis, Dr. J did seem aware that her way of being with Kitty was proving to be iatrogenic. As well, she was aware that her bitterness toward men led her to perpetuate her patient's view of herself as a victim and led Kitty to not examine sufficiently her own conflicts related to intimate engagement with men. Nevertheless, Dr. J was convinced that her nurturing ways would pay dividends in the long run, and besides, it was the only way she felt comfortable being with this and other patient(s). We struggled with our differences until the end of our supervisory year—I, of course, profoundly uncomfortable with Dr. J's and Kitty's interpersonal configuration, and Dr. J silently viewing me as yet another unfeeling and nonnurturing man. When we parted reasonably amicably, we both knew that our respective relational emphases and zones of comfort would continue to be reflected in our clinical work with patients, for better and for worse. These personal factors had much to do with determining our respective theoretical allegiances and our theoretical differences (Hirsch, 2003a).

In contrast with the above relational themes, and perhaps counterintuitively, analysts' self-absorption and/or narcissism can have some potential upsides. The ability to not demand or expect or even desire a great deal of affective involvement from others is sometimes a relief to many patients, and may help them in the creation of freedom to have less than ideal relationships in and out of the analytic dyad (Blechner, 2005a; Dimen, 2003; Hirsch, 2007). Many, if not most, marriages or partnerships require considerable emotional space for them to survive in the long term, and an analytic relationship that is perennially mutually intense and close can reflect an unrealistic expectancy with regard to the schizoid compromises involved in much of interpersonal life. Analysts with a distinct emotionally cool side sometimes have the advantage of being able to function very well in crises. Patients who are threats to fall apart or to make suicide attempts can sometimes provoke highly emotionally engaged analysts into a disorganizing panic, or into measures that fundamentally overprotect or infantilize patients, failing to properly hold the latter, and sometimes increasing the likelihood of suicide gestures or acts.

What I have just suggested is rife with overgeneralization and, as previously noted, probably quite defensive to boot. Nonetheless, I have been trying to make the point that the person of the analyst will inevitably affect patients both for better and for worse, and that all analysts are guilty to varying degrees of willfully enacting their worst qualities, and choosing self-interest in priority to patient interest. If there is a truly valuable analytic ideal, I suggest, along with Wolstein (1954, 1959), Searles (1965, 1979), Singer (1965b, 1968, 1971), Becker (1973), Kantrowitz (1992, 1993), Hoffman (1998), Maroda (1999, 2005), Crastnopol (1999, 2001), Berman (2001), Buechler (2002, 2004), Dimen (2001, 2003), and Slochower (2003, 2006), that analysts fully embrace personal limitations, acknowledging who we are as people and how this impacts others. In this context, analysts ideally are aware of the inherent conflict between being selfishly ourselves and remaining in zones of personal comfort, and stretching or being effort full in order to be optimally useful to patients. This is more likely achievable when analysts optimally encourage patients' transference observations and challenges,* and when we recognize that too comfortable of a dyad with too little anxiety for too long probably means that we are coasting with countertransference, and are insufficiently effort full in pushing toward personal discomfort. However, because analysts are as flawed as everyone else, we will always hurt our patients even when we help them, and awareness of countertransferences does not guarantee their translation into productive and useful analytic engagement.

---

* Wolstein (1954, 1959), Singer (1965a, 1965b), Levenson (1973, 1983), Wachtel (1980, 1982), Gill (1982, 1983), Hoffman (1983, 1998), Jacobs (1986, 2001), Hirsch (1987, 1996), Stern (1987), Friedman (1988, 2006), Mitchell (1988, 1993), Gabbard (1995), Greenberg (1995), Aron (1996), Coen (2002), and Goldstein (n.d.).

# 4

# Preferred Patients, Preferred Relational Configurations*

## Introduction

Back in the days when most analysts believed that strict criteria should be applied to which patients could benefit from psychoanalysis and who were not amenable (e.g., Bachrach & Leaff, 1978), the prevailing sentiment was that such assessments were made with relative objectivity. These were also times, because of supply and demand factors, that many analysts' practices were full, and they had the luxury to choose with whom they would spend 3 to 5 analytic hours per week. If all of one's patients attended with such frequency, one could see only approximately from 8 to 15 individuals each week, and being highly selective about with whom one spends so much time is understandable. However, carefully choosing whom one wishes to be intimate with is not quite the same as the more scientifically toned notion that is evoked when using terminology like the then prevailing binaries, *analyzable* and *unanalyzable*. Psychoanalysis from the beginning has struggled with the absence of scientific validation of either treatment or technique, and efforts to allay skeptics from both outside and inside the mental health profession have led to efforts to use terminology and concepts that appear more respectably scientific. Despite the relational turn in psychoanalysis we can still construct theories of the mind and of therapeutic action that are laden with technical terminology and jargon that are designed to sound either like hard science or like acedemically

* An earlier version of this chapter appears in *Gender and Sexuality*, 2(4), 1997, 469–486.

credentialed philosophy.* Interpersonal and relational analysts once so critical of their Freudian colleagues' tendencies to speak about internal structures of the mind, as if personal psychology operated similarly to principles of physics, now sometimes couch their theories in language that sounds equally complicated, experience distant, and impersonal.** The impression of relatively objective assessment of who is and who is not analyzable is still relevant today to the extent that some practitioners (though very few) still see most of their patients three to five times weekly, and *all* analysts in training must see anywhere from one to three such patients in order to complete their training. The assessment of analyzability is relevant currently more with regard to finding patients who help candidates fulfill their training requirements. Analysts in training who are required to be seen three to five times per week for personal analysis, and their own training cases, though I have no hard data, may very well constitute the biggest bulk of patients who pursue analysis in its most full or ideal form. This is not so much an indictment of analytic process as it is reflective of both a cultural shift in interests, and a drastic decline in insurance reimbursement for even once-weekly, much less multiple-weekly, visits over the course of many years to analytic practitioners.

The affectation of scientific criteria for analyzability is relevant today in psychoanalytic training institutes that screen patients for their analytic candidates, and for that small minority of analysts whose practices are so full that they have the luxury of whom to see and whom to reject, in the form of referral to colleagues. The strong majority of analysts are willing to see anyone who is willing and able to pay their fee, and who will not be too disruptive to their lives, and they will work as analytically as they can even when seeing such patients once or twice weekly. Some will call their work *psychoanalysis* proper (Gill, 1984), and others may use terms like *analytic psychotherapy*. In either type of situation, each analyst prefers to work with some patients more than others, and this, I argue, has far more to do with analysts' personal preferences and tastes than with

---

* This can be seen in the prevalence of highly technical terminology used, for example, by Meltzer (1994), Grotstein (2000), and Newirth (2003), and in the use of currently popular metaphors like "thirdness" (see Gerson, 2004, for a review of this often too intellectualized concept).

** Here I echo critiques already rendered by Greenberg and Mitchell (1983), Levenson (1991), Coen (2000), Hirsch (2003), and Moses (n.d.).

anything that approaches scientific criteria. When in a position to be choosy, analysts will pick patients with whom they feel the most comfortable affinity and with whom they believe they will feel optimally successful. These two deeply personal and subjective criteria often go hand in hand, that is, analysts are likely to believe they will do their most productive work with patients who they most like to be with. Every analyst prefers to be with some patients more than others, and this has only partly to do with questions related to any given patient being amenable or not to psychoanalytic inquiry—the vague concept of analyzability (Hirsch, 1984).

Analysts' preference for one patient over another is far more related to the personal interplay between the two unique individuals than to any external criteria. For example, independent of any other personal qualities, those patients who have suffered the most profound rejections from their caretakers, expect the least from subsequent relationships, and, albeit with much internal conflict, evoke repetition of past destructive relationships are most likely to be rejected for analysis or, when there is a choice, for any sort of analytic engagement. Though analysts may invoke technical explanations for either rejecting or reluctantly accepting such patients, the more genuine reasons relate more closely to the likelihood that any given analyst will enact dislike and/or rejection when with someone who has a long history of misanthropy, first as a helpless victim, and subsequently as an evoker or perpetrator. On the other hand, those prospective patients who have been the most loved and cherished by their caretakers are often adored by others, including the fortunate analysts who meet them in a professional context (Hirsch, 1984). Though many can see the irony involved in analysts' intense and constructive involvement with those who already have the most in life, it underscores the degree to which the person of the analyst overrides so many technical or theoretical questions. In the best of all possible worlds, the heart of analytic inquiry is involved in highlighting those very factors that make a less desirable patient undesirable. This, of course, is the very essence of transference work, though it is all too easy to affectively withdraw from or retaliate toward difficult patients, if not reject them entirely as unsuitable for analytic work, when there is opportunity to do so. The presence of countertransference anger, despair (Farber, 1966), hate (Epstein, 1999; Winnicott, 1949), or boredom is sometimes consuming, and immersion in and coasting with such affective states too often override using such feelings to illuminate transference themes. The *general* characteristics that make a patient desirable or undesirable to work with are not very different from those involved in choosing lovers, friends, or colleagues. Those who are stable, reliable, ambitious, inquisitive, sensitive, caring, generous, intelligent, and physically attractive are more generally sought after in any social context, including the analytic dyad. Such individuals, despite whatever problems bring them to analysis, are likely to do better than their more troubled counterparts in their vocations, in their avocations, in personal relationships, and as analytic patients. The rejected and often more seriously troubled, undesirable patients may be all too familiar with others failing them, and are inclined to hurt or disappoint others as well. They may be prone to miss sessions, drop out unexpectedly, withdraw affectively, and make excessive demands or intrusions, and are less likely to reach analysts' wished for analytic goals. Such encounters may produce expectancy of failure in the countertransference, and it is not uncommon that this prophecy is fulfilled. Unfortunately, even when the range of countertransference experience is used productively to highlight key transference phenomena, patients who have not received much good from others and also have not been productive heretofore in their work are more likely to disappoint their analysts than those who have been deeply loved and have lived rich lives in their developmental years and beyond. This by no means suggests that more personally difficult and less appealing patients can ever be legitimately diagnosed as unanalyzable. Indeed, the binary of analyzable–unanalyzable, like so many other absolutes, is far too simpleminded. One may soberly judge that some patients are more difficult than others, and analysis, like every other enterprise, is more likely to succeed with some than others. When the supply of patients is rich, analysts will tend to choose those whom they like the best, and these are usually also the most likely to provide a feeling of success for their analyst. A continuum of personal difficulty or of likelihood of analytic failure seems more reasonable than do absolute terms that are laden with a pseudo-scientific and pseudo-objective tone (Hirsch, 1984). And, even assuming that some patients are consensually more difficult to be with and less likely to satisfy our analytic aims, one must always take into account the second party in this two-person psychology enterprise—the person of the analyst. If the term *analyzability* still has any contemporary relevance at all, it must be seen as related to the mixture of both participants in the analytic dyad, and the purely subjective personal factors that lead analysts to prefer one patient over another, and to work well with some individuals and have trouble being with others over an extended period of time. To restate, when the factors of supply and demand favor the analyst, he or she will likely choose those patients who represent the greatest possibility of analytic success for the analyst, and with whom one wishes to spend many years in intense affective engagement. These both reflect selfish interests on the part of analysts, and I argue that analysts tend to indulge these interests when they have the opportunity.

The unique individuality of each analyst emerges more clearly in the dimension of personal tastes in people, for it seems universally true that each of us selfishly prefers success to failure. It is the dimension of analysts' personal proclivities and preferences with respect to the personal and professional company they keep to which I now turn. I attempt to further illuminate analysts' tendencies toward pursuit of comfortable relational equilibrium with patients, to develop relationships with patients that are familiar to the analyst and have some parallel to those in analysts' outside lives, and to, with some consciousness, coast in the comfort of these preferred dyadic configurations. To illustrate this point I use qualities of a heterosexual male-to-male construction that I and many of my male colleagues both enjoy, and find familiar and easy to perpetuate. Such analytic engagement may qualitatively resemble external life friendships. Unfortunately, they sometimes may last as long as such friendships and, parenthetically, longer than many contemporary marriages.

In chapter 3, I already described what I called analysts' striving to engage in preferred relational states with patients. That is, each analyst has ways of being with others that are more comfortable than other ways. Some patients may readily fit into analysts' comfortable modes of relating, and this experience could be mutually rich, though it may also lead to interminable analyses. For example, to cite what I believe is a familiar configuration, if a particular analyst is most comfortable when people are dependent on him, a patient who is overly dependent may remain with this analyst for an eternity. The analyst in this situation may well realize that the analysis has proceeded for a mind-boggling number of years, but because this mutual enactment is so comfortable for both parties he or she may find some clinical rationale to keep the process going. Another common example may be seen in a male, heterosexual analyst who looks for affirmation in the eyes of women, particularly attractive women. This analyst may be easily seduced by the Oedipal desire of his good-looking and sexy patient, and she in turn may enjoy the powers she has to win the love of this man of stature. In situations where either or both patient and analyst have unhappy love lives, their Oedipal romance has the special power to sustain each of them for many years. Indeed, the analytic relationship, sometimes for both parties, may become the primary romantic venue. Despite this theme being such a popular one in the literature from the beginning of psychoanalysis, and despite every analyst being warned about such dangers, this configuration may simply feel too good to give up. As with the illustration of dependency, it can be easy to find clinical rationalizations for the perpetuation of relationships that provide significant mutual comfort and pleasure. Romantic or eroticized analytic relationships may create an equilibrium for the two co-participants, both inside the transference–countertransference matrix, and also in each respective romantic relational configuration outside of the analysis (Dimen, 2001, 2003; Gabbard, 1996; Hirsch, 2007). The analytic situation can become a virtual love affair, and complement what might be a tepid romantic existence in the lives of both analytic participants. It is difficult to avoid coasting in the richness inherent in romantic and sexual excitement, and such interactions can be very hard to give up. Even when this transference–countertransference enactment is interpretively addressed and illuminated, if the analyst wishes to remain in this configuration, any interpretations could serve as a rationalization that something is really being done to move on from the enactment. Yet another common personal or analytic configuration that offers mutual comfort and equilibrium for both parties may be seen in the interaction between two withdrawn and/or intellectualized co-participants. Both parties may feel uneasy with or in dread of strong affect in the context of being with a significant other, and both may prefer living in a world of ideas and concepts. It could be that some of the ideas and concepts are *about* affects, but in the analytic exchange those affects are often split off. Because there is always material to address and always dreams to be dreamed and analyzed, such a configuration is sometimes interminable. The dyad can be so mutually gratifying that both participants will find no end of rationales to continue a relationship that provides optimal emotional safety, comfort, and reward. Though I have been guilty of coasting in all of the above forms of relatedness over the many years of doing analytic work, as I have already noted, my focus in the remainder of this chapter is on a less commonly addressed relational configuration—some heterosexual men's pleasure and comfort in engagement with other heterosexual men. In attempting to understand or explain this culturally prevalent phenomenon, I delve selectively into gender theory before returning to two sample clinical illustrations between men.

## Men's Preference for Men

Many heterosexual men prefer the company of other men, in preference to the woman (or women) with whom they may be romantically involved. This phenomenon may be readily visible in the work environment, though it is graphically illustrated in recreational pursuits like drinking, gambling, and sports-related activity. Men's preference for men may be based on a combination of positive identifications with father figures and childhood friends, and a terror of submission to helpless dependence on mother figures and other women. An almost universal fear of confrontation with inherent bisexuality (Freud, 1905/2000, 1915/2000) dictates somewhat indirect expression of male-to-male intimacy. This is frequently in the form of activities that are culturally associated with masculinity and that affirm an often fragile or threatened sense of heterosexuality. For example, a divorced, attractive, heterosexual businessman, very conservative in his manner and his politics, tells me that it is too bad that men must marry women and not men. A never-married, very handsome, heterosexual professional man finds that his most enduring and deeply affectionate relationships are with male friends from his grade school through college years, despite the hordes of women who are interested in him, and with whom he engages sexually. Both of these men are very involved with the playing and watching of sports, and this is often a medium for their contact with men, and has been since childhood or adolescence.

Initially, sports served as a vehicle for identification with fathers who were otherwise retiring, elusive, or preoccupied. Though neither father actively engaged in the playing of sports, both were knowledgeable and avid sports fans. My two patients recall many hours in front of a television with their respective fathers, intently watching or listening to team sporting events. In each dyad there was very little conversation with one another. Nonetheless, all parties were passionate about what was being watched or heard, and they interacted verbally and affectively with the players and coaches on the screen. Both patients do not recall having seen their fathers come alive in quite this way in other contexts. An additional important function of sports interest was in the service of separation from mother and the confines of her home. Both mothers had no interest in or knowledge of sports. One mother is remembered as irritable and nagging, and the other as overwhelming, needy, and infantilizing. The active involvement of playing ball with young male peers served as a legitimate and "healthy" vehicle to remove these two men from their mothers, who were, in various ways, quite restrictive. In one of these two situations, my patient and his mother were so intertwined that his primary gender identity was evolving as female. More details will be presented later, but for now the lives of these two men illustrate my main thesis: The relational configuration between male patient and male analyst can sometimes be so mutually rewarding that maintaining the relationship in and of itself may become the mutually unspoken aim of the analytic process. Such configurations may run parallel to male–male familial and/or friendship bonds.

Men's relatedness to both genders is often driven by dual anxieties. My focus will be on how men are often caught between a fear of overwhelming dependence upon and submission to women and a fear of homosexual desire. Relationships with men around male-affirming activities often help men reduce both these fears, and solidify a sense of heterosexuality. The psychoanalytic relationship between two men can serve as a subtle and unarticulated subtext for both parties to affirm their masculine, heterosexual identity. Due at least to inherent bisexuality, considerable homosexual anxiety is evident in most heterosexual males. Men's preference for men, however, is not a universal phenomenon. It is a significant feature in the life of many males and a dominant theme in a subset of some men, illustrated by the two patients (and their analyst) whom I have briefly introduced. In addition to the realm of recreation and sports, men have interacted among themselves in the traditional gender-splitting domains of the military and, in a different way, the workplace. The culture offers many vehicles and settings for men to connect with one another on relatively exclusive and intimate grounds. It is usually quite difficult, perhaps impossible, to discern which aspect of this male to male interaction might be motivated by one or both of the dual anxieties described, or fundamentally not motivated by anxiety.

The issue of sexual object choice is a very complicated one, and I am not prepared to address it in any depth or detail. Though I am aware that there is no consensus about the development of sexual object choice, my personal belief is that inherent bisexuality is rather quickly shaped by social learning, especially patterns of identification, into strong sexual preferences. In a considerable majority, this is heterosexual, and once established, it is difficult for sexual desire to shift from one gender to the other, except at unusual moments. This can clearly be seen in the futile effort to "cure" homosexual young men of their same-sex desire (Blechner, 1993, 2005a, 2005b; D'Ercole & Drescher, 2004; Drescher, 2002; Frommer, 1994, 2006; Isay, 1989). Indeed, the heart of Freud's (1905/2000) sexual theory refers to bisexual potential in all humans. In addition, he posited an inherent developmental stage in boys of father love, which is usually transformed into identification with father (Freud, 1923/2000). Developmental theory tells us that no important attachments are ever fully given up, even when there appears to be a full heterosexual solution (Beebe & Lachman, 2002; Brisman, 2002; Fonagy, 2003; Freud, 1915/2000, 1920/2000, 1923/2000). Because inherent bisexuality implies that everyone is capable of sexual desire for both genders, I believe that a fair measure of homosexual anxiety is virtually universal among heterosexual men. It is the primary basis for a prevailing homophobia. Aside from the frequent association of homosexuality in the cultural imagination with effeminacy and, therefore, a loss of gender identification, same-sex desire may, as well, disrupt familial identifications. The loss of either can leave a heterosexual man quite vulnerable to a profound void in place of a rooted sense of self. Such anxiety may readily become overwhelming and panic producing. Thus, heterosexual men commonly relate intimately to other men, often through the vehicle of action, frequently group- or team-oriented action (Hirsch, 1999; Hirsch & Hirsch, 2000). Work, sports, and other activities allow for considerable indirect expression of love and affection, as well as a solidification of a sense of male self-cohesion. A perennial wish to affirm and reaffirm a sense of heterosexual maleness can also be a driving force in the more subdued confines of a psychoanalytic engagement between two men. Whereas verbal expressions of affection per se may border too closely to acted-upon bisexuality or homosexuality in most social venues, this is less dangerous in the very strictly boundaried temple of the psychoanalytic situation, where action is absolutely prohibited. In other more fluid contexts, many men's verbal expression of preference for involvement with other men might more frequently slide into sexual engagement, though this behavior is often protected by a frightful dread of the loss of a heterosexual identity. This issue is vividly illustrated in the film *The Crying Game* (1993), which will later be discussed in some detail.

Men's preference for men is grounded, on one hand, in positive identification with fathers and heroes and the familiarity of same-sex friends. Positive factors, such as loving involvement with a father figure, childhood and adolescent attachments to male friends, and the identity-affirming attraction to physically alike others, are obvious crucial variables in understanding men's attachment to other men. Unfortunately, fear of women and of feminine identification is one other strong motivating force that accounts for men's preference for being with other men. The literature associated with relational feminist writing (e.g., Benjamin, 1991; Chodorow, 1976, 1994; Dimen, 2003; Dinnerstein, 1976; Harris, 1991) addresses this anxiety: troubled male–female relatedness as closely associated with men's fear of women. Being born to woman, separation from regressive dependency and feminine identification becomes, to varying degrees, a lifelong struggle.

Obviously, some mothers facilitate separation and autonomy more effectively than others. Identification with father or father figures may also help considerably in this quest for individuation but not sufficiently to counter all symbiotic longings toward mother and then girlfriends and wives. Women, on the other hand, do not feel the need for separation quite so profoundly. For women, the easiest solution is at least enough of an identification with mother so that life is not necessarily a continuous struggle to "not be."

Boys and then men are often quite frightened about "too much" identification with mother, and aggressively countering this becomes one of men's burdens (Hansell, 1998). Many men would not consider working with a female analyst for this reason alone, yet in engaging a male analyst who may share some similar anxieties, these conflicts can easily be overlooked. Identification with mother (or female analyst) may well include effeminacy, interests associated with women, and sexual desire for men (assuming a heterosexual mother). Integral to masculine identity is often a turning of the tables on the weakness–strength continuum. This, too, is reinforced by identification with father, public male heroes, or male psychoanalysts who have ostensibly succeeded in emerging from helpless dependency on women. In striving to transform weakness into dominance, men often devote themselves to maintaining a sense of power and strength in relation to women. There is, however, a circularity here. In disallowing a range of feelings associated with the feminine, many men become dependent on women to express this vital and sometimes dissociated side of themselves (Hansell). Through close association with women via long-term relationships, some men may vicariously experience a range of feeling through the women in their lives. It is not unusual for men to become caught in a cycle of need for physical intimacy and dependence, frequently experienced sexually, followed by efforts at control. A touch of sadomasochism seems built into much heterosexual interaction (Stoller, 1975).

According to authors like Chodorow (1976, 1994), Dinnerstein (1976), and Gilligan (1982), women are commonly willing to cooperate with men's need to dominate. It is sometimes the only way for women to sustain heterosexual relations with men, to raise a family, and to carry on the tradition of their original family. Women have affected the role of the weaker sex and have, albeit with much conflict, attempted to facilitate their men's greater success in the competitive world. Men's stronger musculature has aided in the illusion that men are psychologically stronger than women. Historically, women have been willing to abandon worldly ambitions in order that their men may believe that women are the more fragile and dependent gender. Relations between men and women all too commonly conform, in a variety of respects, to Stoller's (e.g., 1968, 1975, 1979) thesis about the nature of sexual perversion. For Stoller, all sexual perversion is an effort to convert weakness into strength. The man who views himself as insignificant may expose his erect penis to a woman in a public place and achieve some sense of power when she is shocked or frightened. A man may look through binoculars at an undressing woman, and because he sees her in this vulnerable position and she knows nothing of it, he is in control and empowered. Sexual perversion is largely the purview of men. Men's "normal" relations with women, including the not specifically erotic, can be seen to conform to Stoller's formulation of perversion. Control and domination of women are part of the fabric of male–female interaction. In addition to size and muscle mass, it is tradition for men to fight the battles of war, work, and sports, and to protect the admiring and ostensibly weaker woman at home. The role of the woman as cheerleader to the male athlete-warrior has historically been the implicit agreement between the genders. Men's core terror of regressive dependence is transformed into heroism of sorts. Stoller's conception of perversion, as it exists in the fabric of everyday gender relations, is seen in many forms. It may be reflected in being better in math; more worldly, critical, and demeaning; or physically intimidating or abusive.

Nowhere is this theme more graphic than in the cultural norm of male sexualization of women. Like normative sadomasochism, this appears to be ubiquitous among heterosexual men and is not, therefore, usually considered perverse. Very many heterosexual men look at women, directly or through photographs and film, in a manner that transforms the woman into an object of sexual control. Women's physical qualities are the subject of shared fantasy, discussion, humor, and displays of sexual bravado among most men. Topless bars (and the increasingly popular lap-dancing bars), magazines, and an entire advertising and media industry have developed to aid men in believing that, at least through their eyes, they are capable of dominating women. Other men who are less frightened of contact with women beyond the visual may compensate for dreaded submissive helplessness through efforts at sexual conquest. This too, in modest form, is well within social norms. Men who are in a position of being attractive to women because of the lure of good looks or high status are often able to use hands-on interaction with women to reinforce a sense of power and invulnerability. Many men who are highly successful in their work use the same ambitions to "achieve" women. Two men engaging together in a psychoanalytic relationship can implicitly through their shared values and attitudes, or explicitly by the way they may speak or joke about women, counter one another's anxieties, yet avoid addressing these very anxieties and intrapsychic conflicts that may be so central to their respective problems in living. One subtext of some heterosexual male analyst–male patient dyads may be to reinforce and stabilize their respective feelings of heterosexual masculinity.

Emotional disconnection is another normative, albeit often unconscious, way that men are able to dominate women. It is not uncommon for men to be remote, cold, emotionally isolated, or self-absorbed, or in other ways be barely available for personal contact with the discontent significant women in their lives. This frequent female lament may be empowering for the man. In a reversal of the helpless boy's dependency upon mother, the emotionally starved wife or lover pleads with her man to talk to her or to touch her with tenderness. He may be inclined to touch her sexually, yet his love and his erotic desire may be disconnected. The emotionally detached male prototype turns weakness into strength; it is the woman who desires him, and not the reverse. She is vulnerable, whereas he is strong in his isolation of dependence and attachment. Such characteristics may not be in sharp relief for a male analyst who shares these qualities with his patient, and who may be experiencing similar conflicts with his spouse or woman friend. The analyst may be inclined to be empathic with his patient's dilemma while remaining unsympathetic to the aggrieved woman in his patient's life.

The fragmentation of many heterosexual men's feelings—disguised dependency upon, lust for, and control over women, versus no conscious sexual desire but activity-oriented warm or competitive friendship with men—reflects a relatively normal compromise in our culture. This is often replicated in a psychoanalytic relationship between two men who may share similar anxieties, and who are very comfortable relating to other men in prototypically masculine ways. For many men, to feel a combination of sexual desire, intimate longings, affinity, and friendship toward women is often too much—it may run the risk of a loss of boundary to symbiotic dependence (Hirsch, 2007; Mitchell, 2000). To feel all of these feelings for other men could lead to a loss of a cherished heterosexual identity and an undoing of powerful internalized familial identifications. A common solution to this dilemma is to split affections into same-gender love and opposite-gender love. This combination is often the most likely one to help in maintaining anxiety at a reasonable level. A sense of self-cohesion comes from preferred participation in heterosexually confirming male-oriented actions and the ability to feel sexually dominant, in one way or another, in relation to women. This far less than ideal resolution works for many heterosexual men; an equilibrium is established somewhere between two dreads: emergence of bisexual desire and passive submission to the power of women. Psychoanalytic relations between men, despite the unusually wide breadth of content and affect addressed, may readily mirror, in emotional tone, both participants' relationships with other men outside of this professional context.

Much of men's obsessive sexual preoccupation with women is based upon overcoming a fundamental feeling of dependency-based weakness, and a terror of loss of self in relation to them (Chodorow, 1976). A common compromise for many men is to relate to women sexually so as to reinforce a sense of masculine power and to fulfill needs for physical intimacy (Stoller, 1979), and to enjoy the companionship of men, as long as overt sexual desire is reasonably isolated. In the many psychoanalytic relationships where homosexual desire does not emerge in dialogue or even in conscious experience, these male-to-male pleasures are repeated, and may closely resemble such relatedness outside of the analytic dyad. Needless to say, men whose familial experiences are such that they have less reason to be frightened of a loss of self are likely to feel more comfortable being with women in a more egalitarian way. Included in such experience is a strong sense of self-cohesion based on experience with a father figure and a relationship with a mother figure that encourages autonomy and independent selfhood. Nonetheless, I have tried to convey that it is not uncommon for heterosexual men to operate on a delicate balance between two basic anxieties: bisexual desire and overwhelming domination by women.

Because sexual preference is established early, however, the fear of homosexuality is generally not as pervasive, past adolescence, as is what I believe to be a lifelong wish for regression to dependency upon women. The wish for and fear of symbiotic dependency upon women represent significant factors in comprehending men's more conflict-free and comfortable companionship with other men. Indeed, many men prefer the companionship of other men especially when engaged in activities typically associated with maleness and with affirmation of heterosexuality. Some activities, such as sports, are ideally suited to help men negotiate the dual anxieties of fear of women and of homosexual desire.

Involvement in the playing or watching of sports is normally an all-male activity, and holds a cultural association with manliness. It is a vehicle for men to engage physically and often affectionately with one another without the presence of women or of homosexual anxiety. It is an outlet for male-to-male intimacy and sometimes profound connection, without the necessity for direct verbal expression of love. It may be seen as a form of physical and spiritual love, with any sexual connotation adaptively masked beneath a heterosexually confirming activity. This indirect emotional configuration of intimacy is reflected in my patient's lament that he cannot marry a man. As will be illustrated, I am one of those men who he would like to marry, and I as well would not mind such a wedding. Our shared interest in sports, in particular, contributes to our relationship often being as pleasure oriented, intimate (in a fashion), and mutually affirming of masculine independence as are our friendships outside of psychoanalysis. Being with him and others often does not feel much different than the ease with which I engage many of my male friends and colleagues, particularly those who are also involved with or interested in sports.

This thesis is also effectively illustrated in the 1993 Irish film *The Crying Game*, directed by Neil Jordan. It has the trappings of a traditional action movie: terrorism, violence between factions, and romance between a man and a woman fighting together for a common cause. The tradition of adventure stories is then dramatically reversed when a relationship between the terrorist protagonist and his male captive turns into a deeply loving friendship. Simultaneously, the female interest is revealed as a vicious seducer and killer of men. The male "romance" ends when the captive is accidentally killed, and then resumes when the protagonist quits the terrorist organization and falls in love with his deceased friend's girlfriend. It is difficult to distinguish his love for his friend from that for his new girlfriend. When the two are together, the protagonist frequently envisions his deceased friend. These fantasies revolve around his friend playing cricket, with sports having served as a shared passion between the two men. In one of the dramatic surprises in contemporary film, the new girlfriend is suddenly revealed to the protagonist as a transvestite. After vomiting at the sight of his (or her) penis and the recognition of his being romantically in love with and making love to a man, the protagonist recovers his equilibrium, and these two characters proceed to establish a love affair along very traditional romantic lines. Were his transvestite lover not disguised as a woman, the protagonist never would have allowed the love to become overtly sexual and romantic. If his captive and sports-loving friend had remained alive, the two men most likely would have become intimate friends, playing and watching sports together, if you will. In this dramatic illustration of inherent bisexuality, the deception of a man dressing and looking like a woman gave license for a heterosexual man to romantically love another man. The implication is that the protagonist was, indeed, in love with his captive friend, and his transvestite lover was an embodiment of that love. In this expressionist drama, loving male friendship turned into romance when one man allowed himself to be deceived by another man in woman's clothing. One can read this as a statement that men's love for male companions is not very far from romantic, sexual love.

The leading woman in this film is the embodiment of all of men's terror of the overwhelming, castrating mother. In the opening scene, with the background song "When a Man Loves a Woman," she lures a naïve and lustful soldier into a trap where he is captured by terrorists. This is what happens when a man "loves" a woman. While he is in captivity, she tortures and torments him. In contrast, the male terrorist guard is gentle and empathic. The two men form a bond around their shared love of sports. This bond begins to transcend traditional sexual and political allegiances. The male terrorist grows to fear and dislike his lover, the female terrorist, and eventually betrays his organization in an attempt to save his now intimate friend, the captive. As noted earlier, this male-to-male love would have likely been maintained as indirectly intimate, with a focus on their passion for sports. The male terrorist's love for his friend is embodied in sexual love for a woman who is really a male transvestite. During their initial lovemaking scene, the terrorist is seen imagining his deceased friend gracefully playing cricket on a beautiful green field. The song played at the movie's end is "Stand by Your Man," underscoring the depth of devotion and loyalty between the two male lovers. The film rips away the split between loving friendship and erotic love. Were it not for social anxieties and taboos, men could love one another sexually and be emotionally dependent on one another, as well as they could love women and be cared for by them. This split, however, exists strongly in most cultures, and men's love for one another normally stops at the level of shared, heterosexually confirming activities, such as sports. In such activity, inherent bisexuality is further suppressed, and the dangerous woman is isolated and neutralized (Hirsch, 1999). One might think that this would not be the case in a psychoanalytic relationship that is designed to encourage both feeling the widest range of feelings and talking about these feelings. Nonetheless, I observe that many such relationships ring with so much familiarity and comfort that neither participant wishes to consider more disquieting and disequilibrium-producing elements of this relationship. For many male analysts and their patients, coasting in "maleness" comes easily.

There is, of course, a larger body of "boy meets girl," male–female romance themes in film. *The Crying Game* (1993) is anything but typical. However, as portrayed dramatically and exaggeratedly in some of the most popular art and media forms, particularly action and adventure film and television situation comedy, men's affinity for one another can far outweigh interest in women, save for lust. In these genres, reflective of the culture from which they originate, women are commonly important for their caretaking function. Validation of men's potency and heterosexuality is a large part of that function. This potency-confirming function often allows men to achieve self-cohesion through shared activity with other men, while simultaneously escaping from and denying immoderate dependence upon the women in their lives. Indeed, lustful conquest of women is often one of those shared activities. Kaftal (1991) discussed a developmental need for attuned responses from same-sexed others to maintain a sense of self-cohesion. This is especially so for men whose fathers were deficient in providing recognition. Traditionally, the world of work, whether professional or labor, has been a primary medium for shared male activities. Although the workplace is now integrated, it is not unusual for men to prefer exclusive contact with their male colleagues. Considerable prejudice exists toward the integration of women into both professional and blue-collar work. Men often wish to have work as a sanctuary from women, a place similar to a club, the military, or a team where play with and competition against other men are the central activities. Triumph is in the form of money and/or status, and either is likely to make men feel more desirable to women as well as feel like the object of recognition among men. Women's stronger and nonsecretarial participation has led to considerable difficulties in the workplace, anywhere from sexual harassment (Schrier, 1996) to glass ceilings to a decline in the pleasure of playing on an all-male team. Blue-collar workers are often free to voice their virulent displeasure about women's participation in team play. They may be less sophisticated in their efforts to subvert this process, but their often uninhibited vocal expressions capture the sentiments of many of their professional counterparts. Indeed, I know of no literature that addresses male analysts' preference for working with men of shared interests. On the other hand, there is a considerable literature that is sensitive to male analysts' being buoyed and excited by the sexual desire and idealization of female patients, especially those toward whom the analyst is sexually attracted (Hirsch, 1992,

1993, 1994). In this latter configuration, because it is so frequently addressed in psychoanalytic writing and theorizing, it is likely that one or another party will begin to speak at least of the transference side of this attraction. This may serve to enhance the analysts' sexual excitement, or it may detoxify or neutralize it. However, male analysts' preference for male patients in the workplace of the psychoanalyst's office is often not addressed by either party, and the engagement may long persist in resembling that of the analyst's and patient's male friendships outside of the analytic hour.

Work, including psychoanalytic work, like sports, can be a domain where men's preference for men does not carry the fear of homosexual engagement, and where the power of the woman is neutralized. Work, play, and sports are often safe domains within which to fulfill the developmental need to seek out others like oneself. Sports, and sometimes the psychoanalytic work relationship, are more glaring examples of adult men's preference for men, because both are optional activities and the rationale "I must work long hours" cannot apply. This may reflect a continuity with childhood and adolescent escape from mother, into the world of father, heroes, and other boys or men. Sports activity may also be a way of being like father and/or popular heroes, an affirmation of both masculine gender identity and separation from mother. The analyst may serve the patient in this way, and as well the patient may provide for the analyst an affirming male object. In this context, becoming a good player-worker-patient-analyst through hard work may also be fun, and parents are not needed to provide motivation for achievement. The friends that boys make from both formal and informal athletic involvement can be enduring. For boys who develop an intrinsic pleasure in sports, whether in active participation or interest, sports may become a vehicle for male relationships throughout life. Even older men can develop a sense of immediate camaraderie with strangers on the golf course or tennis court or in discussing baseball, football, or basketball. The shared love of sports was one of the initial vehicles for the terrorist and the captive's powerful attraction in *The Crying Game* (1993), and often becomes the basis for powerfully connected male analyst–male patient psychoanalytic affinities. In this latter context, this element of deep personal connection may remain unaddressed by the analyst, for by analyzing this bond and deconstructing it, one risks losing the mutually comfortable and affirming equilibrium provided by this familiar and rewarding relational configuration.

In recent times, male athletes have become far more openly expressive in their affections. The shaking of hands and the pat on the rump have evolved into hugs, kisses, and verbal declarations of love. Teammates and competitors as well have abandoned a masculine reserve for far more open expression. It is possible that one of the unexpected benefits of feminism is greater participation of fathers in the raising of their children. It may be that fathers have become increasingly physically affectionate with their sons, accounting for some of the depth of feeling readily visible to those who watch public sporting events. In addition, boys as well as grown men are increasingly, unabashedly adoring of their athletic heroes because of more media exposure to these athletes than was once the case. Commercial marketing has made uniforms, jackets, shirts, and sneakers increasingly available, and even men of middle age can be seen wearing products identified with their more humanized gladiator heroes. Whether or not all of this reflects a step toward open expression of inherent bisexuality is unclear, though it most likely is not. As noted, once developed, sexual preference is deeply rooted and is, as well, maintained by powerful social and psychological forces. There is no indication that a greater cultural integration and tolerance of homosexuality or a greater affectional freedom of heterosexual men toward one another will alter the fixity of sexual orientation as we know it. Men's preference for men will probably continue to be expressed in shared gender-prototype actions and thereby maintained as a compromise between fear of bisexuality and fear of domination by women.

Probably more commonly than with women analysts treating male patients, heterosexual male analysts may readily enact an avoidance of these dual anxieties with their male patients. As I have tried to stress, it is not unusual for a kind of friendship to develop between a patient and an analyst who share a variety of prototypical, often gender-based interests. Such "friendships" often reflect a genuine intimacy, while at the same time serving to avoid other, more frightening sexual and dependent sorts of intimacy. The analytic relationship may mutually support a sense of heterosexual masculinity yet avoid the spoken conscious experience of homosexual anxiety and the vulnerability of regressive dependency. Such experiences may be highly valued by both parties, and can be preferred by some analysts to other sorts of relational configurations. However, such comforts should not be mistaken for anything approaching objective notions about which patients are more analyzable than others. The patients whom any given analyst deems optimally analyzable are the patients the analyst prefers to be with in the context of a long and intense affective engagement (Gabbard, 1995). I continue with two clinical examples, referred to earlier, of analytic work with men with whom I enjoyed engaging, and with whom I related in ways that resembled my past and present male friendships. As noted, this reflects a further effort to illustrate themes that highlight analysts' inclinations to pursue preferred, familiar, and comfortable relational configurations with patients.

## Clinical Examples

Alan is a successful, "all-business" guy, gray and emotionally detached save for anger. He is judgmental, critical, and rigid in his moral values. He reports truly being love with a woman once (in college), and since then his involvements, including with his recently ex-wife, have been functional. He has always desired children and a traditional family life. When he thought it was time to procreate, he conducted a search for a suitable woman as one would an apartment or a job. He liked having a woman to sleep next to and enjoyed sex, but his marital pleasures ended there. He did not enjoy being with or speaking to his spouse and wished that he could simply meet her in bed and have little else to do with her. They did not have children because of the tenuousness of their marriage, and now he is in the process of searching for another wife with whom to mate. He despises the dating and courtship rituals because they require him to speak to, show interest in, and relate to a woman in some semblance of a socially acceptable way.

Alan's portrayal of his own family closely parallels his quest. His father was dependent on his mother for serving as an obligatory maternal object, and the atmosphere at home is described as perfunctory and lacking in warmth and in verbal relatedness. Alan's enjoyable memories mostly involve watching weekend televised football games with his father and maternal grandfather. When Alan was 11, his mother died, and his father was too desperate and panicked to nurture his son. Alan tended to his father's needs and was unable to mourn. Father very rapidly married a widowed neighbor who proceeded to take care of him, and a stilted equilibrium returned to the family. Alan was angry with his father following the new marriage, and never has mourned his mother. He claims that he did not have a close relationship with her, that he does not recall her as a warm mother, and that he remembers mostly her yelling and her impatience. It is difficult to discern whether she, indeed, was a distant mother or if Alan's memories are exaggerated in order to protect him still from the pain of her loss.

Alan's passions in life were and still are school or work, and sports. His occupation puts him in proximity with many male peers, and he very much enjoys work-related dinners, conferences, and sports outings. He is an avid athlete and fan, and both competes against and attends games with his colleagues. Just as team sports were the basis of his childhood and college friendships, business and sports are now his primary vehicles for personal connection. He has an array of friends who he enjoys in compartments, and no single man toward whom he feels intimate. For Alan, intimacy is in the sharing of moments, and he likes that at the end of the game or workday, the "players" go home by themselves. He can, however, speak openly and intimately in this work–play context, and has not done this with a woman since engaging briefly with the one college girlfriend who left him for another.

For Alan, work and sports represent ideal vehicles for the mediation of dual anxieties: prolonged intimacy with either gender, and submission to both despair and longing for a lost mother. When Alan states that he wishes he could marry a man, he means that he despairs of finding a woman who will ask for no more than economic support, sex, and the persona of family life. Only other men seem to afford him the emotional space he desires. This space includes moments of indirect intimacy in the context of male-affirming activity. Alan is so uncomfortable among women that he is readily irritable, intolerant, and dominating when involved. Intimacy, warmth, and dependency are snuck in through the tactile closeness of sex and the proximity of his and her bodies in bed. It is the absence of a son with whom to share male-related interests that consciously pains him most and motivates him into the excruciatingly uncomfortable domain of what is supposed to be a verbally and affectively expressive therapy.

As might be expected, Alan is engaging with his sports-loving analyst up to a point. I would love to listen to Alan talk about sports (or politics) all session because when it comes to other content, his

warm affability congeals to a cold and dysphoric deadness. Our relationship becomes the empty emotional void that was his marriage
and his memory of his family. In this context, it is difficult for me to
interfere with Alan's opening volleys and my spontaneous wish to
return them. He will normally enter each session in an alert, perky,
and engaging manner and make some note of a piece of sports or
national news. His commentary and analysis are lively, intelligent,
and interesting, and I often find myself encouraging a prolongation
of this social banter. If I finally disengage from this, Alan and I both
seem to disengage entirely. At times he finds a work-related crisis
to discuss, or he may have an "insight" about his family of origin.
At such moments I usually feel present in a nurturing or caretaking manner. For much of the time when not speaking about sports
or current political events, however, Alan is embarrassedly silent,
repeats that he has had no dreams, claims to have nothing on his
mind but work, and/or requests that I ask him questions to help him
get started. When I comply with the latter, again I feel nurturing,
though his answers are normally quite spare. Because of the risk that
a good deal of our time together can be spent in awkward silence,
with both of us struggling to not entirely drift away, I often wish
we could spend the whole session as we do in the lively opening
minutes. I also often find myself wishing that we could go to the
local park together and play ball or compete at tennis. I know that I
could get along very well with Alan were we friends, though I have
doubts about this connection to the extent I attempt to be the analyst
I ought to be for him. Indeed, I spend much more time "playing ball"
with Alan than I know I should. Our silences make each of us very
uneasy, and in my withdrawn state I tend to drift to disquieting elements of some of the affective deadness in my own family of origin,
and to the profound dependence on my own mother from which I
have spent much time in flight. Our sports and political banter are a
good deal of fun for me, and they remind me thoroughly of the quality of both my childhood and current friendships. I value these relationships deeply, though they were often not, and still may be not,
intimate with respect to the breadth of affective experience verbally
shared. Yet I cherish many of these relationships, and even have very
warm feelings for kids or men with whom I played ball over a long
period of time while knowing very little about their personal lives.
This shared interest *is* intimacy for me, as it is for Alan, and when
we are not addressing the analytic themes we are there to deal with,

our bond is a close one. This said, Alan does not acknowledge feeling close to me, though in these contexts I indeed feel quite close to him. With a nod to arrogance, I believe I *know* that Alan shares this affective closeness, and believe that I am more able to acknowledge this based on the benefits of my own personal psychoanalysis. When I bring up how close we seem at various moments of interaction, he likely shakes his head in dismay at what he calls my "psychoanalysis speak," or he makes some jocular illusion to my homosexual problem. He teases that I'm trying to make him gay too, and he can see that I enjoy this banter. Alan is in flight from his grief and from familial affective deadness, and I still have remnants of the latter, and from strong overdependence on my own mother. My own male friendships have helped me immeasurably with these matters, and Alan and I have a nice thing going when we mutually create an equilibrium in the context of a "friendship" that combines flight from anxiety with what has served for each of us as a kind of intimacy.

If Alan's analysis is to further develop, we obviously must find emotional points of contact beyond our comfortable and equilibrium-creating interchanges. Lively involvement in sports or current events is, of course, only a very indirect expression of intimacy and of dependence, and for me it is easy. I am always tempted to coast with this. Indeed, such interaction closely mirrors elements of Alan's engagement with his father and grandfather, not to say his teammates and colleagues. I have not yet helped Alan experience toward me his dissociated longings for love and regressive dependence that lie buried in his history with his mother. This is the hardest part of the analysis for both of us. Our sports-related, compartmentalized, father–son "friendship" may remain, but if he is unable to fragment me in this way, he or we could become quite anxious and disorganized. His desire for me as a maternal object will likely precipitate a dependency and a vulnerability that he finds profoundly difficult, and that raise complicated issues for me. Alan senses that I, like so many of his compatriots, find emotional uncertainty, mutual dependency, and verbal expressions of intimacy somewhat difficult (see Hirsch, 1983). Perhaps this has made it possible for him to stay in treatment with me to this point. I must, however, allow our relationship to deepen beyond the balance he has maintained with me and with other men if we are to progress further into a zone of shared disequilibrium.

Barry is strikingly handsome, with a sculpted body, a writer's wit and creativity, and impressive academic and professional credentials.

He is a renaissance man, articulate and charming with men and women alike, and does far better in the beginning seduction phases of relationships than later on. His passion for and pursuit of women cool precipitously once they are involved with him. He also fares well on interviews and in the early days of new jobs, but his once promising career is faltering because he does not sustain the work at a steady level. Barry's most substantial relationships are with male high school and college friends, and the activities that most bind these friendships are engaging in and watching sports, and drinking and looking for women in bars. He reports that even though he holds back somewhat, he truly loves these guys with less ambivalence than he has ever experienced with a woman. He claims that he would be devastated without these friends occupying a central place in his life. Some of Barry's friends are now married and have young children. Barry is wonderful with kids and longs for some of his own, but fears that he will never maintain a relationship with a woman.

Barry's friends have, since adolescence, helped him differentiate from his mother. She is by far the dominating figure in his family, and she adored her beautiful and brilliant boy from the outset. He *belonged* to her, and many of his lively and creative interests outside of sports come from an identification with her. For some years, Barry was psychosomatically sickly and almost schoolphobic, and his mother loved his company. Barry's father has always been reliable and caring, but a remote and weak presence in comparison with mother. He is a sad figure, quite intelligent yet achieving well below potential in his career, and recessive at home. Barry was the jewel of his extended family, and his charming and seductive ways seem to be both directed toward pleasing his mother, and a way to retain some semblance of control over and differentiation from her. Barry believes he was more identified with his mother than his father, though he now recognizes that some of his unfulfilled potentials in his career, as well as an encyclopedic knowledge of sports, indeed reflect a close connection with father.

Barry has no direct recall of homosexual desire, yet he has speculated that his identification with his mother would have led him to be gay, were it not for a change in schools at age 12. In this much smaller private school and away from the tough kids in his working-class neighborhood, he was introduced to team sports. From this time on, athletics and related male friendships became his primary vehicle for separation from his mother, and a way to connect with his otherwise disembodied father. Indeed, it was also on the athletic fields where he first experienced the admiring glances of girls. He began to learn how to seduce and to control girls (he already knew how to charm), and this too aided his separation from and autonomous strivings in relation to his mother. Unlike Alan, Barry is comfortable with women, enjoys dialogue (with both genders), and appears to be highly sensitive to women's emotional desires. He still attracts women readily, enjoys the seduction, and loses interest. No woman has ever been able to control this Don Juan as his mother did, and he is devoted to reversing his symbiotic longing for her into sexualized power over women.

Not surprisingly, Barry found beginning analysis easier than maintaining it. I was delighted to have this eloquent, vivacious, and charming man as a patient. He entertained me with tales of his involvements with beautiful and interesting women, astute commentary on contemporary culture, and a knowledge of sports that surpassed my own. It appeared to me that we were quite productively engaged when he suddenly decided to terminate because of "financial concerns." I was thoroughly disappointed and perplexed until I recognized that I was a woman or a boss seduced (see Hirsch, 1996, on mutual enactments) and not the enduring friend I had thought. I had failed to recognize the mutually constructed lack of depth in our relationship.

This helped me considerably when Barry returned to analysis one year or so later. I have since tried to be less interested and, therefore, less subtly encouraging of Barry's efforts to speak about mutual interests. Nonetheless, this is often difficult, when, for instance, he begins a morning-after analysis of the New York Knicks basketball game that he attended and I had watched on television some 12 hours before the session. Despite such moments, our current interaction is generally more awkward, less easily flowing, and punctuated by more silence. Since his seduction and abandonment of me, I no longer feel the comfort between us that I used to and that he describes as characterizing his long-term friendships. I had originally thought naïvely and wistfully that I was enacting a long-term friend configuration, for I was not used to these kinds of seductions in my own friendships. I had been more mother to Barry in his transference, and I did not recognize this. His pressure to flee from his mother has some parallel to my own, and, in retrospect, I had been uneasy with being the maternal object of his transference to me, and much preferred being his friend.

Close friendship, for Barry, is a way to express his bisexuality without consciously experiencing sexual desire. It reflects a successful escape from overwhelming dependence upon and identification with mother. Such friendships are based on shared activities, in particular athletics, drinking, and chasing women. Since having been hurt and discarded by Barry, I no longer have the consistent desire to join him in male play. For me, our shared passion about sports and other mutual interests no longer serves to bind the anxiety of our *feminine* dependency-based attachment. My strongest conscious concern is the potential for superficiality in our connection to one another. However, in our work together, Barry is moving closer to the felt impotence of regressive dependency, a "momma's boy" state in which he feels impotent with me, and barely able to be the seducer. It is possible that his growing dependence upon and submissiveness toward me could precipitate homosexual desire for me (or me for him), as well as loss of his hard-won sense of autonomy. He has not stated this, but I believe he also fears that his deep attachments to some of his male friends, like that of the protagonist of *The Crying Game* (1993), might slide into homosexual love. With me, Barry is now risking a reversal of the dominance–submission relationship he has long enjoyed with women post mother, and the liberating camaraderie he enjoys with men. I am risking the reemergence of my own identification with and dependence on my mother, and the dormant homosexual anxiety that accompanies this state, in the presence of this extraordinarily handsome, charming, and seductive man. Barry depends on my ability to approach this mutual disequilibrium and to resist flight into our once comfortable friendship. This is often difficult for me, and there are many lapses and coastings into basketball, football, and movie talk. Despite my injury-fueled wariness of Barry, he can still both charm me and serve as a highly desirable buddy–companion for me (Hirsch, 1999).

## Summary

Barry, more so than Alan, is closer to the theme of bisexuality highlighted in *The Crying Game* (1993). Alan has never experienced the preconscious twinges of sexual desire for the men with whom he plays and works. Such desire, albeit now in a vague and undefined way, is closer to Barry's life historical experience than is the case with most heterosexual men whose closest and warmest relationships are with other men. Like with many men engaged in the battlegrounds of work and sports, it is essential to have a woman in place for nurture, for sex, for dissociated desire for intimacy, and to affirm the credential of heterosexual and familial normalcy. Thus established, my two patients, like so many other men, can take every opportunity to play, work, and compete with other men in male-affirming activity and avoid manifest vulnerability with women. The workaholic, the poker player, the sports fan or player, and the barroom habitué, from up and down the socioeconomic ladder, all may share a fear of women and a vague and unarticulated romantic love for men. The latter is the likely basis for a prevailing homophobia among most heterosexual men. My two patients are high-functioning individuals who have successful work and active social lives, and who look anything but pathological to most of those who know them. They are each variants of what I consider a rather normative personal configuration, a compromise between the dual anxieties of merger with women and sexual desire for men. The fullest intimacy with either gender is often not realized, but a solution somewhere along a dialectic continuum may sometimes allow for reasonable personal fulfillment. Indeed, many men begin therapy when the woman in their life threatens to leave because of excessive sadism, isolation, or overinvolvement with work or play with other men. In majority, heterosexual men do not wish to reduce their action-oriented work and play with their male colleagues or friends, nor are they normally willing to fully and vulnerably surrender in their love for one woman. Very few heterosexual men resolve conflict in the manner of the protagonist in *The Crying Game*, who essentially became the lover to his best buddy.

Despite long and intense personal analyses, many heterosexual male analysts do not transcend these issues and internal conflicts that emerge in the psyches of their male patients. In struggling with similar issues as many of their same-sex heterosexual patients, it is quite comforting to engage as one normally does with male friends, and with men who have been objects of love in the past. Such patients, and the relational configurations established, are often very satisfying to both analytic participants, and can be remarkably free of anxiety for analysts when mutual enactments are allowed to persist. Though engagement of such patients can lead to extended periods of comfort and even pleasure for the analyst (and patient too), as it did with me in my two clinical illustrations, failure to breach equilibrium does not take either analyst or patient beyond what is already comfortable and familiar. It is easy to designate someone as a good analytic patient when we both enjoy each other's company, and are able to coast in relational configurations that mutually are valued and desired. The flow and ease of analytic relationships illustrated here may have the aura of a "good" analytic situation, but sometimes may be little more than a mutual perpetuation of the emotional compromises that are already most comfortable and familiar to both participants.

# 5

# Psychoanalytic Theory and Its Unexamined Comforts*

Contradictions abound when one addresses the question of how theory affects clinical practice and, to stretch the question further, how theory helps analysts be clinically useful to patients. Most analysts from all "schools" would like to believe that they can see patients *as they really are*, free of analysts' memory and desire (Bion, 1967), that they function as an empty container or blank screen, or as a purely empathic observer or as an objective reader of patients' transferences or internalized patterns. Ideally, theory might serve as an anchor, or provide some frame to make sense of what might otherwise be an overwhelming input of confusing raw data. Theory also could guide praxis sufficiently enough to control the influence of both psychoanalysts' personalities and their unwitting participation with patients. It would not, however, bias analytic inquiry, the nature of the data looked for, or ways of comprehending and interpreting each unique individual patient. Yet early in the development of the profession, Ferenczi and Rank (1924/1956) sharply criticized clinical psychoanalysis for becoming excessively dominated by theory, severely compromising the understanding of the unique individuality of each patient and each dyad (see Fiscalini, 1988, 1994; Wilmer, 2000; Wolstein, 1959, 1975, 1983). Especially in psychoanalytic writing, it was hard to distinguish one patient from another. Virtually every patient seemed to have the same underlying dynamics or internal structures, discussion confirmed the universal theoretical constructs of the day, and analysts' interpretations and verbal interventions often sounded stereotyped. Though their monograph has since become a

---

* The original version of this article was published in the *Journal of the American Psychoanalytic Association*. Used with permission. © 2003 American Psychoanalytic Association. All rights reserved.

classic, Richards and Richards (1995) noted, with some irony, that the paper did not win Freud's prize awarded annually to contributions of special significance. There is much basis for criticism about how theory may blind analytic vision still in our more contemporary literature (Berman, 2001, 2004; Coen, 2000; Levenson, 1972, 1981, 1991; Spence, 1982). Some analytic perspectives appear more concerned than others by ways in which theory can narrow the range of clinical perception. Indeed, there is currently a countertheoretical trend toward pluralism and multiplicity, essentially an effort to deconstruct all theory and to neutralize any theoretical hegemony.* This direction in psychoanalysis was initiated by the introduction of Sullivan's (1953, 1954, 1956) key concept of participant–observation (see Conci, in press), refined by early analysts identified with the interpersonal school,** elaborated and blended into relational perspectives*** through epistemological concepts like constructivism and perspectivism, and integrated into the broader contemporary cultural ethos by analysts interested in postmodern thinking and critical theory (e.g., Fairfield, 2001; Gergen, 2001; Layton, 1998, 2004).

The broadest spectrum of interpersonal, relational, and postmodern thinking reflects theories that their proponents wished were not theories. They are theories, in part, born out of the desire to be atheoretical, and they live in contradiction or, at best, in a dialectic between theory and antitheory. It has been recognized ever since Sullivan's application to psychoanalysis of Heisenberg's principal of uncertainty that any analyst's explicit or implicit theory exerts considerable influence on patients, and although analysts are conscious of their theoretical biases, there exists the inclination to ignore this factor and operate as if governed by something that approximates objective clarity. Though aware of the power of theoretical influ-

---

* See Fairfield (2001) for a summary of this controversial issue.
** Particularly Fromm (1941, 1955, 1964), Fromm-Reichmann (1959), Thompson (1950, 1952), Wolstein (1954, 1959), Schachtel (1959), Tauber and Green (1959), Searles (1965, 1979), Singer (1965, 1968a), Levenson (1972, 1991), and Barnett (1980).
*** For example, Wachtel (1980), Mitchell (1988), Morrison (1989), Dimen (1991), Greenberg (1991), Ehrenberg (1992), Benjamin (1995), Aron (1996), Slochower (1996), Leary (1997), Stern (1997), Bromberg (1998), Davies (1998), Hoffman (1998), Layton (1998), Pizer (1998), Grand (2000), Bass (2001), Berman (2001), Knoblauch (2000), Crastnopol (2002), Cooper (2000a), Fosshage (2003), Safran (2003), Seligman (2003), Bonovitz (2005), Harris (2005), and Skolnick (2006).

ence on analytic work, it can be said that analysts, with at least some awareness of what they are doing, tend to coast in the application of preferred theories that are a personal comfortable fit to them. In most analytic moments, analysts will choose to operate within a theoretical structure that reflects their home base, and fail to reflect upon either how this imposes on patients or how a particular understanding may reflect but one of many ways of knowing.

Psychoanalytic theories basically tell us two things: what to look for with patients and what to do with them. The first, general theory has to do with comprehension, and attempts to answer the following questions: What are the universal commonalities among all people, and, in that context, what sense can be made out of individual lives and life histories? That is, how have individuals developed into who they are? What lies out of awareness and serves as the bases for unconscious motivation? The second, clinical theory refers to what to do with patients in order to illuminate unconscious motivation, and to enrich and expand experience so that patients may transcend the internalized constraints, compromises, and rigidities of the past. The two types of theory ought to relate intimately to one another but often do not. The nature of direct clinical work can be so deeply personal that analysts' personalities and idiosyncratic emotional reactions to each patient can readily dwarf guidelines for analytic interaction. Those contemporary psychoanalysts who lean more toward viewing psychoanalysis as a science are normally more troubled by this, whereas those who view psychoanalysis as part of the social sciences or humanities are likely to embrace such contradiction as reflective of theoretical deconstruction. In either case, however, each aspect of theory creates a certain dilemma for a wide range of contemporary psychoanalysts, because any foreknowledge of what to look for, or what activity to pursue, puts distinct constraint on both percepts and acts. Analysts of all stripes prefer ideally to observe with a naïve freshness and curiosity, yet our theories predispose us to what we see.* This is often not reflected on or taken into account, despite awareness of this dilemma. It may be said that in spite of recognizing how our theories bias us, we tend to wear them so comfortably that we normally coast with them, failing to examine fully the impact

---

* Some analysts (e.g., Arlow, 1987; Boesky, 1988) have argued that analysts can observe with a reasonable objectivity and that theory may be used to provide evidence for the accuracy of analytic observation.

on patients, and failing to consider competing conceptualizations. This phenomenon is more worthy of note, because many influential analysts of this postmodern era (e.g., Bromberg, 1998; Davies, 1998; Greenberg & Mitchell, 1983; Levenson, 1972; Schafer, 1983) have convincingly argued the case for multiplicity.* They have maintained that there is no one correct general theory, that people can be well understood with many different narratives (Spence, 1982) or meta-phors, and that a range of styles of therapeutic interaction can be mutative. Others have argued that there is no longer a conception of a singular standard psychoanalytic technique,** and that theory cannot tell us what to do in the context of each unique patient–analyst dyad. Further, and perhaps most significantly, the mutative action of psychoanalysis is seen more as a function of the subtle interactional or relational factors between analyst and patient than of any pro-scribed methodology. Nonetheless, simultaneous to embracing this most liberal and evolved contemporary skepticism about the exis-tence of theoretical absolutes, analysts still normally choose to view their clinical situations through their most familiar and comfortable theoretical lenses.

Analysts representing disparate general and clinical theories help patients change. Theory is an often unexamined context or ground-ing for how analysts understand patients and what is done with this understanding. It serves as an anchor for analyst and patient alike. Using theory as scaffolding and as guiding light, analysts from varying perspectives and within traditional analytic boundaries stand to provide new, salubrious experiences for patients. In the context of a theory of therapeutic action, successful analysts are likely to relate to patients with a passionate commitment (Billow,

---

* Multiplicity should not be confused with eclecticism. The latter refers to the idea that in working with patients, one may choose from a menu of viable concep-tions and successfully apply this mixture to the work. Multiplicity implies that, although each analyst is guided by his or her own preferred theory and tends to apply this with consistency, no one theory can be scientifically demonstrated to be more effective than all the others. That is, there are many ways to understand clinical data, and patients can be helped to understand themselves meaningfully through very different theoretical lenses.

** Wolstein (1954, 1975), Friedman (1988), Greenberg (1991), Levenson (1991), Renik (1993), Gabbard (1995), Josephs (1995), Satran (1995), Aron (1996), M. Ger-son (1996), Mitchell (1993, 1997), Rucker and Lombardi (1997), Hoffman (1998), Kwawer (1998), Richards (1999, 2003), Stern et al. (1998), Imber (2000), Ianuzzi (2005), and Kuriloff (2005).

2000) to understand them. Though this understanding is likely structured by one or another theory, the element of personal caring or even loving (Bach, 2006; Hirsch, 1994; Hirsch & Kessel, 1988) that develops over the course of long and intense relationships has much to do with whether or not personal awareness makes much of a difference for patients. In the final analysis, the quality of the unique individual patient–analyst dyad (Fiscalini, 2004; Stern et al., 1998; Wolstein, 1954, 1975) and, as some suggest,* *the verbal analysis of this dyad* have far greater mutative power than any single clinical theory can account for or explain. However, especially when this relationship is not verbally examined (i.e., the dyadic relationship is not analyzed or deconstructed), as some argue is sometimes preferable (Stern et al.), it becomes easy for analysts to assume that either or both their interpretive theory and their preferred theory of therapeutic action have been responsible for any productive therapeutic outcome. That is, despite the current wisdom that patients change less from theoretically biased insights and procedures than from new and unpredictable (Hoffman, 1987; Stern, 1990, 1996a, 1996b) affective relational experience with their analyst, the reluctance to help patients spell out in words what has been analytically helpful avoids challenging analysts' valued ideas about analytic process. In consciously assuming that our theory of therapeutic action and/or our explanatory theory was responsible for patients' growth, we risk remaining safely embedded in the theories that have become part of our professional identities. Although patients still might benefit substantially in such a context, both analyst and patient may fail to reap the benefit of an optimal understanding about all of the factors that have led to this desired outcome. Analysts' love for preferred theories, and the inclination to coast with these cherished systems, helps provide some predictability and familiarity in the face of a profession characterized by surprise and uncertainty (Hoffman, 1987; Stern, 1990). This can be quite useful to patients, except when it is not, and the idiosyncratic properties of each uniquely individual analytic dyad are given short shrift.

---

* For example, Levenson (1972), Sandler (1976), Searles (1979), Gill (1982), Hoffman (1983, 1998), Jacobs (1986, 1991), Friedman (1988, 1999), Greenberg (1991, 1995), McLaughlin (1991), Mitchell (1993, 1997), Renik (1993), Gabbard (1995), Hirsch (1996, 1998a), Stern (1997, 2003), and Abend (1999).

Theory: A General Discussion

In spite of the analytic ideal of seeing patients with some vision that approaches the unreachable and paradoxical goal of objectivity, every analyst has some sense of connection to theoretical traditions that both structure and bias ideally naïve perception. This may be seen as a home base or a cherished hometown, or as a fundamental identification with a family of origin. Though analysts may appreciate the degree of bias these identifications ensure, for most analysts this remains purposefully unattended to in clinical work, because close examination of this may become disorganizing. I suggest throughout that for most analysts, the predictability of both our developmental theories and theories of therapeutic action fits too comfortably into schemata that are already developed. In the context of quotidian clinical uncertainties, it normally creates some degree of comfort and equilibrium to accept our theories without challenge, and to embrace this apparent knowledge while avoiding the disruptive status of constant reexamination of what is so familiar and valued. Sandler (1983) suggested that although analysts' private theories may differ from their public allegiances to one or another theoretical group, perception that is unbiased by theory is, nonetheless, impossible. One of psychoanalysis's great challenges may be seen as the effort to remain sufficiently aware of our theoretical predispositions so that our range of observation is not profoundly constricted. Fairfield (2001), in summarizing currently popular postmodern efforts to deconstruct all theory, pointed out that this very commitment in and of itself is reflective of yet another theory. Cooper (1985) underscored that it is impossible to live without the structure that theory provides—it gives analysts the sense of grounding and basic security that then may allow creativity to flourish. On the other hand, he argued that theoretical structure inevitably narrows perception. He gave as an example the long-standing division in psychoanalysis between those who conceptualize human development and unconscious process as based on either conflict surrounding guilt or conflict related to tragedy—"guilty versus tragic man." Analysts' fundamental ways of understanding and conceptualizing people may be defined by where they stand on this very basic developmental conception. Brenner (1995) acknowledged that analysts look for data to explain their already preconceived views on the nature of psychopathology. The gathering of analytic material becomes a self-fulfilling prophecy—the data are determined by the questions we are predisposed to ask. Analysts look at the environment for identifiable patterns, and perceptions are organized around these configurations. Tuch (2001) spoke of analysts' "prepared mind," a mind that unwittingly accommodates psychoanalytic data into already existing schemata. He suggested, using Piagetian conceptions, that analysts normally find it difficult to assimilate new psychoanalytic data and to broaden their own internal schemata. Spence's (1982) now classic volume vividly illustrates how patients' life stories invariably conform to analysts' internalized "narratives." Despite the uniqueness of each patient, these narratives consistently reflect analysts' basic belief systems about human development. There is always risk that each patient may sound the same as the next. Nonetheless, some contemporary analysts (e.g., Arlow, 1987; Boesky, 1988) still argue for psychoanalysis as science, minimizing analysts' irreducible subjectivity (Renik, 1993, 1998) in the understanding of patients. Arlow and Boesky are representative of a body of analysts who have believed that the search for consistent patterns in patients' life histories, in the transference, and in the literature and the myths of our culture provides objective scientific "evidence" for certain universal theoretical assumptions. In contrast, Josephs (2001) viewed evidence as nothing more than confirmation of preexisting belief systems, analysts' imposition of both moral and educational goals. The scientist–analyst inevitably discovers the evidence that confirms the theoretical positions already held—accommodation in priority to assimilation. For example, believers in "guilty man" place in the foreground loss of love in a context of conflict over sexual and aggressive wishes. Subscribers to notions of "tragic man" place sex and aggression in the background, as subtexts to highlighting loss of love as related primarily to varieties of insufficient parenting. Theories differ with respect to figure and ground, and analysts tend to find evidence that provides further grounding in the secure home of familiar theory. Once more, even when any given analyst is quite aware of these inclinations, the internal pressure to remain within the secure home of one's theoretical tradition is likely to prevail.

The original interpersonal model of psychoanalysis, participant–observation (Conci, in press; Sullivan, 1953, 1954, 1956), was born as a corrective to a prevailing natural science model that situated analysts in the role of objective scientific observers of patients' minds. From this former perspective, one can look at theory as yet another form of pervasive personal countertransference (Aron, 1991; Barnett, 1980; Fromm, 1941; Greenberg & Mitchell, 1983; Hirsch, 1990; Levenson, 1972; Schachtel, 1959; Singer, 1965a; Tauber & Green, 1959; Thompson, 1950; Wolstein, 1954). Theory becomes part of the analysts' use of self (Jacobs, 1991, 2001), while always acknowledging privately both its irreducible subjectivity and the powerful influence it exerts on patients. Parenthetically, patients tend to identify with and to cooperate with analysts' theoretical structures when the analysis is going well and when they feel understood. Theory that has internal consistency, and that helps patients' lives make sense, provides the same sort of grounding for patients as for their analysts. Patients often accommodate analysts' schemata, and analysts fit patients' lives into familiar and comfortable theoretical frameworks. As repeatedly noted, for the most part this is neither acknowledged nor examined openly in most analytic work. Normally, both analyst and patient, working productively together, prefer to remain safely and quietly in a theoretical home built by the analyst, and inhabited by both participants. Failure to examine this form of countertransference reflects the psychoanalytic norm.

Spence (1982) argued that one cannot view psychoanalytic understanding as representing historical truth but as a mutually subjective narrative (or sensible fiction) that represents one way of understanding a life. Many different narratives may make sense and will vary according to analysts' theoretical countertransference. Schafer's (1983) "storylines" reflect a similar sentiment. He too viewed analysts' theoretical preference as providing the structure that will ultimately accommodate patients' descriptions of their lives. Multiple storylines may help patients make sense of their lives, and much of contemporary psychoanalytic wisdom recognizes the fallacy of theoretical hegemony.*

There are some thinkers who have viewed general theory primarily as something to ground analysts (and patients) but have seen such theory as exerting little influence on how analysts relate to patients. Cooper (1985) distinguished between metapsychology and clinical theory, suggesting there is major disjuncture between them.

---

* Levenson (1972, 1983), Friedman (1988, 1999, 2006), Mitchell (1988, 1993, 1997), Greenberg (1991), Renik (1993), Gabbard (1995), Aron (1996), M. Gerson (1996), Hirsch (1996a, 1998), Stern (1997), Davies (1998), Hoffman (1998), Kwawer (1998), Langan (1999), Richards (1999, 2003), Eisold (2000), Imber (2000), Smith (2001), and Kuriloff (2005).

Wallerstein (1995) agreed, finding more of a "common ground" among analysts in their clinical work or even in their clinical theory than when examining the pervasive polemic among representatives of partisan analytic subgroups. This, however, is a complicated question, because clinical activity can be viewed in two distinct ways. On one hand, it can be argued that each general theory has a logically consistent theory of therapeutic action that should correspond. If otherwise, general theory becomes rhetorical and potentially shallow. On the other hand, analysts' clinical interaction is at least as much a function of the person of the analyst and the idiosyncrasies of each unique analytic dyad than any particular general theory or theory of analytic action. As already noted, I believe that these relational and personal factors have more significance in determining analytic outcome than does any single theoretical disposition. Clearly, analysts' way of being with patients is multidetermined—countertransference ranges from theoretical beliefs to the range of usually unwitting personal affective engagement (Racker, 1968). Before addressing the significance of analysts' idiosyncratic and largely unconscious relational participation, I will turn to a brief discussion about the analytic impact of witting participation—analysts' conscious efforts to relate to patients in line with their theoretical constructs.

Despite the plethora of observations that argue that much of what analysts do is dominated by unconscious relational participation (e.g., Aron, 1996; Epstein & Feiner, 1979; Gabbard, 1995; Greenberg, 1991; Levenson, 1972; Mitchell, 1988; Racker, 1968; Renik, 1993; Searles, 1965, 1979; Sullivan, 1953; Tansey & Burke, 1989; Wolstein, 1954), each major theory has a coordinate theory of therapeutic action. These are largely conscious or witting participations (Hirsch, 1987, 1994) that make sense in light of particular theories of development, unconscious motivation, and psychopathology. These *approaches* (I prefer this term to *techniques*) have considerable influence on how varying analysts work, even though ultimately they may prove less important than the idiosyncratic personal and the unconscious relational aspects of analytic participation. If, for example, ego psychologists attempt to make conflicted sexual and aggressive wishes conscious in order to loosen restrictive compromise formations, it is logical that Freudian analysts focus primary attention on the explication and interpretation of such conflicted desires (Abend, 1999; Brenner, 1995; Druck, 1989; Lasky, 1993). This can be liberating and expansive for patients. If, on the other hand, the core of psychopathology is viewed as the absence of internal

structure based largely on deficient parental mirroring or identifications, articulation of this void takes priority over the interpretation of
conflicted sexual desires within the internalized family. Further, unless
the patient uses the analyst's attunement to repair deficiency and to
build structure, interpretation per se may be relatively useless or even
harmful. Similarly, if one believes developmental psychopathology to
be largely a function of an absence of good enough mothering, it is
only reasonable to view metaphors like *holding environment* as central
to analytic action. Here, verbal interpretation or even description may
be experienced as intrusive and even counter to analytic progress (Slochower, 1996). Yet other witting analytic action is called for when one
views the development of personality, and psychopathology as well,
as based largely on internalized relational configurations (Mitchell,
1988) or dissociated self–other integrations (Bromberg, 1998; Davies,
1998; Hirsch, 1994; Stern, 1996b). Here, the analyst is likely to inquire
into and/or articulate the unconscious repetition of these dissociated
configurations as they recursively emerge in the transference–countertransference matrix (Bromberg, 1998; Gabbard, 1995; Gill, 1982,
1983; Greenberg, 1991; Hirsch, 1987, 1996; Hoffman, 1983, 1998; Levenson, 1972, 1991; Sandler, 1976; Stern, 1987). Insight is focused on
the shifting back and forth between old repetitive and new interactive
moments in the here and now of the analytic playground.

Abend (1999), Aron (1996), Fonagy (1999, 2001), Friedman (1988),
Gabbard (1995, 1996), Gill (1982, 1983, 1984, 1994), Greenberg (1991,
1995, 2001), Hirsch (1996, 1998a), Hoffman (1983, 1991, 1998), Levenson (1972, 1983, 1991), Mitchell (1993, 1997), Richards (1999,
2003), Smith (2001), and Wallerstein (1995) are among those who
have tried to identify commonalities among previously disparate
theories of therapeutic action. Their prevailing sentiment is that current theories are converging around the primacy of analysts' efforts
to examine the affectively laden analytic interaction in the here and
now of the transference–countertransference situation. Nonetheless, although there has been some theoretical convergence along
this line, I believe that many analysts continue to remain quite loyal
to consciously designed analytic interactions that correspond to the
traditions in which they developed as analysts-in-training. However,
whether any given analyst's preferred theory reflects early professional identifications or more recent shifts, this theory becomes one
that is comfortably worn and inevitably imposed on patients. We

coast, as Fairfield (2001) implied, with our more traditional theories as well as our postmodern ones.

## Personality and Relational Factors That Transcend Theoretical Allegiances

The relational turn in psychoanalysis has led to a shift in focus from the study of witting to unwitting analytic action, paying increased attention to what can be called analysts' subjective affective engagement in the analytic dyad.* In fact, because interpretation itself can be viewed as a relational event, the interpretive and the relational are inseparable (Aron, 1991, 2005; Singer, 1977). That is, one can never know if any question, interpretation, or observation is useful because of the insight generated, or because that patient feels seen, understood, or the object of the analyst's passionate commitment (Billow, 2000). The personality of the analyst, what part of the analyst is called into play with any particular patient, and the analyst's degree of personal involvement all may have greater mutative power than consciously designed interventions per se. This is not meant to devalue theory, nor is it meant to imply that either analysts' personalities or their love and devotion in and of themselves represent the essence of the psychoanalytic process. Both general theory and theory of therapeutic action do often provide a desired frame to help patients make sense of their lives, and to anchor analysts in efforts to deal with otherwise confusing data. As much as theory constricts, it may serve as bedrock, and analysts cannot live without it despite many valid efforts to do so. Hoffman (1998) put it well when he discussed analysts' need to be grounded in "the book" while simultaneously having access to spontaneous engagement. The sensitive application of one's theory of therapeutic action is one distinct talent.** Analysts who do

---

* Thompson (1952), Sullivan (1953, 1954), Wolstein (1954), Singer (1965a), Racker (1968), Levenson (1972), Searles (1979), Gill (1983), Hirsch (1987), Mitchell (1988), Greenberg (1991), Ehrenberg (1992), Renik (1993), Aron (1996), Rucker and Lombardi (1997), Davies (1998), Frankel (1998), Hoffman (1998), Layton (1998), Bromberg (1998), Fonagy (1999), Cooper (2000b), Bass (2001), Berman (2001), Crastnopol (2002), Dimen (2003), Seligman (2003), and Stern (2003, 2004).

** It is crucial that any analyst's theory, to be effectively applied, is one that has been reflected upon by and adapted to that particular analyst. Singer (1965b) distinguished between identity (ultimately establishing one's own center of self) and identification (following the lead of respected or idealized others).

this rigidly, however, are likely to compromise the affective elements of analytic work. In this less contentious psychoanalytic era, it has become clear that if theories so different from one another seem to be valuable in facilitating change, both personal and relational factors that cut across disparate theories must have considerable power. Further, it is often that analysts at work in clinical engagement with patients bear greater similarity to one another than they do when they write about their work. In the trenches of clinical interaction, analysts' personalities are dominant over both general and clinical theory. I suggest that differing general and clinical psychoanalytic theories are likely to be effective when analysts are committed toward their own psychoanalytic belief systems, while at the same time are both conscious of this influence and not excessively restricted by this; analysts attempt to be attuned to the unique psyches of each individual patient and are willing to, at any given moment, stretch their theoretical beliefs toward this end; analysts recognize that their own personalities, independent of theory, are bound to play a critical role in the clinical process, and are ready to examine this influence; and analysts over time develop a strong emotional commitment toward, a caring for, or even a love for their patient, and are as well willing to acknowledge this as having considerable impact on all analytic work. I believe that all of psychoanalysis' major theories are potentially valuable to patients when both individual personality and unconscious relational factors supply the fuel to bring these to life. Furthermore, it is always an advantage when analysts recognize and are willing to address with patients the latter's experience of the impact of both the analyst's theory *and* level of personal involvement. It is more the analytic norm to examine the latter in the transference. This normative reluctance to examine theoretical influence makes it easy for even the prototypical postmodern, relational analyst to coast with familiar and comfortable theories.

## Attachment, Personality, and Personal Esthetic

Each individual analyst's theory bears some similarity to an unconscious fantasy, internalized template, or script—some, though not all, of what influences conscious theoretical beliefs is beyond awareness. The more analysts consciously keep in mind this "theoretical countertransference," the more one's internalized theory can be used discretely or selectively, and the more clearly the mutative factors in analysis can be explicated. This internal structure of theory, if you will, develops out of a combination of identifications with personal analysts, teachers, and organized groups and, of course, personality factors and one's personal esthetics or tastes. These intertwined factors are similar to what leads to choices of religious, political, and social groups. In today's more pluralistic psychoanalytic world, one hears less frequently the argument that one theory is clearly better than another. The long-standing hegemony of Freudian theory and ego psychology in the United States has broken down. Though most analysts, at least privately, believe that their own theoretical affiliation is actually better than others, deeper reflection is likely to lead to the recognition that there are multiple ways of understanding patients and of being analytically useful. I believe that any analyst's personality, and how this intersects with his or her engagement with each individual patient, will account for far more of the variance in outcome than anything related to subjective theoretical preferences. One set of metaphors may be no better than another in the effort to help patients see their lives with greater clarity, or to render conscious what has been unconscious. Indeed, most analysts perform rather similar technical operations as one another,* but may use different theoretical terminology or metaphors to describe what is done. Ultimately, the quality of the analytic interaction—and I believe, ideally, the analysis of that interaction—affects therapeutic outcome more so than adherence to any particular theory. As much as this way of thinking meets with much agreement among contemporary practitioners, most of us are not willing to abandon the theoretical scaffolding that affords comfort and a sense of belonging to an analytic family. Although recognizing that our theories are constructs that may truly be no better than those of another colleague, we may still embrace our preferred theory and apply it in our work as if it were the only useful one.

Each analyst's general theory and theory of therapeutic action are determined by a combination of personal factors and semi-accidents of professional environmental exposure. Bracketing personal factors for the moment, I believe that positive transference to and identification with one's analyst and that analyst's *school* often comprise the

---

* See Levenson (1983) and Hoffman (1998) for a discussion of largely agreed upon psychoanalytic procedures or "rituals."

single greatest determinant of theoretical disposition. When analysts, or analysts-in-training, are pleased with their personal analysis, the majority will adopt both their analyst's general theory and his or her mode of interaction. Despite most senior analysts being well aware of this common phenomenon, it is rarely analyzed with vigor, and is certainly less likely to be closely examined than patients' "rebellious" choices. Just as parents are normally pleased to see their children identify with what parents believe are their best attributes,* senior analysts hope for, are gratified by, and tend to coast with patients' professional identifications. These identifications are commonly reinforced by analysts-in-training's choice of supervisors who are friendly and/or theoretically compatible with their analyst. This cooperative effort frequently works to gratify both parties. It may take years before the junior analyst forms a professional identity at least somewhat separate from that of the mentor analyst, though even then there may remain considerable elements of unresolved identification (Singer, 1965b).

This system usually works when the patient-analyst is at least relatively pleased with the more senior analyst. When this is not the case, and there is a choice within the analytic institution (or if the choice is made after training requirements are met), the patient-analyst may very well choose an analyst identified with a different theoretical perspective. The likelihood is that the original analyst's theory is not the problem; it is far more reasonable to speculate that the particular personal mixture had not worked. Parenthetically, this bears out in analytic institutions that represent only one theory and give candidates a choice of individual but not of theory. The chances are strong that the candidate will find a second training analyst representing the same theory as the first, and indeed identify with that theory in the context of a fulfilling analytic experience. In institutions that offer training in more than one perspective, the choice of a second analyst from perhaps a rival perspective is likely to lead ultimately to the belief that one perspective is good and one is bad or even harmful. This is one basis for extreme theoretical antagonisms (Berman, 2004; Eisold, 1994, 2000; Richards, 2003). This may be perpetuated

---

* It is rare that heterosexual parents question why their children become heterosexual. Actually, heterosexual analysts also do not normally examine this development with the same curiosity they might with homosexual patients (Blechner, 1993, 2005a; D'Ercole & Drescher, 2004; Drescher, 2002; Frommer, 1994, 2006; Hansell, 1998).

by senior analysts who may believe that their superior theory forms the basis of analytic change, thereby failing to sufficiently analyze the unique transference–countertransference configurations that are responsible for patients' growth and satisfactory experience. Ideally, awareness of comfort within one's home-based theory will lead to challenging oneself to question the consistent pursuit of internal theoretical equilibrium.

Two examples of colleagues' experience are relevant here. In a psychoanalytic institution known for offering a wide range of theoretical points of view, my colleague early in his training saw a well-respected Freudian analyst and, after one or so years, quit analysis and switched to an analyst identified with the interpersonal approach. He felt no benefit from his initial experience and found the second quite valuable. He attributed the failed analysis to the shortcomings of Freudian psychoanalysis, especially emphasizing his analyst's reserve and relative silence. He referred in particular to his analyst's coldness and compared this very unfavorably with his second analyst's engagement. In speaking with my colleague, my suspicion is that he and his initial analyst did not like one another, and that their work could not get them beyond this. Actually, I think it is likely that his analyst did not like him, and that my colleague responded to protect himself. My sense was supported in subsequent discussions when my colleague repeatedly dichotomized Freudian analysis as cold and surgical, and interpersonal work as characterized by warmth and caring. These characterizations, indeed, correspond to some stereotypes. Nonetheless, it is very clear to me that personality and/or relational factors like warmth and a sense of caring have nothing ultimately to do with theory, and everything to do with the person of the analyst and the particular transference–countertransference matrix in each analytic pair. From what my colleague has told me, it seems likely that neither analyst fully addressed either the particulars of their respective relational configurations that led to first a bad outcome, and then a good outcome, or the likelihood that a good or bad theory was not the key factor in analytic outcome. Both senior analysts appeared comfortable working within the respective theories, and preferred to coast with the belief that in the first case, the patient was not sufficiently analytically minded for the theory, and in the second case the analyst's theory was superior to that of analyst number one. It is no surprise that my colleague thoroughly swallowed one theory, demonized the other, and began to practice his preferred theory in an unquestioning manner.

A second example finds a colleague studying in an institution primarily identified as interpersonal, suffering through 5 or 6 years of a training analysis with a very well-liked analyst, and feeling all of this time that his life was going nowhere. It was not so much that he disliked his analyst, or felt disliked as did my first colleague—rather, he felt no help from the process, and was less than enthusiastic about his own analytic practice. Still feeling quite ambivalent about his profession a few years post graduation, my colleague began a second analysis with a Freudian analyst who was comparable in seniority and stature to his first analyst. He felt immediately liberated, feeling that he finally had the freedom to be himself and to express his uniqueness. In comparing the experiences down the road, he described his first analyst as far too active and intrusive. He felt that this analyst's presence took up too much of the analytic space, and that my colleague was unable to find his private self. Once again, this comparative example captures some of the prototypes or potential difficulties of one particular perspective. The greater license to interact indeed may produce a situation wherein the patient is usurped or overtaken by the all too noisy presence of the other. As in my first example, the initial analysis likely reflected a mixture of two people who did not cohere together. Perhaps in an effort to connect or to be loved, the first analyst asked for too much or maybe even gave excessively, and, in being too focused on being loved, lost the contours of his patient. My colleague's experience, understandably, was to seek posttraining supervision from analysts representing the school of his second analyst, abandoning his affiliation with his interpersonal institution and ultimately identifying himself as an ego psychologist. Here again, a relatively junior analyst is seen to fully embrace one theory and maintain perhaps a career-long antagonism to another. In believing that it was the theory that helped, the younger analyst begins to make this theory into a cherished home, one that is so comfortable that it is viewed as something akin to objective truth. The senior training analyst coasted with the conviction that his theory was proven superior, and this antagonistic system may be handed down to future generations of analysts who may embrace the comforts of certainty, and allow themselves to similarly coast with theories that they are convinced explain all of the productive analytic work they achieve (Richards, 2003).

Every significant contemporary psychoanalytic theory has metaphors that are internally consistent and make intrinsic sense, and a theory of therapeutic action that corresponds, and that has potential to be clinically useful to patients. Although I believe theoretical choice is often an artifact of who one's analyst is or was, theory is also reflective of one's personal esthetic. There are qualities in each analyst that predispose a choice of one or another institution, a particular personal analyst, and where on the spectrum of the institution's or personal analyst's theory to line up. It is not the norm, but it sometimes happens that during the course of training, or more likely after training, analysts explore and/or adopt different theoretical identifications. This may speak well for the personal analytic experience—perhaps the positive transference was, after all, sufficiently examined, and this produced an increased sense of freedom for the patient–analyst. It is very difficult to separate taste or personal esthetic from transference influence. There is, however, one dimension of personality or personal esthetic that I have noticed to stand out above others. This refers to a proclivity toward the scientific and technological, in contrast with understanding the human condition through the lens of the humanities or social sciences. Of course, these general orientations are not mutually exclusive, and the development of these leanings is complicated. Nonetheless, some theories are quite technical in the way people are understood, and perhaps in the specificity of prescribed analytic intervention. Other perspectives' literature reads more like the way people are described in novels and, as well, may advocate a more broad or spontaneously induced range of clinical interventions. I believe it would be interesting research to study the development of analysts and their tastes and interests along these lines, and examine possible correlations with theoretical perspective.

Using myself as an example, from elementary school on I was always both weak and disinterested in the basic sciences, but reasonably strong in literature, history, and, later, the social sciences and humanities. Though interested in both film and fiction, the only genre consistently avoided was and is science fiction. In my pre-analytic clinical training, I gravitated toward humanistic and existential writing, avoiding what appeared to me the very highly technical

Freudian oeuvre.* One body of reading was pleasure, like novels, and the other felt like a chore, like required basic science courses. I could never understand why so many respected peers and teachers seemed to enjoy Freud as a writer—I was never able to get beyond the reductionistic and mechanistic elements of his written work. I began personal analysis a couple of years before I started analytic training, and I think it was largely by accident that my analyst represented the interpersonal perspective. At the time, though I clearly preferred some analytic literature over others, I did not realize that different analytic *schools* existed. I thought all analysts were trained in the same way, though their emphases or writing styles might be different. In the late 1960s Freudian hegemony still existed, and I was not then cognizant of the psychoanalytic minority groups. By the time I began analytic training I was aware, largely through dialogue with my own analyst, of the rival psychoanalytic perspectives. I quickly began to view traditional classical psychoanalysis as the ruling class, finding this attitude quite compatible with an aspect of myself that was rebellious and anti-authoritarian. This was not sufficiently challenged by my analyst, who either may have shared these views or was gratified by my combativeness. At the time it seemed only logical that I choose an institute that fulfilled three basic criteria: My analyst would be accepted as a training analyst, teachers and supervisors existed at this institute who were known to be at least reasonably compatible with the conceptual orientation of my analyst, and the institute would have an available curriculum that was as minimally technical as possible, and that reflected what I then knew to be my preferred interpersonal and humanistic psychoanalytic thinking. My identification with my analyst solidified my original esthetic, and as well, the courses and supervisors that I eventually chose dramatically underscored this. I failed to expose myself to a wide range of theoretical perspectives. I also became quite partisan in my alliance with the interpersonal school, and in my antagonism toward the highly technical Freudians. I am embarrassed to say that, for a time, I believed that only interpersonal analyses were useful. Life events, greater exposure, and, I hope, an element of maturity have brought me to a different place. Though I still prefer what has

---

* I am, of course, aware that these interests or esthetic preferences cannot be understood apart from the development of my personality in a larger sense. Personal "tastes" have considerable developmental significance, though such an exhumation is not my intent in this forum.

now developed into interpersonal-relational writing, I can now enjoy Freudian writing as long as it is not highly technical (and I now see that there is much that is not technical). My witting clinical action is still well within the interpersonal-relational theories of therapy, but I realize now that the way we actually work is usually more a function of our person than our theory (Hirsch, 1994, 1996, 1998a). I also recognize that had I been referred initially to a Freudian analyst, and had been pleased with our work, I most likely would have adopted and identified with the least technical aspects of a Freudian theoretical schema. I suspect that in my efforts to solidify my affiliation, I would have engaged with zeal in efforts to highlight the advantages of my new family.

No theory, regardless of how technical and prescriptive it might be, can ever dwarf the impact of analysts' personalities, and/or analysts' degree of personal commitment or passion toward each unique patient. In the trenches of the transference–countertransference matrix, the technical inevitably breaks down, exposing analysts' personalities and their degree of emotional connectedness and intensity toward each unique individual patient. This does not at all make partisan theory irrelevant, but it places any theory in a context where, ideally, it is viewed as any analyst's most comfortable home base. From this perspective it should be clear that each unique individual analyst prefers to work from within a familiar tradition, and comfortably remain in the warmth of that internalized analytic family. In any given clinical situation, recognition of this may open the possibility of an analysis that may become more fresh, albeit potentially less comfortable, for both the analyst and the patient.

## Some Advantages and Cautions of Theory

Aside from the generally accepted professional boundaries in the psychoanalytic relationship, theory provides analysts with an additional level of border. With theory on one's mind, analytic asymmetry (Aron, 1996; Gabbard & Lester, 1995) is reinforced. The intense and highly personal nature of this relationship can readily transform it into a friendship, romance, or parent–child configuration. Every analyst is tempted probably each day to abandon analytic boundary, and to engage in one or more of these symmetrical ways. Theory reminds us that we are professional, that we have preconceptions that sometimes feel like a scientific body of knowledge, and that we have a repertoire of procedures to give order to a distinctly personal interaction. Freud's strict procedural rules were proffered not only so that an anxious public would not confuse psychoanalysis with sexual engagement. Analysts as well need constant reminder that the intimacy of the analytic interaction is a professionally contextualized intimacy. The more centrally any given analyst keeps both a preferred general theory and a clinical theory in conscious mind during clinical interaction, the more, one might speculate, that this analyst may feel a need for reinforced boundary. At best, because it is well integrated into the person of the analyst, theory is background. It is one way for analysts to stay at least somewhat grounded, while being enmeshed in a mutually affective engagement where the volume and breadth of data can be potentially overwhelming. It is not unusual that younger analysts, perhaps dealing with a greater need for certainty and boundary both, keep theory more rigidly present in their work than their more seasoned counterparts. I have often heard the observation that theory has less of a direct impact on analysts' activity as one accumulates experience. Nonetheless, the term "bedrock envy" (Fairfield, 2001) is reflective of a common if not universal wish for order, structure, and grounding (Becker, 1973; Farber, 1966; Fromm, 1941, 1955, 1964; Hoffman, 1987, 1991, 1998). Many analysts either envy the physical sciences for their more factual base, or try to construe psychoanalysis as science. How many of our institutions refer to their colloquia or conferences as *scientific meetings*? Theory also has an affiliative function. As already noted, one's theoretical allegiance reflects transference to personal analysts, teachers, and institutions. These affiliations are often powerful and can serve as a basis for an analyst's social as well as professional life. It is quite common that one's closest friends (and sometimes lovers or spouses) emerge from affiliation with home-based, national, or international memberships. At best this provides analysts with a rich personal and professional life, and at worst it leads to demonization of alternate professional groups (Berman, 2004; Eisold, 1994, 2000; Richards, 1999, 2003; Smith, 2001).

Sandler's (1983) distinction between public and private theories is reflective of analysts' wish for affiliation. Public theories, often expressed through writing and presentations at professional meetings, may vary considerably from how analysts think and what they do in the privacy of clinical work. Anxieties related to standing alone and to being separate from one's analytic family can lead to psychoanalytic writing that is both stereotyped and impersonal (Coen, 2000). Coen suggested that the aim of much writing is to reinforce institutional connections and to avoid presenting the idiosyncratic nature of each analyst's deeply personal thoughts, feelings, and interactions. He observed that this has led to a rather stilted body of psychoanalytic writing. From a different perspective, Greenberg (2001) has criticized other psychoanalytic writers for emphasizing excessively their spontaneous and personal affective interventions with patients. He believed that these analysts are implying that this kind of interaction is suggestive of a new standard technique. Greenberg argued that this is but another form of affiliative behavior, albeit with a more radical psychoanalytic subgroup.

As much as both general and clinical theory can be used to create needed grounding and professional boundary, as already noted, embrace of theory often goes too far. Theory is commonly used in the service of excessive emotional distance from patients, highlighted by stereotyped responses to them, while at the same time reinforcing deep emotional connection to one's training analyst and "home team." The desire to coast in the glow of warmth and familiarity of internalized others is a temptation for all of us. No theoretical tradition is immune from this problem, though more highly technical theories may lend themselves to it to a greater degree. Levenson (1983) referred to "physics envy," and Mitchell (1997) to "science envy," in their critiques of theories that they believed are overly technical.* Both critics have origins in a psychoanalytic tradition that emerged originally from Sullivan's interest in the social sciences and humanities. It is a theory that emphasizes social interaction (see Stern, 1985), from birth onward, as the basic building block of personality. Ferenczi and Rank's (1924/1956) original criticisms of psychoanalytic theory and technique were similar to Levenson's and Mitchell's, and still apply today to some degree. Coen's (2000)

---

* Postmodern trends in current psychoanalytic writing, and American efforts to comprehend contemporary French psychoanalytic thinking (see Fairfield, 2001), have led to a strong interest in the discipline of philosophy. This emphasis, too, may readily lend itself to overly complicated and/or intellectualized ways of understanding people, via affiliation with a discipline (philosophy) that can be viewed as more respectably academic than psychoanalysis per se. "Philosophy envy" may be one current variation on "physics envy" or "science envy."

observations about stilted psychoanalytic writing are also relevant here. Scientific striving often leads to patients being discussed from a perspective allegedly inside patients' minds. Analysts' subjective experience with patients may be omitted (Coen, 2000), and this may have the quality of talking about people as if one were reading an MRI. In relating to patients, an impression of analytic precision and objectivity may be reflective of both disrespect for patients' subjectivity and a denial of analysts' subjectivity—the excessive hierarchy of a one-person psychology model. It may be implied that the scientist–analyst is not fooled by the superficial outside—the visage (Levenson, 1983, 1991). In addition to the illusion of objectivity, metaphors of complicated internal structures lend themselves to prototypical description, where everyone's "MRI" is virtually the same. Psychoanalytic models that lean toward social science tend to speak about patients' internal structures as based on internalized personal relationships, and emerging in the analytic playground in the transference–countertransference matrix. Highly technical speculations about internal mechanisms are eschewed, and, as Coen (2000) has suggested, the psychoanalytic situation is discussed from the affective personal perspective of both participants, in this most unscientific of relationships.

Despite my preference for a humanistic model, I wish to be clear that any theoretical perspective can be applied in ways that deny analysts' subjectivity, objectify patients, and create inordinate asymmetry. I believe that each of us, even when fully conscious of this matter, is both tempted and inclined to coast within familiar belief systems. Although recognition of this actuality creates the opportunity to expose ourselves to potentially productive chaos (Bromberg, 2006; Hoffman, 1987; Levenson, 1991; Stern, 1990, 1996a, 1996b, 1997), this is, by definition, a most uncomfortable choice to make. I think that both general theory and clinical theory are best viewed as each analyst's personal countertransference or unconscious fantasy, and that this fantasy should be and often is quite accessible to consciousness. Internalized theory develops like all other personal characteristics. It is impossible to not have at least an implicit theoretical template, and for that theory to both shape and restrict analysts' expectancies and perceptions. When theories are too strong they serve the function of creating too much unquestioned comfort and, as well, excessive boundary between patient and analyst. Clinical data may be rigidly accommodated into an already existing schema.* But who is to say what is too strong, for what is one analyst's responsible science is another's rigidity. I think that the best analysts can do is to view all our preferred theories with skepticism. I believe it is most sobering to recognize how thoroughly subjective our theories really are, and how we inevitably impose these on our patients in much the same way we do our other personal countertransferences. Analysts can only strive for some dialectic between naïve curiosity (Stern, 1990), without knowledge or desire (Bion, 1967), and recognition of the restrictions that theory places on assimilation of new experience. Awareness of irreducible subjectivity (Renik, 1993) and of restrictions in vision, like all countertransference recognition, can lead to both humility (Richards, 2003) and more affective use of oneself in the analytic situation. However, the all too human analyst (Racker, 1968; Sullivan, 1953) is always tempted to, or even inclined to, maintain configurations that are most familiar and comfortable, and that produce optimum equilibrium. Awareness of this propensity is recommended, but can never mitigate this propensity entirely.

---

* I have long conjectured that the stereotyped descriptions that have characterized too much of psychoanalytic writing in this country emerged in part from psychoanalysts immigrating to the United States in the 1930s, and working in a language and in a culture that were starkly unfamiliar. I imagine many of these European analysts, in a most disadvantaged situation, looked for contents and configurations already known to them, and were prone to hear data that made them feel more at home. The subtleties and nuances that contribute to unique individuality were all too often likely not picked up, whereas material that was already familiar and compatible with theoretical conceptions was accommodated into comfortably existing schemata. Many of these analysts had been outstanding clinicians, and were brilliant theorists and leaders in the field. Perhaps even more significantly, they were teachers and training analysts to a generation of American ego psychologists. They may very well have set a tone that was in part responsible for a literature wherein patients and analyses tended to sound like facsimiles of one another, and where the unique individuality of both analytic participants was often lost.

# 6

# Baldness

It is difficult to imagine a paper or chapter about male baldness written by anyone who has not struggled personally with this phenomenon. Yet, those of us who know baldness firsthand do not write about it, nor do we normally address it in our clinical work to the extent it is warranted. Indeed, the absence of psychoanalytic literature on the subject of baldness is reflective of the extent that baldness and its psychological impact tend to be socially denied by analyst and patient alike, both inside and outside of analytic offices.* Though there are men who do seem comfortable speaking about their own or others' baldness, such dialogue is often in the context of "locker room" teasing. The good humor in the context of "put-downs" or self-denigrating jocularity, however, tends to be counterphobic in quality. The teaser or aggressor and the butt of the joke both are often attempting to deny the usually mutual highly self-conscious awkwardness about the subject. And, of course, acknowledgment of the curse of baldness and antidotes for it are omnipresent in the popular media, and enormous sums are spent in advertising products to either cure baldness or provide a disguise for it. The extent of this advertising and often dubious product development provides a window into how troubling hair loss is for so many. Nonetheless, serious and intimate discussion of baldness is deemed unfit for discussion by most men, though in apparent paradox, men who cope with the development of hair loss are commonly downright ruminative about the subject. There exists a dramatic discrepancy between the degree to which baldness is often preoccupying, and how much it is spoken of in a way that is deeply personal. This is true in normal social discourse

---

* Remarkably, a search of the Psychoanalytic Electronic Publishing (PEP) CD-ROM finds only one article where the main theme centers on baldness and hair loss in men, and this paper was published in 1936 (see Berg, 1936).

and, ironically, in the unique social phenomenon of psychoanalysis, a venue where one party usually agrees to say most everything that comes to mind, and the other party agrees to uninhibited curiosity. In my own clinical experience, and that which I observe in my work as an analytic supervisor, it is remarkable how patients' feelings about their baldness and/or the baldness of their analysts go unspoken. This profound avoidance is matched by the absence of discussion in the psychoanalytic literature. In my role as analyst I am, indeed, often guilty of not wanting to hear patients' responses to my baldness, and as well not wishing to draw attention to the subject by discussing my patients' baldness. Though I certainly miss some allusions to the subject as a reflection of my own unconscious conflicts, all too often I have avoided the implicit presence of the subject with some consciousness.

There are, of course, many reasons why losing hair and the state of baldness are such delicate and shame-laden matters for so many men, and I'm certain that my observations and speculations are not exhaustive (see Morrison, 1989, for a thorough discussion of shame). Shear (1985) put it succinctly: "Balding is the hammerlock that mortality holds on man's conceits.... It is the final take-down on the fight to stay youthful." These comments capture three significant elements about the phenomenon: confrontation with mortality, the loss of youthfulness, and the conceit of competitiveness. Though the first two themes are quite related to one another, they are not the same.

With the exception of acute onset of serious illness, no other change in a man's life, post puberty, takes place so quickly or is so evident. Baldness is usually the first indication of physical loss and decline, and it often begins earlier in life than most other deteriorations. It stands as a harbinger of inevitably waning physical prowess, even though it often begins at the peak of a man's strength, endurance, athletic abilities, and sexual potency. The beginnings of hair loss often stand in sharp contrast to the feeling of being at the pinnacle of one's physical life, and can readily interfere with the pleasures of being strong, hardy, and in the prime of life. Except to the extent that denial comes into play, a man cannot help but face the inevitability of future physical loss and, of course, ultimately death (Becker, 1973; Hoffman, 1987, 1991, 1998). Absent the onset of baldness, such a gloomy confrontation can usually be postponed for some considerable time, and the exuberant feeling of being indestructible maintained far longer. It is no wonder that so many young men, in particular, become depressed and obsessed when the physical evidence of beginning baldness becomes inescapable. This can be denied only up to a point, and before any adaptation or relative acceptance may be achieved, most balding men suffer through at least a reasonably long period of facing deterioration and death prematurely. Though such a confrontation might have been adaptive at points in human evolution, in this era when the life span is increasing profoundly, facing mortality at a relatively young age has no real practical utility. In a man's 20s or 30s, awareness of incipient decline and inevitable death is likely to impinge on the appreciation of being in one's prime, and I see little that is inherently good or redeeming about this.

The loss of a sense of youthfulness may have significant meaning somewhat independent of facing deterioration and death. In western cultures particularly, youth is closely associated with physical attractiveness, physical and sexual prowess, and athletic ability. More recently, with the advent of profound technological advances, youth too is associated with both inventiveness and optimal utilization of contemporary tools of communication, learning, and pleasure seeking. There is often a profound sense of well-being in feeling sexually attractive, physically strong and capable, and intellectually nimble enough to be comfortable with complex innovation. Although there is obviously no physical link between physical capacities or intellectual dexterity and baldness, any loss of a sense of being young can detract from the fullest appreciation of one's strength and potency. To the extent that physical attractiveness is indeed associated with looking young, and hair loss invariably makes a man look older, the loss of feeling like the object of sexual desire is often profound. Indeed, hair loss may have more impact on men who are used to feeling good-looking, for they are in a position to see the decline in gazes that communicate both admiration and sexual desire. For men who have relied on such subtle or sometimes obvious communication from others in order to feel good about themselves, the relative loss of such nonverbal responses can be devastating (Morrison, 1989). For men who have not been used to being the object of sexual attraction, hair loss can reinforce other feelings of inadequacy. Though this is ineffable and virtually impossible to document, many balding young men in particular seem to lose a certain "bounce" that comes with feeling young and potent and at the height of one's sense of power and confidence. Something appears to be taken away prematurely—youth and its benefits ought to have a longer shelf life in a western world where life expectancy keeps rising.

Though it is difficult to imply universal or general phenomena, competition among men certainly seems more normal than extraordinary. The fact that physical beauty in the context of looking optimally young is so central to western women cannot neutralize how important this is to many men as well.* Men, too, compete on this dimension, as well as on the dimensions of athletic accomplishment, intellectual achievement, and economic success. Hair loss commonly is associated not only with looking less handsome than men with a full complement of hair, but also with feeling somewhat crippled in comparison with another who is physically whole. Irrational as this might appear to an outside observer, there exists in many bald and balding men a sense of shame that can be compared to, for instance, not having a limb. Though the severity of the deficiency is incomparable, the feeling of having less than other men often has profound psychological meaning and impact. If not taken literally, the traditional psychoanalytic conception of castration anxiety is an excellent metaphor for this phenomenon. That is, taken out of its context of literal fear of physical castration by one's father, *castration anxiety* refers to the feeling of having less than another man or men—less height or muscle mass, a smaller penis, or less hair. In both my clinical work and my social contexts, I have rarely encountered men who were deeply disturbed in an ongoing way because their penis allegedly was deemed small. Having less hair than other men, and the competitive inadequacy that accompanies this, may very well more profoundly capture what the concept of castration anxiety has been meant to symbolize in the history of psychoanalysis. Fundamentally, baldness is frequently experienced as an indication of being less of a man than those competitors with more hair, notwithstanding that baldness is almost exclusively a male gender phenomenon.

Berg (1936) interpreted anxiety about baldness as reflective of an upward displacement of castration fears. He referred to the Samson myth to support the association of long hair with potency and exhibitionism, and the loss of hair with castration and depressive

---

* It is worth noting how male protagonists in film inevitably have a full head of hair, whereas it is not uncommon for antagonists to be bald or balding. I have observed similarly that male candidates for high elected office in the United States have a distinct advantage when they have optimally full amounts of hair on their heads.

affect. His connection of hair with phallic virility is supported by the observation that both facial and pubic hair develop at puberty, corresponding in the animal kingdom with lions' development of manes and stags' growth of antlers. Berg noted that discouragement of phallic sexuality in prisons and in monasteries is historically associated with the shaving of heads.* He viewed male hair as distinctly phallic in nature, and the tradition of maintaining control over hair growth by cutting, trimming, and shaving as a function effort to tame instinctual expression and to adapt to and compromise with societal norms and demands. Berg cited a number of clinical examples to support his thesis that hair loss in men can be traced directly to castration anxiety in the Oedipal context. Levin (1957), in the only psychoanalytic article that I was able to find that addressed the Samson legend, affirmed the association between hair and vitality. The name *Samson* refers to the sun and, in mythology, to the power of the serpent (hair as writhing snakes), whereas *Delilah* means night, calamity, and to become feeble. Samson's phallic potency is lost with his hair, and, like Hercules, he is both weak and bald when imprisoned. However, when Samson is further castrated by the removal of his eyes, his hair begins to grow back, and enough of his power returns to exact revenge on the forces of darkness and castration.

Though I am very far from a heroic figure, a personal clinical example might well capture some of the significant elements of the meaning of baldness as it relates to issues of mortality, loss of youthfulness, and competition among men. I began my personal analysis at age 28, and my analyst was some 15 years my senior. The year was 1968, and long hair for men was at its height of fashion. For me, this was a mixed blessing. On the one hand, I grew my hair long to both

---

* Note that this hypothesis is complicated, because the shaving of heads in contemporary times is also associated with the physical strength and potency of soldiers and athletes, particularly American football players and basketball players, and international soccer players. The tenor of this contemporary phenomenon, however, is that the war (or the game) has more urgency than explicit sexual activity. That is, the masculine power expressed through potent competence in battle becomes the vehicle to elicit sexual attraction. As of this writing, male head shaving is quite fashionable, and in my estimation has become a highly popular and effective counterphobic means of dealing with hair loss. Indeed, the shaving of heads has become so popular that it is not unusual to see young men shave their full and healthy heads of hair as a way of emulating some contemporary cultural icons. In this latter circumstance, of course, there is always the comfort that baldness is thoroughly elective, and hair will return at a point when fashion shifts.

cover up and distract from what was indisputably the beginning of male pattern baldness. This also helped me to deny the full extent of my hair loss. On the other hand, more than in any other era in my memory, abundant hair was both a fashion value and integral to what were considered to be good looks and sexual allure. I was, at the time, both unmarried and unattached, and, indeed, preoccupied with my growing baldness. My analyst was a good-looking man, and although he wore his hair far less fashionably long than my own, he showed no indication at all of any hair loss. In the early months of my analysis, sitting face-to-face with my analyst, I spoke little about my concerns related to declining physical appearance. However, because my analyst was older, married, and more conservative in his physical appearance, I did not experience conscious competitive feelings. As soon as I began to lie on the couch, however, I was excruciatingly self-conscious of the bald spot at the crown of my head. My analyst, with his full complement of hair, was sitting above me at a perfect angle to look at my baldness. I quickly felt a loss of the competitive edge I had felt toward this older and more settled man. The sense of youth that propelled me to pursue women, sports, and adventure seemed sullied. My married-with-children, relatively conservative analyst now seemed more youthful than me. I felt a deep sense of shame in a three-times-per-week display of my humiliation and inadequacy in full view to a man who now appeared to me as more potent than me. It seemed so profoundly unfair that in addition to being more professionally established and earning far more money than me, he was also, in my eyes, younger and more vital. I had fantasies of his outliving me, and of my exhibiting yet other "diseases" related to aging before he did. My competitive edge was gone, and I was confronted with this in a way that felt merciless.

Now, short-run unhappiness sometimes aids long-run workings through, and this period of my analysis proved ultimately very useful to me. I am also grateful that my analyst encouraged me to talk about baldness and related issues, for as noted earlier there is often collusion to avoid this subject. For example, had my analyst been sufficiently uncomfortable with his own sense of competitive superiority, he might have been supportive of me in a way that "combed over" the intensity of what I was experiencing in my transference to him. For my part, although there were many ways I manipulated my physical appearance so as to deny to myself and others the reality of my hair loss, I was so obsessed with this matter that I believed I could not avoid speaking about it with my analyst without making the process into a sham. In this regard it is both surprising and dramatic that in my position of analyst to men who are balding, I have not always addressed this issue to the extent it was dealt with in my own analysis, or to the extent it has reflected profound feelings of loss, weakness, and shame in a number of my own patients.

The most glaring example of mutual avoidance of confronting baldness occurred with a young man (Ted) who began analysis while a 19-year-old college sophomore. Ted had some therapy as a young adolescent, precipitated by academic underachievement. His parents became concerned because this issue was reoccurring in college, where Ted's grades were passing, but far below his capacities. His lack of objection to beginning treatment suggested to his parents that there was more that was troubling their son. Indeed, Edward's life was dreary, and consisted of going to classes, watching television, and getting drunk at bars on Friday and Saturday nights. He had made no friends at college, belonged to no college organizations, and had been avoiding his old childhood friends. Ted did the minimum amount needed to pass his courses, and found none of them exciting or interesting. Throughout his life Ted had been an excellent and passionate athlete, and had a wide repertoire of sports to enjoy. He reported to me that he had played competitive basketball and soccer in particular, with much aggression and fury, and did not understand why he had stopped. At his college there were abundant possibilities for pickup, intramural, or, for Ted, perhaps even varsity-level competition, and Ted was well aware that most of his friendships had come through athletic engagement. Further, the good feelings generated by competent athletic performance helped this otherwise shy young man feel more relaxed in the pursuit of women. He had had no girlfriend for some time, was doing nothing to meet young women at school, and avoided them at the bars he visited on the weekend.

It is fair to say that Ted was significantly depressed, and sitting with him in sessions often felt dull and empty in a way that reflected his current life. He attributed his depression to an identification with his father, whom he described as socially incompetent, friendless, and a masochistic castrato in relation to Ted's mother. Ted's most intense affective expressions were reserved for the rage he felt toward his father for the latter's legacy of low self-esteem and profound social awkwardness, and for taking the abuse he received from his wife.

Despite his father's considerable success in business, Ted viewed his mother as far more intelligent, vital, and socially attuned, and believed that during periods in his life that he deemed more rich, it was his mother who gave him the emotional equipment to appreciate such experiences. That said, he also was highly critical of her for living the life of a wealthy housewife while enacting scathing criticism toward the husband who enabled her to shop and travel at her whim. Ted believed that his mother should have been more sensitive to how her marital sadism would affect her son. In his transference comments Ted suggested that I was a more balanced man than his father, and that he would have benefited from having a father like me. He stated that I seemed to be at neither extreme on the continua of sadomasochism and of social comfort. I tried, desperately I thought, to deflect to me some of his fury toward his father, but this was to no avail. Ted's response to me, though overtly positive, was restrained, and I always had the feeling he was concealing a good deal. I conveyed this to him, and he denied it repeatedly, though in retrospect I did not push enough. I believe I feared my patient's capacity for the aggression he described on the athletic fields and the sadism attributed to his mother.

Concealment and my collusion with this proved to be central to this clinical relationship. Ted was tall, muscularly thin, and reasonably attractive. The most distinctive thing about his physical presence was the constant presence of one or another baseball cap he wore for every moment that I saw him. For a period of one full year, I never saw him hatless. Now at this time in the culture, baseball hats were at the height of fashion, particularly among men of Ted's age range. I certainly asked Ted why he always wore his hat, and whether he wore it everywhere else. He replied that he wore it everywhere because he never bothered combing his hair, and besides liking the way his hats looked, it saved him the trouble of grooming. I was suspicious that Ted's hair might be thinning and that he was trying to hide this—his response to my questions was flimsy. I would try to look at the hair that showed at the sides and back of his cap, and once in a while I saw some hair protruding from the front of it. I could not determine anything from this *silent* deliberation. What is most remarkable here is that I never came right out and asked Ted if he was shamefully hiding thinning hair. This is even more worthy of note because I had often worn hats in contexts that I would ordinarily not, in order to cover my own various stages of baldness. Ted could plainly see the status of my own baldness, and though he never commented on it, he had to know that this was something about which I had some knowledge and sensitivity. I later learned from him that he was perplexed why I seemed to buy his weak reason for wearing a hat, and why I didn't push him more to reveal the secret he kept from everyone except his family—he had begun wearing a toupee at age 18.

It took me one full year to learn this, and to find out that Ted's father was also bald as a young man. Perhaps it was the one-year anniversary of working together that inspired me to finally break through my inhibition about raising the subject of baldness, but there is no escaping that I chose consciously to avoid pursuing a theme that I knew aroused discomfort for me. Of course, I did ratio-nalize that Ted might not have "been ready" to address whatever he might be concealing under these baseball caps, though in retrospect it was I who was not ready. Ted was telling me plainly, albeit nonver-bally, that among the reasons he was depressed and started analysis in the first place was to deal with the myriad of issues his early hair loss provoked. On the most pragmatic level, Ted stopped engaging in sports because in doing so his toupee would be exposed, and, even worse, it could fall off or become displaced in the context of physi-cal contact. The loss of what was Ted's greatest passion, source of esteem, and vehicle for friendship was emotionally very costly (Han-sell, 1998; Hirsch, 2007). Similarly, the key manifest reason Ted was thoroughly avoiding young women was based on his fear that he'd have to remove his hat at some point, and in the vigorous context of sex, like with sports, his toupee might be moved around or fall off entirely. Ted described avoiding seeing his old friends because he knew they would notice his toupee, and undoubtedly inquire about it. He had shaved off most of his remaining hair in order to have his toupee fitted, and believed that wearing it inhibited whatever natural hair growth might have taken place. It turns out that Edward was distraught about the radical decision of purchasing a toupee at such a young age, in contrast with the more usual option of living with gradual hair loss. He was ashamed and humiliated by both his early balding and the solution he chose to help him deny his baldness. His toupee and the hats that covered it were a double attempt to deny his hair loss to the public, though Ted himself was preoccupied with and depressed about his premature baldness, his faulty antidote, and all he was giving up to help deny his status to the external world.

It goes without saying that even early baldness does not affect everyone to the same extent. Ted's pursuit of a toupee was a radical solution, and the extent to which he avoided both social and athletic contact was extreme. It was also quite unusual to not raise verbally such a subject in the context of analysis, in spite of my powerful collusion to keep this matter hushed. For Ted, baldness symbolized being his socially inadequate and ineffectual father who could not be anything but a castrato with his wife. The part of Ted that identified with his father was symbolized concretely by the deficiency of having no hair. At the height of his physical and mental prowess, Ted saw the beginnings of what he took to be his destiny—his decline into weakness and subservience. He saw the inevitable path of decline, and what this would look like, in the form of his father, when he got there. Ted's growing baldness gave him a view of an anticipated future, an all too early confrontation with his mortality, and with the absence of youthful vitality that he saw as characteristic of his father. Where he once felt aggressively competitive with male peers, Ted now believed he had lost. He believed that his friends and fellow students were better looking, more youthful, and more appealing to women, and had brighter and longer futures. Ted became preoccupied with both this decline and his felt impotence, and his efforts to deny this by concealment only turned out to compound the problem.

Though Ted was comforted by my collusion with his denial, it was harmful to him that as the analyst he sought to help him address these miseries, for too long a period I had silently helped his suffering compound. If I, who knew something firsthand about baldness, found the subject unspeakable, Ted's worst fears about his future were reinforced, or even enhanced (Fromm, 1964; Singer, 1968). I later learned that Ted did assume that my own baldness had caused me sufficient pain that I did not wish to broach the subject. Indeed, Ted's experience of his own baldness and the losses that it represented were still alive for me, and I anticipated correctly that his overt verbal immersion in this would touch uncomfortably on many of my own feelings. I assumed that Ted's reflections about our shared baldness would include his linking of me with his father in all of the shame-laden and humiliating ways he both saw him and identified with him. I had been the object of Ted's manifest admiration, and he always claimed my superiority to his father. In part, he wished to maintain his idealization of me, and I had some awareness of how I benefited from this. I do not think either of us wished for me to become de-idealized, and to be confronted with the aspects of me that literally and symbolically bore some similarity to Ted's father.

Of course, during the period of Ted's analysis that I have discussed I did not have the benefit of all the awareness I now exhibit. However, I had enough self-reflectiveness to know that there was something I was not speaking about that warranted being put into words. I knew that once opened up, the words that would eventually follow would make me more uneasy than the state I was in at the time, and that an unsatisfying but comfortable enough mutual equilibrium would be shaken. As a psychoanalyst I know that this must occur in order for the process to work, but as a fallible human being indulging my self-interest I chose to prolong an equilibrium that produced some relative comfort for both Ted and me. Ted's life began to get better when I risked our life together getting worse.

It is not unusual for balding men to think that they have more hair remaining than is truly the situation, or perhaps to deny that a hat is worn to conceal significant baldness. As already noted, over a period of time I had tried to conceal from myself (and others) the extent of my baldness by combing my hair in ways that I believed gave the impression to me of greater abundance. Though the mocking term *comb-over* reflects an extreme example of this phenomenon, and has become the butt of humor because it can be so exaggerated,* modified and far less outlandish versions of this are quite common among balding men. In most situations self-deception is more weighted than deception of others. That is, it is more likely that the baldish man has the illusion of having more hair than does the observing population. Usually, nobody else is fooled. There are, however, moments of confrontation that make the bald truth inescapable to those who prefer to engage in self-deception. For example, looking at a mirror head-on may give one the impression of having more hair than looking at multiple-angle mirrors (like when trying on clothing for a tailor), and mirrors without direct overhead lighting attached give less accent to the top of one's head. A windy day will likely disarrange thinning hair and readily expose the extent of one's baldness. It is common to see balding men walking with their hand on their head to keep wind-blown hair from exposing greater baldness.

* Former New York City Mayor Rudolph Giuliani was a public figure who served as a poster example of the "comb-over" phenomenon. In more recent times, like so many bald men now, Giuliani has shaved his head, and his coping mechanism for his baldness is no longer mocked.

Photographs can be jarring to one's narcissism in many respects, and I know of many instances where the angle of the camera conveys the extent of a man's baldness beyond what represents one's day-to-day physical self-image.

Peter (discussed in chapter 3) began analysis in his mid- to late 40s, and he seemed to be unaware of the extent of his baldness. As already noted, he was tall, thin, and pale, his dull and stilted demeanor enhanced by what little remained of his graying hair and the way he combed it over the crown of his head. No hair remained on the front of his head, and his efforts to affect hair on his crown made him look both awkward and pasty. Parenthetically, I have come to believe that natural baldness usually is more attractive than those futile efforts to arrange one's hair to conceal this. Peter had good facial features, and I believe he might have been considered handsome were his face more balanced by a relatively full head of hair. As he was, though, Peter experienced himself as more physically attractive than I did or, as I suspected, most others did. He was a pretty child, and had been the object of his mother's absolute adoration. The internalization of being the object of strong desire often endures beyond the point where it matches the gaze of contemporary others. This can be enhancing to one's self-esteem, as I believe it was for Peter. In fact, Peter had few current sources of feedback that could lead to enrichment of feelings about his physical being. He was a closeted gay man, and the only sex he had was with young men whom he paid in some direct or indirect material way. He was not flirtatious with men who were his peers in any way, nor did he ever hang out at gay meeting places. I never got the impression that women were particularly interested in him or pursued him, despite his being a very wealthy, eligible, and ostensibly heterosexual bachelor who traveled in affluent banking circles.

As described in chapter 3, I was the only current peer on whom Peter had a crush, and though he was inhibited about describing his sexual fantasies, it was clear to me that he felt in some state of being in love with me. I felt from him some of the unconditional adoration he experienced in his relationship with his mother. Unfortunately, this was not reciprocated, for I experienced Peter with a physical aversion somewhat akin to how I imagine his father responded. Like his father, in comparison with Peter I felt handsome, athletic, and vital, though his facial features were far better than my own. In an objective sense he was a reasonably attractive man, and I believe that it was his tightness, awkwardness, and discomfort with his body that detracted considerably from his physical appeal. At the time I focused privately on Peter's baldness in trying to account for this, though the topic virtually never entered our conversation. Indeed, I think that I projected distaste about my own baldness, and Peter was sufficiently masochistic to both idealize me and help me feel like his handsome father. Peter both denied the extent of his own baldness and said nothing about my much longer hair that, in part, served the function of attempting to cover up the obvious truth of gradual male pattern baldness. I believed at the time that I had much more hair than Peter, but looking back this might have been my illusion. Indeed, the two of us likely shared a similar distorted sense about our respective pates. I believe that I made Peter the bald guy who was not physically attractive, so that I could maintain my preferred vision of relatively youthful good looks. In my eyes Peter was old, dry, bald, and dull looking, and I think that I maintained him in my mind as so physically unattractive so as not to face these concerns about my own self. This was a position that was all too familiar for him from what he had internalized in relation to both his father and his brother.

There was one moment that was especially striking as a missed opportunity to address Peter's sentiments about his baldness, and his physical attractiveness in general. He opened a session by describing walking past a large store window and seeing his reflection. It was a windy day, and Peter said that he was shocked to see how bald he looked. He spoke some about his surprise and his sense of aging, but this dialogue did not go very far, and we did not return to this. In far retrospect, it is all too clear that I did not want to address the variety of losses associated with Peter's baldness, for such issues were too close to home. It was, however, decidedly hurtful to my patient to facilitate his denial about both his physical appearance and the urgency of his social situation. Peter was proceeding in his pursuit of young men as if they were likely to be attracted to him and, perhaps, desire more than a paid-for sexual encounter. Some of the young men were potentially dangerous, and a few had robbed him after he fell asleep. These pursuits also dictated a life of smoking, some drugs, much alcohol, and very late nights. Though he had protected sex, Peter was placing himself in considerable physical jeopardy. In another vein, Peter was most decidedly not in the immediate future looking toward a life with companionship. In the context of his distorted sense of youthfulness and good looks, he operated as if he were still his mother's beautiful boy, and the object of desire in the eyes of sexy young men. Addressing the baldness he perceived in the store window reflection was certainly not the only opening given to me to help Peter confront his avoidance of male peers more tangibly.

At the time I had some awareness that I desperately wanted to avoid feeling the potential revulsion about myself that I felt toward Peter, and that he might have begun to feel about himself had we dealt with his internalized unattractiveness in any meaningful way. I believe I feared both identifying with his own anxiety about no longer being the object of anyone's desire, and the likelihood that I would lose the gaze of desire I received from Peter. In order to deny the extent of his own baldness, Peter needed to be blind to my own. In worrying about my own physical declines, I felt reassured that I was both more attractive and healthy than Peter, and Peter's vision of me as highly desirable was particularly reinforcing of some of what I preferred to deny. Though much of what I now reflect upon is with the benefit of considerable hindsight, I was well aware while seeing Peter that I avoided the subject of baldness. Indeed, I knew that focus on this matter and all that it meant and symbolized to both of us would be mutually destabilizing, and I opted for maintenance of both personal and mutual equilibrium. I knew that the passive and masochistic sides of Peter's character would prevail and allow me to do this.

Maury was another story entirely. He was highly competitive and cocky, and if the term *masochism* is to be used in regard to him, it would apply to the others who entered his world. We began analysis when Maury was in his mid-60s and I was some 12 years his junior. I felt junior in many respects—Maury had worked himself up from poverty to attend Ivy League schools, accumulate great wealth in business, make a name for himself in philanthropic circles, sire a large number of children (and grandchildren), and maintain a prodigious extramarital sex life with any number of much younger women. He was brilliant and had many interests and talents, both cerebral and athletic. One could say that Maury was manic, but to use this term categorically seems to me a way to write off his many abilities, and to feel less inadequate in comparison with him.* Indeed, it was difficult for me and for others to experience a sense of competence in Maury's presence. He was a gentlemen—overtly mild mannered, respectful and even self-effacing, and rarely competitive in any overt manner. And, of course, he had some problems that brought him in to see me in the first place. Parenthetically, I believe that there is always a danger that we (therapists) accent our patient's problems in order to enhance our own comparative sense of esteem. I'm certain that I did this with Maury, especially because I found it difficult to feel strong in relation to him, though his sadistic use of power was most subtle and elegant. Maury initiated analysis because his wife, after discovering one of his sexual dalliances, threatened to leave him if he did not. Although this was a bogus reason for me to engage him as a patient, shortly after beginning our work Maury was challenged by some legal problems and financial setbacks that thoroughly began to preoccupy and depress him. With the onset of these issues, I was relieved to have a bona fide reason to work with him, and to feel less inferior to him.

Even before Maury's miseries began, there was one way that I did not feel overshadowed by his presence. Though in excellent health and physically very active, Maury was in his mid-60s; had developed a gut, albeit in an attractive avuncular way; and took good care to comb his thinning hair back in a way that exposed a receding hairline but concealed some of the baldness on top of his head. He was a tasteful man and would never stoop to a "comb-over" strategy, though his hair did have a tonic that kept it strictly in place to avoid wind-blown exposures of areas of baldness. Some 12 years younger and distinctly more trim, I initially believed that we had a roughly equivalent quantity of remaining hair, denying that mine was still thinning while his hair loss had reached its endpoint. I experienced some edge over Maury with regard to my very relative youth, and that my hair was worn more informally, not slicked down and impervious to breezes. Through the years we met, Maury spoke a good deal about his concerns regarding weight, bowel function, and sexual performance, but he never talked about his hair, or about concerns with dying. Maury claimed to be unconcerned about dying per se, fearing only incapacity or prolonged pain and illness. He

---

* I believe in general that diagnoses are often used to make practitioners feel that they are in competitive ascendancy with patients.

reflected that he had accomplished much in life already, and though he would like to stay alive to do more, he'd die satisfied with what he had achieved and contributed.

Over the years that I saw Maury, it became evident to me that my hair loss had exceeded his, and that I no longer had the advantage of this element of youthfulness. I began to think that I perhaps fooled myself from the beginning—that Maury had always had more hair than me. In the context of my years together with Maury, there existed a tangibly physical measure of my aging. It felt to me that I had caught up with Maury in age, or even passed him, and that I would become ill or infirm, or even die, before him. I believe that Maury's avoidance of the subject of his and my own baldness reflected his wish to cover up his vulnerable bald spots, both figuratively and literally. Though Maury did speak about other perceived weaknesses such as weight gain and erectile dysfunction, he saw these as matters that could be altered (e.g., by diet and Viagra). This manically energetic man had some power to influence these declines, and this gave him a sense of potency. The gaps of baldness on his scalp were something that he was powerless to alter—he could only conceal these as best he could. He had lost something, and this not only was immutable but also symbolized other losses and those to come in the not too distant future. Maury did not wish to discuss baldness, but neither did his analyst. I was well aware that Maury's hair was the only part of his body that remained unaddressed, yet I never put these thoughts into words with him. Were he to address the significance to him of the loss that left him powerless, I too would be forced to face this full within myself. Perhaps even more significantly, I feared Maury's potential competitiveness about the subject. Though this was not initially conscious, I was afraid that Maury would explode my deception that I had more hair than he. Further, I worried that he'd challenge my reasons for raising a subject that he never brought up. He would confront me about projecting my personal concerns onto him, and I would become the manifest object of his sadism. We had dealt with his sadism in some transferential discussions, though it is clear that I wanted no part of his sadism in relation to the competitive theme of which of us had more hair. In retrospect it is, indeed, remarkable that Maury omitted only one part of his body from our conversations, and that I never overtly noted this glaring omission. These two facts only underscore the power that baldness often has on men, and my thesis that analysts' self-interest in combination with a mutual fear of the destabilization of the transference–countertransference equilibrium generally impede the analytic process in some way or another.

Warren is roughly 20 years my junior, and someone who I have seen now for about one year. He is not as refined as Maury, and his anger and competitiveness are palpable. He exudes manifest self-confidence, apparently full of himself based on considerable success with women and in business, and generally gives the impression of someone to not get on the wrong side of. Though exuberantly outgoing, friendly, and congenial, it was clear from the outset that like Maury, Warren strives to dominate and control those in his world. He seeks analysis in part because his periodic anger toward his wife and children has become hard for them to endure, and this same anger has made it difficult for people to stay in his employ. The latter situation has hurt his business tangibly. In addition, Warren acknowledges that he drinks and gambles to excess, and as a younger man used recreational drugs habitually. Further, Warren has a history of panic experiences in relation to perceived physical disease. It takes little for him to interpret symptoms as potentially fatal, despite all of his medical reports assuring him that his health is excellent. His wife, his physicians, and now I are the only ones whom he allows to see this frightened and dependent side of himself. Indeed, he does acknowledge strong dependence on his maternal and somewhat masochistic wife, and he dreads the thought of losing her. Though it feels to me that Warren can explode toward me if I make one wrong move, he has so far been quite respectful toward me, and vulnerable in his articulation of his fearfulness.

Warren has exhibited total male pattern baldness since his early 20s (I had seen him for a consultation roughly 15 years ago). I do not know when his hair loss began to become obvious, because neither he nor I have raised the subject to date. From the time I initially met him some time ago, until now, Warren wears his hair in the traditional manner for bald men. He has never affected coverings of either any sort of comb-over or hat variety, and does not shave his head as so many of his bald contemporaries now do. He presents his baldness as matter of fact—in a sense conveying an almost arrogant "Take me or leave me" message. As well, in the way he outfits himself Warren appears prideful about being traditional, informal, and no frills. I read his implicit message as conveying that he does well in the world without the accoutrements needed by most others.

Again, his implicit communication is, for instance, "Women usually like guys with hair and who keep current with styles, but I am so compelling that I can get all the women I want doing it my way." His overt arrogance does bear some resemblance to what has been patented as a "Frank Sinatra" attitude. On the other hand, Warren is very self-conscious if he gains a few pounds, and exercises almost daily in order to both keep trim and prevent disease. In this context, his absolute absence of self-conscious concern about his baldness is both striking and unusual for someone who lives in an active social world, and is very conscious of interpersonal nuance. Indeed, I have never met anyone this young, outside of those who could be considered schizoid or socially oblivious, who appears as untroubled by his profound baldness as this man.

In this context I feel some concern, similar to what I felt with Maury, that Warren will see my inquiry about his baldness as an intrusion of my own personal concerns, because for him, such superficial matters are allegedly not even worth thinking about. I fear that I will become the object of his forked-tongued sadism for my being weak and insubstantial, and for presuming that he is as superficial as I am—at my more advanced age, no less. I think that Warren likes the idea that he has overcome deficiencies, and that despite baldness perhaps inhibiting people like me, he has paid it no heed, and seduces women more successfully than those who wear fashionable accoutrements. Indeed, Warren speaks eloquently about the pride he feels in having evolved from a very troubled and fractured family to an individual who has achieved a great deal in many dimensions. Warren's family of origin is and was a mess. At some point or another both parents were psychologically dysfunctional, and they had always barely subsisted economically. When they divorced in late middle age, both parents became physically decrepit based on both illnesses and emotional breakdown. Both of Warren's siblings have made very little of their lives, and one has been in and out of psychiatric hospitals since adolescence. To the extent that Warren dissociates all significance to his baldness and relies on manic denial to flee from any meaning of inadequacy it might symbolize to him, I expect to be severely attacked for any effort to puncture his mania.

On one hand, Warren is preoccupied with his mortality and potential demise, in the form of panic attacks related to hysterical illnesses. He is, however, able to externalize this by confabulating disease as entering his body from outside. I suspect that Warren's baldness is more reflective of what he has denied as being on the inside—some internalized sense of weakness and inadequacy embodied by all others in his original family. Warren flees desperately from his identifications with his parents, though some of his self-destructive, addiction-like behavior flirts with an embrace of them. Both Warren's mortality and loss of youthful vigor are associated with his family, and this drives him to overcompensatory endeavors. Like his internalized family, baldness is something that emerges from inside, and Warren is not keen to address this side of himself. In complement, I have not been sanguine about Warren's potential for competing with me and annihilating me. I anticipate a transference configuration where he and I struggle to disidentify with his family, and I fear that I will lose this battle and, in the context of my own baldness, feel this profound weakness in lieu of my patient. In our relationship currently, Warren is able to be weak and vulnerable with me and dependent on me, and he seems to be benefiting from analysis. This equilibrium feels good to me, and I feel like a competent analyst. To the extent that I push baldness and its symbolic meanings, I believe that Warren's attack will precipitate in me considerable feelings of weakness and inadequacy, and I cannot be certain that I will be able to get him to rescue me by himself embracing these latter feelings.

Tony, also 20 or so years younger than me, seemed as well to be unaffected by his early baldness, though his similarities to Warren pretty much ended there. Tony was genuinely unconcerned with his appearance, and tended to look dumpy, sloppy, and totally out of touch with current fashion. Like many schizoid men involved with technology since childhood, Tony warranted the label *nerd*, and he had little sense or concern of how he appeared to others. He was generally lost in his own thoughts and interests, and although cordial with me, fundamentally showed little recognition of my existence. This quality was leading to both marital and business difficulties. Tony's wife wanted more of his affective presence and less of the anger she received when she tried to intrude into her husband's private existence. Tony's business had some social components to it, and his failure to engage with clients counteracted his intelligence and his technical competence. The concept of personal analysis was very foreign to Tony, and he was highly skeptical that this enterprise had any potential. He was concrete in his thinking and unreflective, and most of his dialogue was related to how other people were messing up his life. He had little conception of how he influenced others, or why others found it so difficult to be with him. Indeed, I initially found him quite tedious, and I rarely looked forward to our sessions. I was, on the other hand, very comfortable with Tony, and I felt it easy to say whatever I wished to him. As a way to get beyond my boredom with him, and as an effort to connect with him, I became very challenging and provocative. I especially prodded Tony with respect to his ways of withdrawing into schizoid oblivion, and his inclination to pay little heed to how he impacted others. I was active in informing him how he affected me, and he was generally responsive to this approach. He did argue with me a good deal about my observations, yet I had the sense that he was hearing me to a reasonable degree. Needless to say, by this point, part of my comfort with Tony was based on my feeling quite vigorous, vivacious, and "with it" in relation to him. In addition, despite our age difference I felt youthful and physically vital and attractive in comparison with him. I actually felt that I looked younger than he, though I doubt that this was objectively the case.

Tony was raised in a home where his slightly younger brother was the apple of both parents' eyes. This brother was clearly better looking, much superior at sports, and socially more adept from an early age, and his interests seemed more in tune with those of his parents. The discrepancy between his parents' gaze upon his brother and upon Tony only became more accented by the latter's adaptation of schizoid indifference. Tony never let himself consciously experience the pain of so patently losing out to his brother, and the price he has been paying is reflected in the repetition of this loss and trauma. That is, in most social contexts my patient managed to become less appealing than his male counterparts.

Though I was pleased that Tony benefited from my forthrightly addressing these themes both historically and in the transference, we failed to go anywhere with the issue of baldness per se. I was very open in showing my surprise that his baldness never troubled him, particularly because both his brother and father were never bald. He shrugged whenever this was raised, and I believed him to the extent that on a conscious level, he barely gave a second thought to what I and most men become downright ruminative about. Indeed, I felt jealous that he was able to escape a form of misery that, during the period I worked with Tony, still plagued me at times. I admired how "inner directed" he was, in contrast to my superficial preoccupations with appearances. Despite these feelings, I always felt the superiority of being more in the world than Tony, even after I had helped him be more awake and alert than prior. I was aware of not pushing the baldness issue as much as I would ideally, for I wished to maintain the comfort I felt in my still feeling more young and vital than Tony. Were he to feel all that his baldness represented, particularly in the context of his brother and father, Tony would likely have confronted a greater depth of both dysphoric and angry affect related to his perceived inadequacy in his family's eyes. He might have softened his schizoid shell and, as well, become more aware of how comfortable I was with my ascendant feelings in relation to him. He conceivably could have more fervently embraced his dissociated competitive feelings, and if so, no doubt some of them would be turned toward me. I think I helped Tony a good deal, but had I been more willing to assume with him the "loser" competitive position with which he was so identified, I might have helped him more.

I have tried to illustrate through clinical example the degree to which an issue as important as male pattern baldness can go unaddressed in the course of long clinical analyses. Though this cannot possibly be a universal phenomenon (note my own personal analysis), the almost absolute absence of literature on the subject of baldness does serve to dramatize that this is a subject matter that receives remarkably little psychoanalytic attention relative to its affective significance among many men. Though avoidance of speaking about baldness in clinical work and in clinical writing is often unconsciously motivated, all too often there is a mutually conscious decision to remain silent about this subject. In each of my clinical illustrations I made a somewhat conscious decision to avoid addressing some elements of this issue, and for different reasons, each of my patients not only was relatively comfortable with this but also joined me in my reluctance to speak openly about the subject of baldness. To address this subject matter would have therapeutically destabilized each relationship, and in each situation, my own and my patients' sense of safety and comfort prevailed. Ted did not wish to see me as his castrated, masochistic father, and I did not wish to experience the powerful sense of inadequacy that both he and his internalized father lived with. Peter did not want to face how both aging and undesired he was, and, as well, lose me as an idealized and heroic paternal figure. I did not wish to identify with Peter's profound sense of competitive failure and his feeling of deterioration. Maury did not want his manic exuberance and competitive edge punctured symbolically by the empty spaces on his scalp, and I did not wish to be the target of his sadistic assault on my own inadequacies. Warren wished to believe that he had transcended his family's incompetence, and I feared that he might turn his internalized incompetence toward a detailed explication of my own. Tony preferred oblivion to acute feelings of competitive loss, and anger in relation to having been the object of disdain. I feared both identification with his loser status and the impact of his discovery of the competitive aspects of himself.

In each illustration, my patients benefited from our work together, but did not benefit as much as they otherwise might have had I addressed *everything* that I had seen. They each allowed me to omit the particularly delicate area of hair loss because of their own discomforts with the subject, and I exploited their anxiety in the service of reducing my own. Though this interaction, on a moment-to-moment basis often operated beyond my conscious awareness, I was often enough consciously aware of not raising the subject of baldness. I do not uniformly and across the board avoid this with all of my male patients. Indeed, some of them raise the subject themselves and do not permit me to avoid it, even if I would sometimes prefer to. The clinical work illustrated here accents how the subject of baldness can readily be avoided when the symbolic meanings attached to it for *both* patient and analyst reflect extreme feelings of shame, competitive loss, personal weakness and inadequacy, loss of youth and vitality, and confrontation with aging, physical decline, and mortality. The profound absence of a psychoanalytic literature on the subject of hair loss and baldness reflects that it is far from uncommon that this subject is given very short shrift in clinical work.

# 7

# Money and the Therapeutic Frame

## Introduction

Quite a number of years ago, shortly after I began full-time independent practice, I ran into a former hospital-based supervisor of mine whom I had not seen for some time. She was with her lawyer husband, whom I had met, and after she congratulated me for making the bold move to private practice, something that she had always been reluctant to initiate, he asked me bluntly how I deal with the conflict between my patients getting better and leaving, and the loss of income that follows. He implied quite clearly that his psychologist wife, senior to me and more qualified, had chosen the professional higher ground by continuing to see her patients while on a hospital salary basis. His commentary was pithy, but profound and jarring both, and a distinct departure from the normal congratulatory, well-wishing responses to which I had grown accustomed. I had no intelligent answer to his question, and I recall mumbling something about recognizing that this was a problem, and that I hoped my successfully discharged patients would be satisfied consumers and refer others to me. A similar encounter was repeated some 30 years later while I was in Germany for a conference. At a dinner with a few German colleagues whom I had just met, I learned that their national health insurance pays 100 percent of psychotherapy and multiple times per week psychoanalysis fees for prolonged periods of time. I was further told that because of this coverage, virtually every analyst has a full practice and a waiting list for new patients. My envy was palpable, though tempered by their lament that the fees I and other analysts in the United States were charging were roughly two to three times what they received. Parenthetically, the issue of fees and busyness of practice is a primary subject of discussion wherever I travel, as soon as a drink or two loosens tongues. One of my German colleagues, when learning from me that the practices of the vast majority of U.S. analysts were not full, and that the competition for patients in the marketplace of supply and demand was often considerable, asked the same question put to me 30 years earlier: Essentially, how can you try to help patients when an ultimate positive outcome will lead to loss of income? This time I was more prepared and had a better answer, because I had already coauthored an article (Aron & Hirsch, 1992) identifying economic conflict as the single greatest problem in our profession, and was in the planning stages of this chapter and had been doing some reading on this subject (e.g., Josephs, 2004; Lasky, 1984; Liss-Levinson, 1990; Myers, 2008; Whitson, n.d.). I essentially told my astute German colleague that I believed his system created far better conditions for productive analytic work, and that despite my enjoying much higher fees than they, I think I'd be both less anxious and a more useful analyst in their system.

Economic anxieties plague all but a very few analysts I know, especially in large American urban areas like New York City, where the supply of trained analysts is voluminous and the relative number of potential patients who can afford preferred analytic fees creates considerable competition among analysts. Most colleagues are elated when a new referral comes, and depressed when a patient leaves prematurely. Sadly, even after a successful analytic experience, it is often difficult to feel satisfaction and pride only, without this being tempered by anxiety and regret in relation to lost income. As one colleague responded to my "How's it going?" after running into him in the street, "It's been a great month—none of my patients have left." The degree to which we are dependent on our patients to both exercise our skills and create economic security is powerful, and although this is preoccupying, it is rarely addressed in the literature or as part of formal panels and conferences. Analysts' economic dependency on patients leads to an inherent and profound conflict between self-interest and patient interest, and this conflict always has the potential to severely compromise analytic work. Indeed, I believe that analysts' financial concerns reflect the most vivid example of this conflict, and I still suggest that analysts' anxiety about income is the single greatest contributor to compromised analyses.*

Emotional greed disguised as economic greed undoubtedly has something to do with the degree that analysts ruminate about money, though greed often has its primary source in deprivation and fear of subsequent deprivation. I know of no literature that has studied the psychogenetics of such worries among analysts, though it is plausible to assume that those among us who have greater internal expectations that they will have enough in life are less frightened than their counterparts. However, regardless of inevitable individual differences among analysts, dependency on patients, on multiple levels, is very real and pragmatic. As Singer (1965a, 1971) suggested, we are dependent on our patients, in addition to our need to earn a living, in order to practice a profession that we presumably like and value, and for which we have trained long and hard. He further noted that analysts often grow very fond of and attached to patients, and each separation may hurt along the same lines as separating from friends or family. When patients leave prematurely, this inevitably tells analysts that they have not done very well, and most probably that they were not liked and valued both as a professional and as a person. Independent of the need to earn a living, patients saying hello and goodbye to us bears close similarity to both loving and rejecting experiences in our personal life. Whenever a patient remains with us, the experience lends itself to feelings of being loved (Racker, 1968), and this theme of staying or leaving can be played out multiple times with multiple patients during each workday. Searles (1965, 1979) also appreciated the multiple forms of analysts' dependency on patients. Searles was one of the early analytic writers to grasp the true nature of a two-person psychology, with both analysts and patients sharing all of the same emotional needs and desires vis-à-vis the other, usually in equal measure (Racker, 1968). As well, both Singer (1971) and Searles (1979) wrote openly about

---

* Though I write throughout this chapter as an analyst and about psychoanalytic work, I wish to make clear that I believe similar conflicts surrounding financial self-interest exist in the practice of all forms of psychotherapy (and psychopharmacology). Indeed, though my interests and knowledge base are restricted to the practice of psychoanalysis and psychoanalytic psychotherapy, I believe that such conflicts are likely relevant in all of the professions where individuals earn their income to at least some degree as private practitioners.

analysts' wishes to be not only loved by their patients but helped by them too. Both authors were sensitive to patients' inclinations to be of help to caretaking figures, first to parents and then to analysts. If analysts are unreceptive to patients' helpful strivings, they run the risk of diminishing patients, conveying to them that the latter are greedy, dependent, and immature only—that the analyst is strong and sufficient, and the patient weak and deficient (Goldberg, 2007). Sullivan's (1953, 1954, 1956) shift from a more authoritarian one-person model to one of co-participation* precipitated the democratization of the psychoanalytic process, the view championed by those identified with the interpersonal school, that the analytic dyad is composed of *two* flawed individuals (see also Racker, 1968). Relational perspectives in psychoanalysis** begin here, with the view that the personal subjectivity of both analytic participants is visible within the dyadic field, and that each party, at least unwittingly, has some influence with the other. Racker's (1968) proclamation that the analytic relationship is not one between a well analyst and a sick patient mirrors Sullivan's declaration of the shared and compromised humanity in every analytic enterprise, and these are the sentiments that have grown into prominence in much of contemporary psychoanalytic discourse, especially those perspectives now under the conceptual umbrella referred to as *relational*.

---

* See Fromm (1941, 1955, 1964), Fromm-Reichmann (1959), Thompson (1950, 1952), Wolstein (1954, 1977, 1983), Schachtel (1959), Tauber and Green (1959), Searles (1960, 1965), Singer (1965a, 1965b, 1968), Farber (1966), Levenson (1981, 1988, 1992), Barnett (1980), Hirsch (1987, 1990), Ehrenberg (1992), Blechner (1992), Eisold (1994, 2002), Fiscalini (1994, 2004), Satran (1995), M. Gerson (1996), Stern (1996), Kwawer (1998), Guarton (1999), Langan (1999), Imber (2000), Wilner (2000), Brisman (2002), Buechler (2004), Aron (2005), Ianuzzi (2005), and Kuriloff (2005).

** See Wachtel (1980, 1982), Hoffman (1987, 1991, 1998), Mitchell (1988, 1993, 1997, 2000), Morrison (1989), Aron (1991, 1996, 1999), Greenberg (1991, 1995), Stern (1990, 1997), Frommer (1994, 2006), Davies (1994, 2004), Davies and Frawley (1994), Benjamin (1995), Slochower (1996), Bromberg (1998, 2006), Layton (1998, 2004), Pizer (1998), Frank (1999), Grand (2000), Bass (2001), Knoblauch (2000), Crastnopol (2002), Beebe and Lachmann (2002), Cooper (2000b), Dimen (1991, 2001), Fosshage (2003), Safran (2003), Seligman (2003), M. Hoffman (2004), Bonovitz (2005), and Harris (2005).

The fact that analysts are dependent on patients is not a problem in and of itself. This normal human quality becomes an impediment when it is either denied by analysts or exploited by them. The recognition of our fragility and dependency, economic and otherwise, can be very facilitating of analytic process when such recognition leads to the effort to contain these self states of the analyst. For better or worse, however, analysts' flawed humanity works to sometimes defensively help deny that dependency on patients is powerful, and at other times to not curb dependency when we can see that exercising this is more in our own interests than in patients' best interest. Because dependency experienced through economic need is such a powerful force in most analysts' lives, analysts' temptation and inclination to choose self-interest in priority to patient interest are woven into the very fabric of professional life.

The tangible and practical need to earn a reasonable living makes anything approaching a relatively objective attitude about which patients to work with, and how long to keep them, nearly impossible. As noted, this dilemma of self-interest versus the interest of clients or patients is not, of course, unique to psychoanalytic practitioners. Based on the laws of supply and demand, professionals and businesspeople are inclined to enlist potentially interested consumers, even when a hypothetical jury of disinterested peers might easily judge that the consumer either does not need the service or would be better served elsewhere. Newman (2006), for example, wrote pointedly of his experience searching for medical treatment for a life-threatening malignant tumor. Each physician consulted seemed convinced that his own specialty was best suited to address this urgent life-or-death matter. None were inclined to refer him to rival colleagues, despite the fact that one well-known specialist colleague in particular clearly turned out to be the most appropriate one to address this unusual cancer. Newman concluded that most of those he consulted for his health crisis were interested in their business primarily, and did not consider with due equanimity if their special skill was the one most likely to save his life. His story confirms the conventional piece of wisdom that suggests that if one is considering surgery, consult first with a physician who is not a surgeon. "First, do no harm" (if applied to psychoanalysts as well as physicians) is a worthy ideal, though this is difficult to adhere to in a context where competition with peers for needed income is a very practical force.

Though greed and competitive feelings toward rival peers* may be powerful motivating forces for many or most analysts, it is *needed* income that creates the most serious difficulties and conflicts. Greed and competition are luxuries when compared with the desire to support oneself or one's family in a manner that approaches what is anticipated by those aspiring to upper-middle-class or professional-class ways of living, and, as well, what is expected by others in the community whose gaze is evaluative. From what I can see, the considerable majority of psychoanalysts in the United States are quite anxious about earning sufficient money to live comfortably without worrying about their economic future. Because all of our work is referral based, analysts are often anxious even when practices are relatively full, for who can know when the next patient might leave, the next referral call might come, or what might happen the following year, or even 5 years down the road, when children's college tuitions may be due or health insurance fees skyrocket? It is the quotidian and pragmatic nature of financial concern that makes this issue so powerful, and that leads to such great difficulty in placing what might be best for patients in priority to analysts' own interests. It is for these reasons that I reiterate the belief that analysts' economic concerns create a most vivid example of inherent conflict of interest, and represent the most serious problem in any effort toward productive clinical work.

In what follows, I will attempt to state some major consequences precipitated by analysts' anxiety about money, and subsequently discuss these and present clinical examples that are illustrative of such problems. Perhaps the most predominant consequence of analysts' financial concerns is keeping patients in treatment too long, and the development of patients' excessive dependency that inevitably arises from this (Renik, 2006). I have no research data to support this, but my own anecdotal observation is that many patients remain in analysis for a staggering number of years, and that it is more common than it was in other generations for patients, many of whom are

---

* Though the focus of this chapter is on financial needs and economic greed, selfish and harmful competitiveness in helping professions, of course, goes beyond money matters solely. For example, Gabbard (1996) and Gabbard and Lester (1995) addressed the problem of psychotherapists' sexual involvement with patients; and for a powerful description of destructive competitiveness and egregious pursuit of selfish interest in religious circles, see Frawley-O'Dea and Goldner (2007).

analysts themselves, to remain in analysis for 10, 15, 20, or even 25 years with the same analyst. A related effect of analysts' economic interests emerges in the number of times per week that patients are seen. Though, as most analysts, I believe that at least three sessions per week are optimal for analytic work, analysts' motives for seeing patients multiple sessions each week can be unrelated to this analytic ideal. Some patients who are seen many times each week, indeed, are not necessarily being seen in an analytic context with analytic aims. That is, some analysts are doing supportive or maintenance-oriented work, yet seeing patients who can afford this as if they were conducting an analysis. Similarly, many patients who can pay high fees will be seen multiple times per week for many, many years, long after it is easy to rationalize that analytic goals still prevail. One colleague has said to me, without shame, that a couple of his patients are so troubled that he anticipates that they will be "patients for life." Another very well-respected colleague proclaimed at a clinical meeting that she and all of her colleagues have their "lifers," patients who allegedly "need" to be in analysis for literally their entire lives. This statement was not challenged by others at this meeting. In the above situations, "analysis" becomes a vehicle for the creation of mutual attachment and of dependent ties, and the rationales for this may center on biased assessments of patients' degree of psychopathology. The very idea of adhering to the patients' original analytic goals or aims is forgotten. Maintenance of the analytic relationship may become an end in itself (Renik, 2006). A third compromise precipitated by analysts' anxiety about money is the striving to be liked by patients, in order that they remain in treatment. In this respect, analysts may be overly supportive and complimentary; strive to be helpful in ways that do not correspond to the analytic aim of facilitation of autonomy; avoid challenging patients when this would seem to be potentially useful; avoid uncomfortable transference themes, particularly themes related to anger and disappointment; engage too tentatively in order that patients' anxiety, even productive anxiety, be kept to a minimum; and use deliberate self-disclosure in order to gratify patients' wishes (in contrast with self-disclosure being used to open up areas for exploration). I also believe that certain theoretical points of view are sometimes embraced more because they are gratifying than because they are the most likely to effect ultimate separation and autonomy. Both analytic reserve and analytic challenge can be eschewed for fear that these attitudes may provoke patients to quit, whereas measures that were more traditionally associated with supportive psychotherapy may maintain patients in prolonged attachment. I contend that analysts are more likely to conduct briefer analyses, and analyses that try to create significant independence, when the analyst is more willing to let patients leave and to lose income. Unfortunately, this does not occur enough in our current analytic culture, and when it does, it may readily be a function of an analyst's practice being full, the analyst having new patients waiting, or the patient's fee being low enough that the analyst does not wish to prolong this commitment at a reduced fee. I am not suggesting that the willingness to see patients leave is always good for patients, for this too can easily be based on the wish for a higher fee, or the wish to see someone new, or perhaps more interesting. And, the wish to keep patients for many years and see them as often as possible can be based on what is believed best for patients, or even on a strong and ultimately fruitful attachment. However, as with Newman's (2006) surgeons, our (analysts') financial needs carry much weight in the myriad of judgments and choices we make in our clinical work, and these choices are very often quite conscious on our part. I intend to use clinical examples in this chapter and in the next, to illustrate this delicate and controversial theme, and the often enormous impact that it has on many aspects of psychoanalytic practice.*

## Clinical Illustrations

I saw Norman, with him "kicking and screaming," for 11 years, initially twice per week and then three times per week. He complained almost daily, often quite nastily, that this was a profound waste of time and a futile exercise with a profession full of charlatans. He had been in therapy with a nonanalyst, and then in a prior analysis, for the previous 14 years before beginning with me, and concluded that both treatments had been total failures. He lamented that he had "lost his mind" while in college and, though functioning as a successful graduate student and then professional for much of his post-college life, claimed that he has never had full use of his cognitive

---

* Once again, I feel compelled to note that these conflicts are not at all peculiar to psychoanalytic practice, though this is the only profession with which I have firsthand experience and am qualified to examine.

faculties since. Because of this rather vague complaint, he insisted that he *needed* to see the likes of me, despite his conviction that psychoanalysis is fraudulent. "What alternative was there?" he argued.

Norman described his prebreakdown self as powerfully focused and astute, brilliant both academically and in his comprehension and awareness of social and cultural phenomena. He was the favorite child and the prized possession of his mother, and he was being groomed by her to follow in the footsteps of her ancestors, many of them esteemed rabbis in pre-Nazi Europe, and more recently in the United States as well. Until his college years Norman was a good boy, a straight-A student, and a serious Jewish scholar with a glorious future in the Orthodox Jewish world of his mother and her ancestors. Though his nonreligious father mocked his "momma's boy" existence, Norman did not fight him, or push away from mother until his senior year in college. At this point Norman discovered that he was attractive to women and began masturbating at a more frantic pace than during the years that he buried himself in his books and did not notice that he was good-looking and desirable. Simultaneous with this, he recognized that he was passionate about science and began to wish that he could pursue a career either in clinical medicine or in medical research. Both his interest in women and his veering away from Jewish studies put him on a collision course with his mother, and at about the time he was graduating he had his "breakdown." After getting to know Norman somewhat, I interpreted that what he called his breakdown was actually the only way he felt could get out of being a compliant boy. This alleged loss of the ability to think straight allowed him to postpone going to seminary, and to take a break from his studies. As part of his recovery he began to travel and to live independently for the first time, and in this context, he began to enjoy women and initiate the active sex life that still characterized his life at the time I met him.

By the time Norman returned to New York City, after 2 years of "recovery" via odd jobs and travel around the world, he had already applied to medical school and was prepared to pursue this career. Although by the time I met him he was a well-respected researcher and teacher, Norman was still insisting that his mind never has worked as sharply as it had earlier, and that he wanted his mind back and needed to be in therapy for this reason. Though I have heard clinically psychotic individuals talk of "not having my mind," Norman was anything but crazy. His professional life was productive, and his interests were rich. He had no intimate friends and preferred serial monogamy with women to marriage, but he was not certain if this situation troubled him, for he reported liking his space and his autonomy. It did not take very long for me to recognize that what Norman meant by not having his mind was that he was in considerable conflict about having defied his mother, and that he felt that he could never be all present in any career or in relationships that excluded her. In the good old days of mother–son symbiosis, Norman had a unity of mind with mother, and in this partnership, there was no conflict. There was virtually total presence in their relationship, and in the intellectual pursuits that were aligned with her. As an adult performing independently, he was very angry with his mother and maintained a distant physical connection. Nonetheless he was still strongly dependent on and attached with her, and could not feel unambivalent engagement in either his work life or love life.

This same angry dependency characterized Norman's connection with me, as it had over the 14 years with his two other therapists. He would attend sessions reliably, invariably attacking me in the same mocking and incisive way that his father castrated him while growing up. He was relentless, never giving me any credit for saying anything worthwhile, or for whatever movement existed in at least his professional life. Though I was committed to doing better than my predecessors, whom I assessed as engaging in a mutually constructed symbiotic dependency with my patient, Norman would not acknowledge my superiority to them. His sharp criticism kept me very alert and wired, and I believed that I was both very present with him and attuned to him. I believed that my observations and interpretations were astute, and that I dealt directly with his anger-dominated transference in a way that his other therapists ignored. As much as I experienced that I was my most capable analyst self, I was confronted with my being as much of a charlatan as my rivals, and with Norman's stated facts that he did not feel fully present in his work, and that he was still cynical about being in loving and intimate relational configurations with anyone. I felt close with him despite his porcupine ways, though he never acknowledged reciprocal feelings. At best, he mocked me with some warm teasing for my girly desire to have him love me. My interpretive emphasis was on Norman's fear that his loving bond with me would leave him totally subject to my will, and masochistically submissive to me in ways similar to his connection with both his parents. Were I not the object of his castrating aggressions, he would be the good boy of his youth, and forced to abandon any semblance of self-direction and personal freedom. Though he acknowledged to some extent the relevance of these transference themes, he never admitted to caring about me in any way, and we struggled over this theme for what seemed like an eternity. It was only in the 10th year of our work that I began to stop talking with him about love and attachment and shifted to the term *dependency*. Under manifest protest, Norman visited me for years in spite of his busy schedule, just as he had my predecessors. He earned a good living, but he paid my highest fee, and at the rate of three times per week our time together cost him a great deal of money. Though disguised by consistent aggression, Norman *was* a very dependent man, and my failure to emphasize his dependency in the transference was, indeed, the same mutual enactment of dependency exploited by his previous therapists. I had early on diagnosed his previous therapies essentially as dependency operations, and because I was so active in addressing transference themes I was able to deceive myself into believing that I was engaging in a distinctly higher-level therapeutic enterprise. Norman's dependency on me was lived out, and was not sufficiently pointed out. I knew how dependent he had been with his mother, but I did not let myself fully articulate this in his transference to me. We engaged in an extended enactment that reinforced both his dependency and his denial of dependency. Norman did not consciously feel love for me or for anyone else, and he readily could tell me that I was off base in addressing this sort of attachment in the transference. When, very belatedly, I began to speak with him about his dependence on me, and use as evidence the many years he had visited me (and others) and the many thousands of dollars spent on the psychoanalysis he so damningly criticized, Norman was able to relent somewhat and give me credit for finally pointing out something salient to him. He began to see the impact of his dependency and the disguises he used to protect him from feeling this acutely, and this awareness had some salubrious impact on his life, his love life in particular. This also signaled the beginning of the end for our work together, though Norman was angry that it had lasted so long.

It seems awfully clear in retrospect that I exploited Norman's dependency instead of clarifying this much earlier in our analysis. I felt alive (though battered) in my work with him, and enjoyed my alertness and having *my* full mind when with him. The years went by quickly, and Norman's existence in my life, two to three times weekly, was both emotionally and intellectually stimulating and financially rewarding. Though I did not articulate this clearly to myself, I knew that dependency was at the core of Norman's involvement with his mother and in his two previous "dead" therapies, and that it had to be, certainly after the years went by, the heart of the matter between us. How could this not be evident? Indeed, it was quite evident, but I did not articulate this to myself beyond fleeting private thoughts, nor did I spell this out with Norman. In an unformulated way I knew that once this theme was worked through, our analysis would end. I was dependent on Norman in a variety of ways, though were I seeing him in a clinic and money were not an issue, I have little doubt that the theme of dependency would have been center stage much sooner in our work together. Though I consider this analysis ultimately a productive one, it should have had a far briefer duration. I believe this illustration is emblematic of all too many of my own and my colleagues' analytic work, where patients' dependency is either facilitated or subtly fed in order that we are helped to maintain some economic security.

This analysis lasted 11 years, though for Norman, his total years in therapy added up to 25, and 19 of those years were in multiple times per week analysis. This is not unusual in our current psychoanalytic culture, where it is not only difficult to find patients outside of our profession willing to come for three or more sessions per week, but also hard to find enough people who have the money to pay at least some approximation of analysts' preferred fee. That is, when analysts are fortunate enough to be referred people who both are interested in attending multiple sessions each week and have the financial resources to do this, it becomes especially conflictual to facilitate their successful termination. Unconsciously and with some consciousness both, analysts find rationales to hold on to such individuals as long as possible, as I did with Norman. I have observed in myself and among supervisees and colleagues that this phenomenon exists even with patients who pay reduced fees, sometimes significantly reduced. My informal discussions with colleagues have supported my private observations about how difficult it has become to attract patients into three or more times per week psychoanalysis in the United States, especially since the stark decline in the numbers of training candidates at analytic institutes. If one's practice is not full, it may be quite appealing to be in a position to practice the standard analysis one has been trained for, and this may be rewarding despite the lower than preferred fee schedule. As well, reduced fees multiplied three to five times per week still usually add up to substantial income. The combination of this factor and the appeal of working analytically in the optimal fashion often leads also to the co-creation of dependency and to unnecessarily prolonged analyses. For example, analytic candidates in training commonly pay considerably reduced fees, yet remain as highly desired analysands, and from anecdotal observation many spend an inordinate number of years in analysis. In this era of fewer analytic candidates for senior analysts to see as patients, extended analyses have, indeed, become more common.

Mitchell was an economics research scholar who received his doctorate but never worked as an economist, choosing instead to manage his investments and to engage part-time in his family business. When he first came to see me, shortly after achieving his degree, he believed he wanted an academic job and, indeed, searched for one. He found nothing available in New York City, where he wished to live, and after one year he no longer pursued this. However, shortly after beginning four times per week analysis with me, at my full fee, Mitchell did get an offer to teach in a relatively rural town a few hours outside of New York. This was far from his ideal situation, but he was considering it and talked with me a good deal about this. This job was a decent opportunity, and one that could conceivably be a first step to a traditional academic career in perhaps more interesting geographic locations. My patient was single, struggling with his sexual identity, but claimed to wish to settle down with a Jewish woman. At the time, his love life was totally barren, though this had also been the case for virtually all of his life. Indeed, this was primary among his reasons for entering analysis. He acknowledged some conflict about the direction of his sexual desire, though insisted most of his masturbatory fantasies were directed toward women. Already in his late 20s, he had had only the scantiest sexual experiences with women, and he claimed to have had none at all with men. I was quietly skeptical, sensing in him an attraction to me, and a strong prohibition toward homosexuality, which was internalized from his family of origin and from his subculture. Much of his stated reservation about accepting this academic job revolved around the lack of availability of suitable women, though I thought that it also reduced the likelihood of fulfilling his homosexual desires. While he wrestled with this decision, I was quite clear that I did not want to lose this interesting man who paid my full fee, and even asked for four sessions per week, one more than the three sessions that were the rule of thumb of my own psychoanalytic culture. Though I knew he would not likely find a full-time academic position in New York, and thought the offer he had was a decent place to launch a career, I was quite supportive of the parts of Mitchell who wished to stay here. I did see these pro–New York arguments as credible to an extent, but I knew that I was nowhere close to neutral on this issue, and that I withheld myself from fleshing out some of the talking points in favor of accepting this academic post. Indeed, one of my arguments referred to the absence of trained analysts in easy commuting distance from this college campus, and Mitchell's early devotion to the analytic process and to the goals he hoped to reach through this commitment. Though his concerns about finding a wife and continuing analysis, and my sense that he wanted homosexual opportunity, all had validity, despite some rationalization, I knew what I preferred. Mitchell was undoubtedly influenced by my desire to keep him as a patient. This set the tone for a long analysis that was fueled, in part, by Mitchell's dependency on me and unarticulated homosexual interest in me.

Were Mitchell coming once per week and/or not paying my highest fee, I suspect he may very well have taken this academic position. Though after some time he did eventually enjoy managing his family business and his investments, I always believed that he may have had more satisfaction following his scholarly and academic interests. In retrospect, Mitchell clearly sensed that I wanted him around, and though he knew that I was heterosexual, he experienced my wish to be with him as an opportunity for both a dependency-dominated and a sexually intimate involvement with a somewhat older man.

Mitchell did begin to acknowledge his dependent attachment to me, but never admitted homosexual interest, despite reporting periodic homosexual fantasies about other men. He insisted that he was heterosexual and wished for marriage and family, and consistently focused on anxiety about sexual performance and feared impotence as reasons for not following up with women after their initial date or two. He linked his previous impotence and heterosexual anxiety to feelings of diminished self-worth, in the context of his relations with his dominating and competitive father. Mitchell believed that his father wanted him to remain his personal castrato, and that he had internalized this. Indeed, Mitchell's place in the family business, as lucrative as this was for him, kept him attached to his father in a perennially subordinate way. His presence persisted in helping his father feel competitively strong. He hoped that I, as his analyst, would offer a new experience that would help make him strong and sufficiently competitive in order to become potent with women. Unfortunately, however, I had already helped steer my patient away from an independent career pursuit, and I was cooperating with his coming to see me one more time per week than my psychoanalytic tradition dictated. In some parallel with his father, my own self-interest took some priority to that of Mitchell. I was perhaps, like his father, getting more from being with him than he was from his analysis with me. I enacted with Mitchell a facsimile of this father–son configuration—like his father, his subordinate position was rewarding to me. Indeed, this was not unknown to me in my conscious reverie.

I was reluctant to be candid with Mitchell and tell him that I believed he was gay, and that he should come to terms with this and allow himself to enjoy sex and companionship, instead of continuing his futile dating patterns with women. I rationalized that I did not know this for certain, for Mitchell kept denying his homosexuality each time I questioned this. By not telling him forthrightly what I believed, he and I lived out a homosexual engagement. I became the relationship that Mitchell denied himself from having outside the transference, and our currency in his staying with me was his wish for me to help him overcome his anxiety with women. He was dependent on me as a lover and as an ostensibly more benign paternal presence. This went on for 6 years, with Mitchell achieving some sense of potency in taking over many of his father's functions in the business, after some of the latter's health problems began to limit him. He began to enjoy the business at this point, and I felt less guilty over my having supported this career choice, in part for my own economic benefit. At one point I even confessed to Mitchell that I had wanted him to stay in New York and that I had been biased in my analysis, though I stressed my enjoyment in working with him, failing to mention the economic element. Despite his dependence on me, Mitchell began to feel stronger. I believe that he ultimately sensed how dependent I was on him, and that in some respects I was the economically struggling son to his wealthy father self. It was in this emotional context that Mitchell began to confess to me that he had all along had more homosexual fantasies than he admitted and, with increasing frequency, had been having brief sexual encounters with men for the past couple of years. He claimed to still want a wife and family, but acknowledged that integrating his preferred sexuality with this would be difficult. He explained that he failed to tell me the extent of his homosexuality because he did not want it to be real, and as well, if I knew, I'd have given up on his efforts to grow comfortable with women. At the time we terminated, Mitchell had grown to enjoy his place in the family business, and developed a knack for investing his money via day trading and other vehicles. His sex life was more open, and he engaged with increased frequency. He had had a few short-term relationships beyond anonymous encounters, though he did not think he wished to develop a serious relationship with a man. He still believed that he might be able to develop a heterosexual marriage and a family, while perhaps maintaining a secret homosexual erotic life. He was convinced that there were women out there who would be happy to be married to a wealthy man who was gentle, caretaking, and devoted to his children, and that these women would be able to tolerate a barely existent sex life. I was not in a position to challenge this, and actually believed that Mitchell was probably correct. I knew firsthand how easy it was to be dependent on Mitchell—how willing he was to be a caretaker both emotionally and financially. I was, however, disappointed that I had not helped him be more comfortable in his homosexual skin, and that shame and internalized familial desires continued to constrain him. He, on the other hand, seemed relatively pleased with our work together, and did not have the sense that our 6-year, four-times-per-week arrangement was either excessive or a function of my own self-interest. Mitchell was a sweet and generous man, and he was raised to make others feel good.

Though I am somewhat pleased with the ultimate outcome of this analysis, I am also convinced that it could have been both briefer and equally useful at the three times per week rate to which I am accustomed, and which corresponded with my own experience as an analytic patient. I am also not convinced that Mitchell would have not been better served had he taken his academic job, experienced accomplishment and independence outside of his family business, and commuted to a local analyst an hour or more from his college. Further, I feel certain that if I had been more candid about my belief that he was gay, and that it was a waste of time to keep talking about his wish for intimacy with a woman, we would have saved considerable time.

Though 6 years is not especially long in today's analytic culture, my relationship with him was an enactment of the homosexual, dominance–submission one with his father, and it served to keep him more tentative about pursuing other gay relations. Indeed, I was aware that I believed the fourth weekly session unnecessary, and I felt some ambivalence about my patient embracing his sexuality and moving on from our relationship. Even though I and many of my colleagues have engaged in much longer analyses, even ultimately fruitful ones, the troublesome element of my selfish interest in the economic rewards in my work with Mitchell is unmistakable. I believe that it is more common than otherwise that patients like this one, who pay full fees and are willing to come as often as analysts prefer, have analytic experiences that are prolonged and/or can be facilitated at a lower weekly frequency. Under circumstances like the one I have just described, it is difficult for analysts to avoid the self-deception that long analyses at an optimum* weekly frequency are invariably best for each given patient. There is no doubt that this configuration is invariably beneficial, on an economic level, for each analyst.

## Discussion

It must also be noted that there are many circumstances where the obverse is true, that is, where a given patient is seen fewer sessions per week, or for a shorter duration, in order that the patient may be able to afford the analyst's preferred fee. In fact, this is a common dilemma faced by most analysts. As is evident, most analysts, financial interests aside, prefer to work with most of their patients multiple times per week for an extended period of time, the exact preferred number of sessions per week determined by the particular analyst's theoretical identifications. Most every contemporary analyst in the United States is aware of the unfortunate circumstance that only a small percentage of patients are interested in pursuing three or more times per week treatment. Of those, only a tiny fraction can afford these multiple sessions for a significant number of years at our preferred fee scale. When a patient is willing or is interested in pursuing an optimal analytic experience but cannot afford to do this at the

---

* I wish to reiterate that I saw Mitchell at a weekly frequency beyond what I normally consider optimal.

analyst's preferred fee, the analyst is confronted with the choice of seeing this person under ideal circumstances at perhaps a sharply reduced fee, or seeing the patient twice or once weekly at a much higher rate. Analysts' economic realities make it very difficult, in this frequently faced conflict, to choose patients' interest in priority to their own.

For example, if a particular analyst is low on filled hours, this analyst may be more likely to encourage patients to attend as frequently as possible, inducing them with a sharply reduced fee. Although this structure may be a blessing for the patient, the analyst's offer may have been more related to self-interest (filling unbooked hours) than to the patient's interest per se. If it has not been clear to this point, I wish to underscore that there are, indeed, many instances where analysts' self-interest and patients' self-interest are aligned. However, in the illustration just given, which in practice comes up quite often, there are some potential risks. If, for example, this analyst's practice becomes more busy, he or she may resent this reduced-fee patient and begin to see this individual as a burden. This anger may be subtly communicated, and in extreme, the analysts' unconscious motive might be acted out so as to undo the multiple session–reduced fee arrangement or, even worse, to induce the patient to leave treatment altogether.

Another common resolution to the equation of fee and sessions per week is to agree to see a given patient once per week at the analysts' preferred fee, while in full awareness recognizing that this patient might be both better served and willing to be in a more ideal, multiple sessions per week analysis. This situation is likely to evolve when the analyst in question may have only a few free hours, and/or believes that he or she already sees enough long-term psychoanalytic patients at reduced fees. This matter is complicated by the viewpoint articulated by Gill (1982, 1983, 1984, 1994) that the intrinsic factors, particularly analysis of transference, define what can be called psychoanalysis, and although multiple sessions per week over a number of years are an analytic ideal, they comprise an *extrinsic* factor in defining psychoanalytic treatment. I have always been in full agreement with Gill's argument, and have often used this to rationalize my choosing to see a patient in once per week psychoanalysis (with the expectancy that this will run for a significant number of years) at my preferred fee, rather than either reducing my fee or referring this person to someone who would be willing to work at a reduced fee for multiple sessions per week. I, and many of my colleagues, are faced with this dilemma on a regular basis—in today's analytic culture, it can be seen as a quotidian situation. In some such moments, especially if I find the patient interesting and/or appealing, I will offer a referral to someone who might see him or her more frequently at a reduced fee, but I may not strongly emphasize the potential advantages of such a pursuit. Parenthetically, if, for instance, I were an analytic candidate in need of a patient to meet my requirements, I *would* likely make a strong effort to sell the patient on the advantages of multiple times per week analytic work. In my current professional situation, if I sense that the patient and I have made a good connection and he or she is someone with whom I'd like to work, I am likely to convey the optimism about our analytic future that I genuinely feel, emphasizing with less enthusiasm the patient's other options, and the potential advantages that may lie in these alternatives. I would be far more reticent about acknowledging this blatant pursuit of self-interest if I did not believe that it is normative among colleagues at all levels of experience.

I might add, perhaps in order to shade my own selfish behaviors, that I know of far more egregious pursuits of self-interest, ones that fall closer to ethical borders. I know of analysts who advise their patients to come every other week, expressly because they can charge double for each session. They explain to their patients (and sometimes rationalize to themselves) that attending every week is not a serious advantage, though privately and to like-minded colleagues they acknowledge that they feel that they do their best and least compromised work when feeling well compensated. I am acquainted with other analysts who see patients for double sessions, implying that this constitutes two times per week psychoanalysis. One common motive for these double sessions reflects an accommodation to some patient's unwillingness to disrupt their schedules by making two trips each week to their analyst's office. However, in condensing two sessions into one longer one, the philosophical basis of multiple visits is largely negated, though the analyst is technically justified in charging for the time involved in two independent sessions. I believe every analyst knows that encouraging patients to commit to the inconveniences of attending sessions is a part of the devotion necessary for productive work, though this shortcut, for obvious economic reasons, may be difficult to resist when offered by patients. One can say the same for telephone sessions, an increasingly common practice among contemporary analysts (Richards, 1999). Though there are some situations when sessions over the phone may be unavoidable, more frequently I observe this phenomenon to be devolving into a convenience for both parties. Like double sessions, the convenience of the telephone might reflect an absence of full commitment to do the hard work of analysis on the part of the patient. I believe that most analysts would agree that a certain level of commitment is needed in order to maximize the likelihood of success, and the too easy or too convenient way might make the outcome of a treatment more dubious. Nonetheless, when faced with the prospect of a patient leaving treatment because he or she is finding it too difficult to attend, many analysts are tempted to work in a way that is knowingly a severe compromise.

A qualitatively different but also questionable practice is an analyst's willingness to see patients who are related to one another either as family or by close friendship. This has long been frowned upon by psychoanalysts representing all of the major traditions, though once again I observe anecdotally that this is a more frequent phenomenon in today's professional culture. Indeed, a certain percentage of most practitioners' referrals come from current or past patients. When the referral source does not specify that he or she does not wish for the analyst to see the referral, and the referred-to analyst is anxious about the economics of his or her practice, it may be very tempting to see a new patient who has a close relationship with a current or past one.* It is not relevant for the purposes of this chapter to review all of the reasons why this has consensually been regarded as poor practice. Were economic needs not a factor, I believe it would be hard to find an analyst who would not agree that referral to a colleague is the reflexively appropriate procedure, and clearly in the best interests of both the old or current and the prospective new patient. It is actually difficult to find a rationale that might support doing otherwise, though I have heard from a few colleagues and supervisees that they believe that it may be an advantage to have knowledge about a patient from information received from a close acquaintance. I think that this very weak rationale can only be an effort to save face, and to cover up an analyst's shame that is inevitable when a thoroughly conscious pursuit of self-interest so obviously conflicts with the prevailing professional culture.

---

* Unfortunately, I know of some analysts who actively encourage their patients to refer significant others to them (e.g., spouses or children).

The economic realities of psychoanalytic practice create choices that I believe very few would take were we working for a salary at a clinic or under the German national insurance system referred to earlier. Some analysts opt for therapeutic configurations that constitute or come close to constituting unethical conduct, though I believe that most every analyst makes some decisions about the basic physical structure of the analytic relationship that reflect compromises that fall far short of analytic ideals. Such decisions can only be controlled when they are acknowledged, and made without self-deception. However, even in full consciousness, I believe that most analysts will make some basic framework decisions that are affected by financial self-interest.

# 8

# Money and the Ongoing
# Therapeutic Relationship

Beyond some basic analytic frame matters focused on in the previous chapter (who is seen as a patient, the number of years that therapy lasts, and the weekly frequency of the sessions over these years), financial interest may also influence the very fabric and texture of the ongoing treatment relationship (Aron & Hirsch, 1992; Josephs, 2001; Lasky, 1984; Liss-Levinson, 1990; Myers, 2008; Whitson, n.d.).* In addition to the obvious avoidance of examining co-created excessive dependency developed in the analytic dyad, therapists may engage patients in any number of other ways that are most likely to keep them from leaving treatment, and such engagement may run counter to the ultimate aims of patients' autonomy, independence, flexibility, and resilience (Aron & Hirsch; Renik, 2006; Whitson). As noted in the introduction to the previous chapter, this compromised interaction can readily include the avoidance of addressing anxiety-laden issues because these might provoke discomfort and possible flight, and/or the provision of what had been, in another era, called *analytic gratifications*. As Mitchell (1988) has pointedly suggested, these omissions and commissions can be rationalized as sensitivity to what the patient allegedly "needs" at any given moment. They can also be purported to conform to the highly respected theoretical contributions of psychoanalytic pioneers like Winnicott (1958) and Kohut (1984).** Indeed, there are times when any given patient may be far from ready to hear something, or when a supportive comment, an exclusively empathic

---

* As noted in the previous chapter, everything I write about can apply to all fee-for-service relationships in and out of the mental health professions. I refer to psychoanalysis and psychoanalytic therapy only for the obvious reason that this is my purview.
** See also Summers (1999).

stance, a piece of parental advice, or a sharing of some personal data is genuinely in a patient's long-term interests. Nonetheless, I am arguing that many, if not most, choices to not inquire into disquieting issues, particularly issues related to transference themes, are motivated more by analysts' interests than by those of patients (Aron, 2005; Coen, 2002; Gill, 1982, 1983, 1994; Friedman, 1988; Gabbard, 1995; Greenberg, 1995, 2001; Hirsch, 1998b; Hoffman, 1983, 1987; Jacobs, 1991; Levenson, 1972, 1981, 1992; Poland, 1992; Searles, 1965, 1979; Singer, 1965b, 1968, 1977; Stern, 1987, 1996b; Wolstein, 1954, 1977, 1983). This may be rationalized as adherence to an empathic stance as advocated by practitioners of a self-psychological approach, or a holding and containing function as represented by some analysts identified with a middle school object relations tradition. Indeed, I believe that many analysts' efforts to be warm, nurturing, and gratifying to patients go well beyond the wish to create safety for them, and instead are intimately linked with analysts' worries that patients may leave treatment if they become too angry in the transference (Hirsch, 1983). Though most analysts would agree that a timely and discreet pursuit of deconstruction or shake-up of the patient's self-experience and experience of the world is fundamental to meaningful change, many of us instead pursue the maintenance of a relatively safe comfortable equilibrium within the analytic dyad, and in the patient's life. Though there are self states (see Bromberg, 1998, 2006; Davies, 1994, 2004) within each patient that fight the process of change, and that wish to maintain familiar internal and external representations (equilibrium), I do not believe that anyone begins analysis without some hope (Cooper, 2000a, 2000b; Farber, 1966; Hoffman, 1998; Mitchell, 1993) that their rigid and familiar compromises will expand (Levenson, 1983, 1988), and their comfortable though constricting certainties (Frie, 2002; Fromm, 1941, 1964; Hirsch, 1998a, 1998b; Singer, 1965a; Stern, 1987, 1990, 1996a, 1997) will be challenged. Patients may become angry at an analyst for provoking these disquieting moments in the treatment, but, needless to say, without some reasonable disruption at some point significant change is unlikely. A therapy that goes too smoothly without patients' display of anger, criticism, or disappointment to the therapist is likely to be stagnant, even if it is experienced mutually as pleasant, warm, or comforting. When the analyst aligns primarily with those aspects of the patient that pursue equilibrium, it becomes unlikely that meaningful character change will evolve, and the process of repetition may become interminable. In this context, the therapy sometimes proceeds more like a benign parent–child relationship, or like an old and comfortable slipper/friendship. It is not unusual for long analyses to take on the quality of close friendships, and for this phenomenon to be mutually enacted and remain unanalyzed.

Mutual pursuit of equilibrium can take two basic forms. As just noted, one configuration may be that of the analyst acting consciously as an exclusively supportive and benign other, perhaps a presence opposite to that which seemed to characterize the patients' allegedly* deficient developmental years. The other form, of course, refers to unconsciously formed mutual enactments. Despite analysts' conscious efforts to be for the patient either a neutral other or a new and "good" object, therapists will invariably become unwittingly caught up in patients' old repetitive patterns before this becomes conscious to either party (Black, 2003; Bromberg, 1998, 2006; Friedman, 2006; Gabbard, 1995; Gill, 1982; Greenberg, 1991; Hirsch, 1993, 1996, 1998b; Hoffman, 1983; Jacobs, 1986, 2001; Levenson, 1972; McLaughlin, 1991; Mitchell, 1988; Poland, 1992; Renik, 1993; Sandler, 1976; Stern, 2003, 2004). Indeed, we cannot evolve into new configurations unless we reach them first through the vehicle of living through old and familiar experience. Though many mutual enactments do not take the form of the benign and loving aspects of parent–child relatedness, when they do, unless this is addressed by the analyst, these enactments have the potential to endure for years. And when these enactments are not warm and mutually affectionate, such as a replication of a sadomasochistic parent–child configuration, they still may well persist for years because of their comfort and their familiarity to the patient. That is, both old and "bad" transference–countertransference experience and efforts and new and "good" analytic interaction, if not examined and addressed explicitly, can endure for a very long time. The "bad" configuration can provide a patient with

---

* I say *allegedly* because the view that early experience may simply be deficient does not characterize the thinking of all analytic schools of thought. For instance, it is more than semantic to characterize an emotionally absent parent as providing a distinct experience for a child, with that absence characterizing an *active*, albeit harmful, way of being for a parent. Neglect, therefore, may be seen not as producing deficiency, but as creating a personality characterized by such experience, and perhaps anticipating or even inviting parallel neglect from others as life proceeds. Deficiency implies that there is no experience and that the patient has virtually no identity, though being ignored is, indeed, a powerful experience and may produce a self distinctly defined by the wounds of absence.

a comfortable and familiar home, and the "good" configuration may be both highly gratifying, and replicate early self states characterized by feeling "held" or "mirrored" (Kohut, 1984; Slochower, 1996; Winnicott, 1958). The implicit quest for comfort and familiarity of either dimension may dominate and obscure any of the therapeutic aims or goals originally expressed at the beginning of treatment (Hirsch, 1983; Mitchell, 1988, 1993; Renik, 2006).

Economic considerations may be one motivating force behind analysts' willingness to maintain with patients ways of engaging that maintain both forms ("good" object and "bad" object) of equilibrium. In one form, a patient's old (and "bad") comfortable intra- and interpersonal integrations are repeated as unwitting and subtle mutual enactments. The therapist may fail to point this out even after becoming aware of this repetition. One fear may be that the patient may become angry toward the analyst for enacting "bad" old object experience, and that this anger might lead to a premature termination. Another, perhaps more subtle anxiety for the therapist is that an analysis of an enactment may represent a step toward the evolution of a mature termination. The second type of equilibrium places the therapist in the consciously determined role of the new, benign or "good" object, perceived by the therapist as counter to the patient's significant internalized self–other configurations. In such a formulation, the therapist may discount that holding and mirroring have played some role in a patient's life history (Goldberg, 2007; Searles, 1965, 1979), that the patients' parents were not only "bad" objects and therefore that such "good" engagement is not entirely new. Though an analyst's wish or therapeutic strategy may be the provision of salubrious new experience to the patient, this is often not the only motive. As treatment proceeds these apparently benign and caring integrations may readily become institutionalized, and maintaining this form of mutual comfort may become the unstated aim of the therapeutic endeavor. This, too, will undoubtedly help stretch out the length of the analytic work and, as well, reduce the risk at any given moment of an overly dependent patient's flight from disquieting disequilibrium. Further, this form of therapeutic engagement may make it quite difficult for many patients to be openly angry and critical to their apparently benign and loving analyst (Coen, 2002).

As I have noted throughout, analysts sometimes engage both these equilibrium-maintaining ways with some elements of conscious awareness. The sometimes failure to address uncomfortable transference themes and enactments in my own clinical work has been discussed throughout this text. I also see this phenomenon of avoidance quite often in my supervisory work, where a relatively young analyst may be dependent on a fairly small number of patients to both practice the work he or she loves and to earn at least some facsimile of a decent living. In a number of such situations I have observed, in particular, the tendency to preserve a benign and supportive therapeutic stance in order that the patient stay comfortable, not become angry in the transference, and maintain the therapeutic dyad for as long as possible. This is most commonly rationalized as responsivity to patients' needs, and/or patients' absence of readiness to begin to integrate disquieting new experience. As already noted, what had once been ambitious analytic aims can readily erode, and maintenance of a supportive and dependent parental relationship, or one that resembles a warm friendship, can morph into the implicit yet unstated mutual goals of the work. In essence, the psychoanalytic structure of multiple times per week treatment may obscure the practice of what in my mind dissolves into long-term (mutually) supportive psychotherapy.

## Clinical Illustrations

Dr. M consulted me for supervision because he had been feeling stuck with a couple of his long-term patients. He believed that he had helped them expand their lives to a point, but for some time the work has not succeeded in moving these individuals forward. Dr. M felt that he understood the psychogenetic factors in his patients' lives quite well, though he sensed that there were unseen transference and/or countertransference factors that were responsible for the absence of movement in the work. Nick was his most troublesome patient in this regard, and Dr. M could not understand why an analysis that had created such expansion in Nick's life had hit a proverbial wall.

Nick, now 26, had originally consulted Dr. M some 6 years earlier, shortly prior to Dr. M beginning analytic training. Nick seemed to know that he had a strong intelligence, but he never had pushed beyond a year or so of community college, and a series of union apprentice construction-related jobs. He came from a lower-middle-class, Hispanic, blue-collar family, and had always been in some conflict about following in the footsteps of his father, uncles, and older brothers, or pursuing academically an interest in psychology. His family was close and seemingly supportive of his difference, but Nick would never engage school with a total commitment. He believed that starting therapy could help him pursue a more directed course in terms of career and, as well, expose him firsthand to a profession that he had intermittently aspired toward. Nick was also worried about his love life, even though he was still quite young. All of the men in his family had settled into their long-term commitments during or just after high school, and Nick felt uneasy with his desires for "screwing around" for a while, at least.

Dr. M, himself from a more educated upper-middle-class family, found this "diamond in the rough" young man quite charming, and was thrilled by how responsive he was to therapy. He proved highly intuitive and insightful, and progress was palpable. Nick resumed school, got his bachelor's degree, and began considering master's- or doctoral-level graduate school, with an eye toward becoming a psychotherapist, or even a psychoanalyst like his own useful doctor. Fairly early in their work together, Dr. M began psychoanalytic training, and enlisted Nick as his training case. He seemed to continue to be a satisfying patient in this context as well, and soon completed his master's degree in social work and was considering pursuing a doctorate. Dr. M was less pleased with developments in his patient's love life. He had had a series of monogamous relationships, but they all were with women who were either far less educated or quite troubled emotionally. More than one of these young women had histories of serious drug use, and/or were currently using drugs or drinking to excess. Addictive behavior had never been an issue with Nick. After completing his degree, Nick was slow to pursue professional licensure and to look for work in his field. When he did find work, it was in a setting that did not lend itself to doing psychotherapy, his purported interest. Dr. M completed his training hours with Nick, and reverted back to seeing him twice per week at a somewhat reduced fee. It was in this context, after feeling a cessation of progress, that I was consulted.

In speaking to me about his patient, Dr. M emphasized his disappointment in Nick's choice of women, in his persistence in staying in what Dr. M felt was a dead-end job, and in his failure to pursue further education. He would find himself counseling his patient about these matters, though he also described being cautious about *questioning*

Nick about these choices. Dr. M noted to me that Nick had become generally more irritable with him in the last year or so. When given advice by his therapist, Nick would tend to brush him off, but when presented with challenging inquiry he might become angry. He was sensitive, in particular, to anything that might reflect a difference in values between them, or that touched on the distinct differences in their respective backgrounds and in their racial and ethnic composition (see Layton, 2004; Leary, 1997). In reporting therapy process to me, it also emerged that Nick sometimes spoke to Dr. M with his childhood blue-collar, outer-borough New York accent, and when he did this he could butcher grammatically the language he normally spoke with elegance. This was not consistent, though it became a highly salient variant on his transference engagement to his soft-spoken, upper-middle-class analyst. We both agreed that this way of speaking both symbolized and reflected Nick's conflict about continuing to move in a direction that would create further disparity between himself and his internalized familial integrations. I viewed his speech patterns as an implicit request to Dr. M to address this central theme (see Singer, 1968). Though Dr. M did not disagree conceptually, he conveyed to me quite clearly that he dare not broach this. The one time he did so, ever so gently, Nick became furious with him, emphasizing the imposition of his fancy doctoral-level and "upper-class" Manhattan private school background on his own more earthy, Hispanic, "real" self. Dr. M understood Nick's reaction to reflect that his patient was not yet ready to address this key conflict in this particular form.

It seemed reasonably clear to me, as it must be to readers, that Nick was in considerable conflict about going beyond those in his heritage, and was holding on dearly to cherished identifications. He viewed his analyst as trying to make him into someone with whom his analyst felt more comfortable, and this usually silent transference–countertransference struggle became more salient than Nick's internal struggle to actualize his autonomy from his internalized family. I suggested to Dr. M that he should address Nick's choice of job, girlfriends, and use of language in this context, and to stop avoiding these themes just because it made him angry, and because it raised the delicate issues of race and socioeconomic status. When I questioned why Dr. M was so reluctant to anger his patient, he was candid in letting me know that he feared that he might drop out of treatment if pushed on this matter and, as well, that perhaps Nick needed further holding before feeling sufficiently ready to deal with this core theme. Given the length and the productivity of their work together, I conveyed that I doubted Dr. M's feared outcome. I also speculated that his patient might be ultimately more angry at him over time if he were to stay stuck in place, the treatment dragged on, and this key theme were never resolved. In addition, I suggested that Nick would not be speaking to him in his old speech patterns if, implicitly, he did not want to show Dr. M this conflict, and wish for him to bring it explicitly into their work together at this time. Finally, I conveyed that I could not see any other way to get past the equilibrium they had created together, and the stagnancy that had set in. Though holding is indeed useful at times, I argued that Dr. M's current position did not reflect holding, but instead was emblematic of "delaying." In retrospect, I was challenging Dr. M in a parallel way that I hoped he would his patient.

Despite much back-and-forth dialogue, Dr. M, with trepidation and tentatively, began to agree with my vision of their transference–countertransference configuration. In this context he confided to me that his practice was still fairly small, his wife was a full-time student whom he supported, and they were hoping to start to raise a family. Fundamentally, Dr. M let me know that at least on an economic level, he could not afford to lose this patient. It was also clear that in the context of his relatively small practice and his long-term attachment to Nick, the risk of his terminating made Dr. M vulnerable in multiple ways. Nonetheless, I pushed him and I reassured him, and he ventured forward one day with direct efforts to address Nick's use of language, and more. As he had predicted, Nick became enraged at Dr. M during each session for a number of weeks. He absorbed his rage and was appropriately undefensive, but quietly with his patient, and vocally with me, he was convinced that Nick would leave treatment if he did not back off from pursuing this line of inquiry. Indeed, I encouraged him to not back down, and argued that this disequilibrium was both needed and productive for his patient despite the discomfort it caused both of them, and the anger that erupted as a result of this. Dr. M gathered his courage and told me that he was too anxious to continue to raise this issue, even though he did not disagree with my analysis of the transference–countertransference situation. Dr. M hoped that he would be able to return to the themes we had discussed at some time in the future, and essentially asked me to stop challenging him to do what he did not feel ready to do. He and I were now at an impasse, and we resolved this (or avoided it) by mutually deciding to no longer discuss Nick. My supervisee began to present other patients, and though we were quite amicable, I was disappointed; I felt that I understood his dilemma. I knew that I had been in many similar situations as his, and also had encountered such moments as a supervisor with much frequency. It is still possible, of course, that there was much that I missed about Dr. M's work with Nick, or about parallel process factors in our work together in relation to this patient (see Frawley-O'Dea, 1997). Even if this is so, and it probably is, I do believe that Dr. M's financial concerns were one driving force in maintaining this therapeutic impasse. This in part dictated for him which issues were approachable and which were not, and, in particular, the degree to which his patient's anxiety and anger could be activated in the transference, and tolerated in the countertransference.

Though I believe that patients who maintain comfortable equilibria at levels of living that are significantly compromised will ultimately become angry at their analysts for not helping them move beyond this, there is invariably much dyadic pressure to remain with what is both familiar and comfortable. For patients this usually reflects ties to cherished, internalized familial others, whereas for analysts it may suggest a wish for prolonged and (on the surface) benign ties to patients (Coen, 1992). Though many patients, like Dr. M's patient, warn us to not push them too hard, it is worth assuming that no one would remain in analysis *just* to maintain a status quo, and that each patient will ultimately be dissatisfied if sufficient change is not actualized over a long period of treatment. It is impossible to discern objectively what reflects good timing or bad timing, for so much of this concept depends on analysts' readiness at least as much as patients' willingness to be less held in place (Farber, 1966; Fiscalini, 2004; Frie, 2002; Fromm, 1955, 1964; Gill, 1982; Hirsch, 1987; Hoffman, 1998; Singer, 1968; Wilner, 2000; Wolstein, 1975). However, I find it difficult to seriously consider notions of holding and of timing in therapy relationships that already have endured a significant number of years. I am often suspicious that there will never be a right time to address certain uncomfortable matters, and that this will result in a process that no longer has goals, and that may become interminable. Further, I believe it is impossible for therapists to feel any reasonable sense of professional satisfaction or of accomplishment when they help maintain patients in a compromised but familiar station over a significant period of years. Though analytic engagements characterized this way may provide analysts with needed professional attachments and income, I suggest that such compromise can also make an analyst both personally depressed and despairing about his or her profession (Buechler, 2004; Cooper, 2000a, 2000b; Farber, 1966; Mitchell, 1993). As just noted, though one may reason that any given patient may not be ready for challenge, how many years can such a explanation be offered while still conceptualizing this endeavor as psychoanalytic? Currently influential theoretical perspectives that emphasize the value of analysts containing and creating a holding environment, or of facilitating identifications through self–object transferences, may provide theoretical bases for years of extraordinary patience, but as noted earlier, the originators of these perspectives (Kohut, 1984; Winnicott, 1958; also see Summers, 1999), and their most articulate advocates never have viewed the psychoanalytic process either as interminable or as akin to what used to be thought of as supportive psychotherapy (Fosshage, 2003; Gabbard, 1995; Hirsch, 1983; Slochower, 1996). In order for holding or self–object transferences to have a theoretical clout in a psychoanalytic context, these ways of being with patients must have a statute of limitations. That is, there must be a moment when both analysts' and patients' equilibrium begins to be challenged. It is too easy to misuse theory to help us disguise our wishes to remain attached to our patients for as long as we possibly can, while deceiving ourselves that we are engaging in something that we can still call psychoanalytic praxis.

Dr. I, a freshly minted psychoanalyst, is faced with many debts and expenses in relation to her analytic training. Alice, her patient of 5 years, now in her late 30s, has had a long history of failing to live up to her potentials in both love and in work. Alice is very bright and creative and physically attractive, but since early adulthood has consistently withdrawn from experiences at a point when her life stood some chance of becoming enriched. For example, the patient, an aspiring actor and writer, left college a few credits short of her degree, has often not followed up auditions, has failed to take editorial suggestions on written work that might have been publishable, and has been comfortable only with men who are not interested in long-term commitment. Alice persists in claiming that she wants to reach contentment in work and in love, but in a very concrete manner uses some situational anxiety to account for each instance of withdrawal. Dr. I clearly sees a pattern and, as well, has a sense of her patient's dynamic history that sheds light on her stagnation. However, each time she links a current withdrawal to previous regressions, or tries to make sense of this pattern by interpreting it in a historical or adaptational vein, Alice reports that she feels like she is being blamed for her problems. At such points she is likely to miss or to come late to sessions for a period, and her analyst fears that Alice is about to quit, as she has done with so many other ambitions. Dr. I tends to coax Alice to attend sessions more regularly, and backs off from questioning her most current retreat, or her withdrawal in the transference. As Dr. I explains it, she is trying to "regulate" her patient's anxiety, for Alice, she believes, is still not yet ready to take sufficient steps to move forward. Dr. I is aware that her patient is inclined to regressive dependency, and that she, Dr. I, has become the parent from whom Alice fears separation. My supervisee can readily see her patient's anxiety about separation, and her patient's mother's anxiety about her daughter moving beyond her, and she can acknowledge that she herself fears losing Alice because of her own attachment to her, and for economic reasons as well. Further, she can see this enactment of mutual dependency, and the likelihood that Alice will leave if eventually she is more successful in work and/or love. In addition, Dr. I also fears that her patient might abandon her if Dr. I becomes consistently more challenging about the ways Alice compromises her own progress in life. I challenge my supervisee by predicting that she and Alice can continue like this forever, and in this context, Dr. I is likely to evoke a psychoanalytic theory that suggests her patient needs more holding, mirroring, and regulating, and is not yet ready to be pushed to endure new challenges within the transference and outside of this. A distinct parallel process can be seen between our relationship and the one between patient and analyst, though I refuse to back off from challenging Dr. I.

Recently Alice returned to school in order to finally finish her bachelor's degree, in a program that also offers a combined master's degree. Were she to complete this, a whole new venue would open up for her with regard to career opportunities. However, as Alice is getting into this program she is feeling great pressure and anxiety in relation to what is being demanded of her, and she is missing classes, getting colds and sore throats, and provoking her school to ask her to take leave. At my suggestion Dr. I was pushing her patient to see this experience as part of a chronic repetitive pattern, and that if she withdraws yet again, she will remain still longer in a dysphoric and dependent configuration vis-à-vis her old internalized family, and her relatively new one, in the form of her psychoanalyst. In this context Alice once again has started to miss sessions and to come late to others, and Dr. I, fearing once again that Alice will abandon her, has herself withdrawn from addressing the parallels between transference withdrawal and retreat from the challenge of this new academic experience. I, in turn, fear that Dr. I will stop presenting this patient in the same way Dr. M did in our supervisory work. Indeed, once any therapist sees that economic forces may be a factor in driving the tone of the analytic relationship, it is difficult to continue facing this with another person watching, while at the same time not being willing to risk losing the patient and the income derived from this work. Actually, so many of the stagnant analytic dyads that I am called upon to consult about have this pattern: Patient X is depressed and/or anxious, the analysis reached a plateau some time ago, currently the therapist listens with empathy to reports related to the slings and arrows of life, and neither party feels much hope or optimism that anything beyond this soothing and mutually dependent relationship is very possible. In many such situations the analyst feels affectively attached to the patient but finds the work quite boring, and is willing to endure the absence of satisfaction and accomplishment in order to maintain this attachment accompanied by some economic security. Of course, this situation is more accented and may be more entrenched when the income derived is *needed*, and/or when the therapists' practice is not very full.

I too, of course, am guilty of coasting in status quo analytic relationships where omission of challenge and the failure to address mutually uncomfortable transference–countertransference themes characterize the process. Laura is a physically beautiful full-time mother of two, and formerly an up-and-coming young partner in a major corporate law firm to which she plans to return at some point. She is in her mid-40s, educated in the Ivy League, and from an affluent upper-middle-class family characterized by high achievement athletically, professionally, and financially. Indeed, she, her two brothers, her two sisters, and her father had all been competitive athletes, and are now highly successfully practicing professionals or businesspeople. Only Laura's mother has deviated from this pattern. She was never athletic, nor has she used her education to enter the competitive world of work. Laura describes her mother, with much contempt, as a typical suburban housewife, devoted to running her family, doing charity work, and socializing in the country club. Though grateful that she was a dedicated mother to her five children, Laura believes that she set a bad example, in particular to her three daughters. She portrays her mother as mindless, spending inordinate hours on the telephone with friends, and catering to Laura's father as if he was a king. Though Laura admires and respects her father's considerable accomplishments, she is competitive with her mother and cannot understand why her dad remained with a woman so unchallenging and subservient. Long ago, Laura had resolved never to allow herself to be so masochistically dependent on anyone, and most decidedly not a husband.

Laura began analysis 3 years ago, depressed with her life as a mother and homemaker only, and stuck with a husband who more often than not repelled her. She was committed to raising her children in an intact family, and on a full-time basis until they reached age 10 or so. Though she adores her children and has much satisfaction from them, she felt insufficiently challenged, and too far removed from the dynamic and competitive life in which she had always engaged. As well, she did not know how she could last in her marriage for another 6 years, feeling the contempt and disrespect that she did toward her spouse. Laura had always been able to fix her problems with acts of resolve and will, but now she felt trapped with no way out. Laura acknowledged that her marriage had been a pragmatic one, and that romance and sexual passion had never been strong features of this relationship. She had had any number of very passionate sexual relationships, though her loss of control in these contexts was often with men whom she knew were unavailable. On two occasions she was passionate about men with whom she dated for some period, and hated the degree of vulnerability that she lived with in these relationships. She ended one of these relationships for this reason, and had her heart broken by the other lover. She characterized her husband as a decent man with a strong sense of commitment, a good family background, and an excellent work ethic. She expected from the beginning that he would be devoted to her and to their children, earn a very comfortable living, and never challenge her dominance in family or in personal matters. He represented a safe choice. She had felt fond of him and warmly toward him, and she never expected she would feel so trapped and oppressed by his consistent presence. It is not that he attempts to dominate his wife so much as she feels the boredom of an absence of freedom to pursue the excitements of competitive work and passionate sexual encounters. Over the course of her marriage Laura has had a number of brief and exciting sexual engagements, mostly with married men whom she met in some business context. She believes this helped her sustain her marriage, and she misses the opportunity for erotic one-night stands that were facilitated by her immersion in her profession, and by the frequent business travel that characterized her work.

As one might expect, after not too long Laura experienced the quiet steadiness of our analytic work as oppressive and dull. She recoiled from the dependence she had begun to feel toward me, and all of the talking we did reminded her of her mother's deadly telephone conversations with her depressed friends. She hated feeling dysphoric about her life and, even more, hated speaking about this. As bright as she was, Laura preferred action to quiet reflection, and with some contempt, she conveyed that she felt caught in a Jewish psychoanalytic cliché (Laura was a secular Jew whose grandparents on both sides were born in the United States). There was no erotic charge at all in her feelings toward me; indeed, I felt that like her husband, I repelled Laura. Although she reported some value to the far greater understanding of herself that developed from our work together, the claustrophobia of our relationship almost neutralized this value. She believed that though she saw her current situation and its historical antecedents with marked clarity, there was no obvious physical solution to the dilemma she faced.

Laura had always physically controlled the pacing and the intimacy of our engagement by rather often coming late and/or canceling sessions. Because of the exigencies of mothering two young children and traveling to me from the suburbs, she had reasonable excuses, but we both knew there was more to this. Further, at times when I sympathized with, for instance, her needing to tend to her children's illnesses or school conferences, and I offered makeup sessions, she would rarely be interested in availing herself of my apparent generosity. After one-plus years into our analysis Laura began to drop her excuses, and at times would either forget her appointments or decide that she did not wish to come. Sometimes she would explain that she needed her space from me, and other times she claimed that there was nothing new to say. She and her husband together had plenty of money, and Laura did not at all seem to mind paying for sessions she did not attend. I saw her twice per week, and there were a few months where she missed in the area of half of her sessions. Though it was articulated that, like her husband, I had become stifling, oppressive, and boring, she was never quite comfortable conveying to me verbally that she could not stand being near me on a regular basis. She also held back from me spelling out the degree of her disappointment with me, in the context of having hoped that analysis would provide more of a tangible and concrete vehicle for both physical and psychic liberation. Instead, she felt dependent on and pinned down by two unexciting men, and her tame equivalent to liberating sexual encounters in the transference was to become repeatedly unfaithful to our scheduled appointments.

Though I felt awful as the object of my good-looking and vital patient's profound disinterest, I colluded in the failure to articulate all such sentiments and to sufficiently challenge her infidelities to me. At times I was able to rationalize the latter as a function of my respect for her wish for space and for pacing. At some point in our second year of work, I managed to mobilize my courage and to push her to speak about how dramatically similar her feelings were for me and for her husband, and she was able to begin to see that the contempt she felt toward both of us had meaning beyond our respective personal shortcomings. That is, Laura perceived more clearly that any relationship that constricted her freedom and evoked dependency wishes began to smell rotten, and stimulated fears that she would live out her mother's mindless and masochistic subservience. She began to attend sessions more regularly, and I felt more respected. However, as one might expect, this pattern reoccurred, and after periods that seem to me like meaningful steady work, Laura will lose interest, forget her appointments, cancel sessions, and convey to me that she wants a break from me. "We repeat the same things over and over," she will say, and add, "It is sooo tedious." We have come out of these phases, but are in one currently. Laura insists that she needs a *formal* break for one month or so, and she wants me to keep her hours open, and will of course pay for them. She is aware that if she gives these hours up, given her routines with her young children, it will be difficult to find alternate appointment times that are nearly as convenient for her. I feel encouraged that she does not wish to dump me altogether, though I fear that if I insist that she keep coming and finally work through her aversion to dependency, she will quit. My clinical sensibilities tell me that I should push her to try to resolve this core theme, which so vividly appears in our transference–countertransference mix. We have been at this place two or three times previously, and if we do not get through it, we will be here once again within 6 months at most. As well, I have a queasy feeling about the ethics of collecting fees for keeping time available while my patient acts out her wish for dominance and for emotional distance. Nonetheless, I am concerned that if the alternate hours I have available are inconvenient for her at the point she wishes to return, she just might not come back at all. I am leaning toward not "going to the mat" with her about this, though I suspect that if I were supervising a colleague's work, I'd suggest just that, leaving me with the feeling that I've been unfair to both Drs. M and I. I believe that the decision I am about to make is for my own best interest rather than for what will be ultimately optimal for Laura. By avoiding this struggle I am avoiding the full power of my patient's sadism and contempt, and I am insuring that I will keep her as a patient until the next time we cycle back to this familiar configuration.

As my illustrations suggest, the avoidance of patients' contempt has meaning beyond the degree to which such feelings are most unpleasant and difficult for analysts to bear affectively. Though an analyst's past experiences in addressing such affects might have been largely fruitful, it can still be difficult to not associate challenging patients to articulate these feelings with the risk of losing patients. Analysts' efforts to be empathic only, or holding only, may have clinical value in many instances, but at other times it reflects a wish to keep patients in treatment by being unchallenging, and by muting areas of inquiry that may prove disquieting or disruptive to both parties. Though concepts such as "timing" or "readiness" can be argued (for critiques of this, see Barnett, 1980; Coen, 1992; Farber, 1966; Fiscalini, 2004; Fromm, 1964; Gabbard, 1995; Gill, 1982, 1983, 1984; Goldstein, n.d.; Greenberg, 1986; Hirsch, 1983, 1987; Hoffman, 1983; Kuriloff, 2005; Kwawer, 1998; Mitchell, 1988, 1993; Searles, 1965; Singer, 1965a, 1965b, 1968; Wilner, 2000; Wolstein, 1954, 1959), as I have tried to illustrate, equilibria characterized by tentativeness and avoidance have the potential to go on for years. In many cases that I have consulted as a teacher or supervisor it seems to the therapist like it is never the right time to address difficult transference themes, and, indeed, this position can be maintained for an eternity. As I have suggested, when tentativeness, avoidance, and being unchallenging and supportive have characterized a treatment situation for a long time, it is difficult to shift gears and introduce a somewhat different mode of relatedness. The patient is likely to be comfortable in this nurturing and dependency-dominated relationship where the analyst is always experienced as being in the patient's corner. The analyst may, in fact, be uncomfortable with the stagnation, and the inhibition and caution required to maintain this relationship, but fears that any shift in engagement will result in the patient leaving, and income lost (Aron & Hirsch, 1992). Though once a relationship of this sort has persisted for years it will likely be disruptive to shift, there are times even in new analytic relationships where being too unchallenging and unquestioning may backfire, and the patient may ultimately leave treatment because it is *insufficiently* stimulating. Patients are often more resilient than their dependent analysts expect.

Bob, in his late 30s, was referred to me at a time when I had too many gaps in my schedule, and I was uneasy about my economic situation. He had never been in treatment and expressed much skepticism, and conveyed that he'd give it 6 months to see if it seemed worthwhile. He sought analysis because yet another relationship with a woman had broken up and, as well, because his marketing career had failed to progress as he had hoped. He spoke to me in a vague and platitudinous manner, and I found it difficult to feel that I was getting to know him. Though he recognized a string of failed relationships and career disappointments, he tended to blame others and to have little sense of his participation in the difficulties. When he described his background, he was so general and fuzzy that I was emerging with little sense of where this man came from, and how this contributed to who he was. I knew that he was hurting because of the failures he had encountered, though his suffering did not at all show in his demeanor. In fact, Bob tended to have something close to a chronic smirk, as if this was not a serious engagement, and I was no one who could be significant to him. Though I was well aware that his absence of personal and emotional presence and his condescension and his vagueness must be related to his troubles in life, I decided to be with him in a way that reflected my being on his side, and empathic with the hurts suffered at the hands of others. At the time I believed that this was the most likely way to keep him in analysis, and I rationalized that once my 6-month trial was over, I would begin to point out to him more of what I observed about him. In a sense I gambled that Bob did not want to be challenged at all, and that he would quit treatment were I any way but supportive and tentative. I gambled wrong, for when my 6 months' trial was up, Bob conveyed that it had been pleasant, but that he had derived nothing. I could not disagree with him. I had been so concerned with keeping him by being a nonrejecting "good object" that I wound up mirroring his nonpresence with me. In retrospect, he had very good reason to stop seeing me as his analyst.

Sometimes efforts to win patients' loyalty by omitting all challenging or potentially disruptive inquiry may work to maintain them in treatment. Similarly, efforts to be helpful in concrete ways, or to gratify certain of patients' wishes, can work to develop a tie to us, or a productive dependency on us. Analysts may reason that this is a beginning phase, and what a patient needs to help be settled in the analysis. And, sometimes this is so, and once the patient is comfortable the analyst may introduce interventions that are less equilibrium producing, and begin to deepen the analytic work. At other times, omissions and efforts to win a patient's affections may characterize an analysis for many years, and the only benefit may be reflected in the analyst's economic security, and perhaps a mutual sense of interpersonal safety.

James came to see me in a panic. He was married with three children, and his lover was pregnant and wanted to have the baby. He had been struggling to maintain his family intact, though he felt far more in love with his lover than he did with his wife. He was a devoted father, yet between his business travel and his serious affair, his children did not always see much of him. He himself had been a child in a divorced family and vowed never to put his children through the pain this had caused him and his two older brothers. James' marriage had settled into a pragmatic, child-focused partnership, though he expected his wife would also be shattered were he to leave. His lover was at the outer edge of her childbearing years, and believed this would be her last chance to have the biological child she had always longed for. My patient believed it was unfair of him to ask her to abort this child, though he was clear within himself that this was his preference.

James had been in analysis for relatively brief periods on and off since college. He invariably came with a crisis, experienced some situational help with this, and terminated the treatment. He told me that he had never really been helped "deeply" in analysis, but could not put his finger on why this was so, beyond concluding that he was a very stubborn individual. He seemed to have no rancor toward any of his previous analysts, shouldering all the blame for the absence of character change on himself. With this information it should have been apparent to me that if I helped him with his crisis and placed his characterological issues on the back burner, he would soon leave. Indeed, one of his enduring personal themes was to periodically generate crises in his life, and to seek help in resolving them. He was comfortable being dependent in spurts, though not in the long run. Nonetheless James' crisis and his panic were compelling, and with considerable consciousness I responded to his pleas for a pragmatically oriented helpfulness, placing his more enduring characteristics in the background. I believed that James would not stay in analysis were I to prove unhelpful with regard to his immediate situation, and I did not want to lose this wealthy, interesting, and influential man as a patient. Fortunately for both of us, I did not have an opinion about whether it would be best to leave his wife, or to remain in his marriage and support his lover and their child, seeing them when he could. He had the financial resources to do this without any strain. After a couple of months of meeting together, he decided to choose the latter path, and believed I had helped him come to a decision of his own. I was, however, more directly or concretely "helpful" in answering his many questions about the possible effects of divorce on children, and the potential well-being of a child being raised in the unusual circumstances that he had decided to arrange with his lover. I told him my views on the dangers to children of James living a life of deception, the risks to his children of eventually finding out about his double life, and the importance of spending more time with the three children he had already sired. I suggested to him that the life he was choosing would place significant physical and emotional strain on him, and he would have to cut back on work and on golf, at the very least.

   We met for approximately 6 months, and when he had made his choices and his plans he stopped coming. Fundamentally, he conveyed that as I had told him, he had too much in his life to do anything with sufficient commitment, and our time-consuming appointments were one of the activities that needed to be cut. For example, our early morning appointments directly interfered with his having breakfast with his children, and sometimes taking them to school. When I noted how the two of us had just repeated an old therapy pattern and an old familial pattern as well,* he agreed. James thanked me for helping him come to some profoundly difficult decisions, and for my attention to his relationship with his children, and he agreed with me that I had not touched him on any deeper level. He admitted that he was disappointed, though concluded that his intransigence made him an unlikely subject for the more profound aims of psychoanalysis.

I knew better—I had chosen to be gratifying and pragmatically helpful because I believed James would stop coming were he not to receive this help. Further, this was in spite of my being acutely aware of his repetitive patterns in previous analyses. I rationalized to myself that by noting with him that I was aware of this pattern, and some of its characterological roots, and that we would get to this core material post crisis, this would hold him in treatment. However, I know as well as anyone that we are judged by what we do, not what we say. James would have been better served had I focused less on being helpful and more on the roots of his character. Perhaps he would have left analysis sooner had I pursued this course, though in retrospect I think these deeper themes could have been better integrated with examining his current crisis, and he might have felt more helped in both the long and the short run. In the final analysis, my "helpfulness" was motivated more for my benefit than for the benefit of my patient.

I am by no means arguing that all of the generous and kind things analysts do are not in themselves motivated by the wish to be useful to patients. This certainly holds for the practical advice all analysts give at points in a long treatment, and for tried-and-true analytic attitudes of holding, containing, and empathy. All such engagement is present and is genuinely helpful over the course of any analysis. I am, however, suggesting that such analytic engagement can exist for multiple reasons, and sometimes analysts' motivations are tilted toward the pursuit of maintaining patients in treatment for the analysts' own personal and economic well-being (Aron & Hirsch, 1992; Renik, 2006; Whitson, n.d.). It is awfully difficult for an outsider to discern, for instance, if being pragmatically helpful, or being empathic and hold-

---

* Without going into much historical detail, James' affectively volatile parents relied on his competence and stability, and he had very early in life become a "parentified child." Surrendering to his own dependency had always been difficult for him, and he did this only in brief spurts. Indeed, he often stirred in me the wish to be dependent upon him.

ing one's observations, are genuinely motivated by the wish to deepen the analytic work and/or to be generous, or to prevent a patient from becoming angry and quitting. This can only be known by each of us when we candidly examine our work, for anything "good" on the surface may be motivated by private selfish interest.

To illustrate another analytic intervention, we can look at the phenomenon of deliberate self-disclosure. I cannot here go into any reasonable discussion about the history of this most controversial of interventions. Suffice it to say that where once there was an analytic taboo, in current times self-disclosure is viewed by many as anywhere from one of many legitimate interventions to perhaps a necessity for analytic progress (for thoughtful discussions of this issue, see, e.g., Aron, 1996; Bromberg, 2006; Davies, 1994; Epstein & Feiner, 1979; Frank, 1999; Gill, 1982; Greenberg, 2001; Hirsch, 1995; Hoffman, 1998; Maroda, 1981, 1999; Mitchell, 1993; Renik, 1993, 2006). It should be apparent by now that I view the potential therapeutic value of any analytic activity largely as a function of whether this is motivated *primarily* by the desire to be of use to the patient or to ourselves as individuals. Though there are numerous reasons why deliberate disclosure can be beneficial to patients, there are times when analysts disclose information or feeling states so that a particular patient will feel less deprived or more gratified, and look kindly toward the analyst as a person. More often than not, the wish to be liked by a patient has embedded within it the fear that we will be abandoned. Of course, in the context of this chapter, abandonment is more than personal loss, for it is always accompanied by economic loss.

Barney is an affable and gregarious man until he feels wounded. At those moments he can be incisively mean and hurtful. Indeed, he comes to see me because of the disparity between how well liked he is in his social world, and how tyrannical he can be at home toward his wife and children, and in the workplace toward his underlings. In the early stages of our work together I have seen some of his rage, specifically around his being charged for a cancelled session. I note this only to convey that I have some firsthand knowledge of what it is like to be on his wrong side. This is enough to make me both more cautious with him than is optimal, and take measures to please him, for he is someone who can easily walk out and never return when he feels crossed. I have addressed this theme with him, but it does not always stop me from efforts to stay on his good side.

In Barney's dominant affable mode he is a raconteur, telling me interesting stories from a life that has been filled with drama and adventure. He knows many luminaries, and has numerous interesting avocations that take him to elite segments of all corners of the world. When in this mode, he might turn to me and ask if I've ever traveled to a particular country, if I have eaten at a particular restaurant, or if I ski, and if so had I ever skied at a particular resort. At such moments I find it more difficult than I do with others to examine what he imagines, or to ask him why he might be asking. I also know, for example, how competitive he is, and how aware he is about his wealth in comparison to my own, though I am often tentative about broaching this as a possible motive for his questions. I feel slow on my feet, and I wind up answering more of his questions than I think I ought to. I would like to say that this is part of an analytic openness or spontaneity, or meeting some need of my patient, but I know this is not true. Fundamentally, if I do not match his manifest friendliness in some reasonable way, I believe he will view me as the stereotype of the analytic cold fish, and fear he will fire me with the same abruptness he does his employees, and, like them, I will be out of a job. As with the provision of empathy or pragmatic advice, any form of self-disclosure may be motivated to help patients and expand the analysis, or it may be for our own interest in keeping them as patients. Indeed, the same can be said for a very wide range of analytic procedures, interventions, and attitudes.

I am certain that the reader can think of many more specific ways that analysts' economic concerns may impact analytic work. For example, are we inclined to give more desirable analytic hours to patients who pay our highest fees? Do we pay more attention to these individuals, that is, do we work harder to be optimally alive and present with them, in contrast with lower-fee patients? If this is so, it is likely that we may try to keep these patients in analysis longer than patients who pay a lower fee, and whose time we might wish to clear up for someone paying more. Indeed, this may be a mixed blessing. That is, when we feel less compelled to maintain a patient in long-term treatment, we may work more efficiently to help this patient reach his or her aims and separate from us. Analysts' fears of losing a patient are normally inhibiting and constricting, and we may feel greater freedom and spontaneity with patients toward whom we have less investment in keeping in long analyses. If an analysis becomes stagnant after a significant number of years, we may be prone to persist too long with a patient paying a high fee and, perhaps responsibly, refer a lower-paying patient to a colleague. As already noted, my anecdotal observation is that in our current analytic culture, patients are seen for an increasing number of years. I would wager that this is largely a function of the patient supply-and-demand ratio for any given analyst, and, in addition, that those patients paying analysts' highest fees are generally seen longer than their lower-fee counterparts. Indeed, analytic fees are largely a function of supply and demand. For example, those of us who are more in demand are likely to charge higher fees and, as well, have a more strict policy for payment of missed sessions, because the risk of patients becoming angry and quitting has less economic consequence.

Though the picture I have painted in this chapter and in others may appear bleak and cynical, as I have suggested earlier, one advantage that psychoanalysts may have over others in the professions or in commerce is the profound valuation of self-awareness. As I have underscored, the only way to curb or to modify the naturally unabashed pursuit of self-interest is by recognizing these very normal inclinations. The act of recognizing and embracing or accepting our selfish desires allows us to make conscious choices. At many junctures these choices are likely to result in placing some of our patients' interests ahead of our own, though I do not believe that we ever abandon all of our selfish desires and actions. To the extent that analysts deny the centrality of self-interest, they will not have the choice to change themselves in any given clinical context, and unless the analyst is able to change in the analytic interaction, the patient will probably not change either.

# References

Abend, S. (1982). Serious illness in the analyst: Countertransference considerations. *Journal of the American Psychoanalytic Association, 30,* 365–379.

Abend, S. (1999, February 28). Summary of conference: Concluding remarks. Speech presented at Reflections on Analytic Hours: Good, Bad, and Ugly symposium, New York.

Arlow, J. (1987). The dynamics of interpretation. *Psychoanalytic Quarterly, 56,* 68–87.

Aron, L. (1991). The patient's experience of the analyst's subjectivity. *Psychoanalytic Dialogues, 1,* 29–51.

Aron, L. (1996). *A meeting of minds.* Hillsdale, NJ: Analytic Press.

Aron, L. (1999). Clinical choices and the relational matrix. *Psychoanalytic Dialogues, 9,* 1–29.

Aron, L. (2005). On the unique contribution of the interpersonal approach to interaction: A discussion of Stephen A. Mitchell's "Ideas of interaction in psychoanalysis." *Contemporary Psychoanalysis, 41,* 21–34.

Aron, L., & Hirsch, I. (1992). Money matters in psychoanalysis: A relational approach. In N. Skolnick and S. Warshaw (Eds.), *Relational perspectives in psychoanalysis* (pp. 239–252). Hillsdale, NJ: Lawrence Erlbaum Associates.

Bach, S. (1995). *Narcissistic states and the analytic process.* Northvale, NJ: Jason Aronson.

Bach, S. (2006). *Getting from here to there: Analytic love, analytic process.* Hillsdale, NJ: Analytic Press.

Bachrach, H. & Leaff, L. (1978). Analyzability: A systematic view of the clinical and quantitative literature. *Journal of the American Psychoanalytic Association.* 26: 881–892.

Barnett, J. (1980). Interpersonal processes, cognition, and the analysis of character. *Contemporary Psychoanalysis, 16,* 397–416.

Basescu, S. (1977). Anxieties in the analyst: An autobiographical account. In K. Frank (Ed.), *The human dimension in psychoanalytic practice* (pp. 153–163). New York: Grune & Stratton.

Bass, A. (2001). It takes one to know one; or, whose unconscious is it anyway? *Psychoanalytic Dialogues, 11*, 683–702.

Becker, E. (1973). *The denial of death*. New York: Free Press.

Beebe, B., & Lachmann, F. M. (2002). *Infant research and adult treatment: Co-constructing interaction*. Hillsdale, NJ: Analytic Press.

Benjamin, J. (1991). Identification with difference: A contribution to gender heterodoxy. *Psychoanalytic Dialogues, 1*, 277–300.

Benjamin, J. (1995). *Like subjects, love objects: Essays on recognition and sexual difference*. New Haven, CT: Yale University Press.

Berg, C. (1936). The unconscious significance of hair. *International Journal of Psychoanalysis, 17*, 73–88.

Berman, E. (2001). Psychoanalysis and life. *Psychoanalytic Quarterly, 70*, 35–65.

Billow, R. (2000). From countertransference to "passion." *Psychoanalytic Quarterly, 69*, 93–119.

Bion, W. (1967). Notes on memory and desire. *Psychoanalytic Forum, 2*, 271–280.

Black, M. J. (2003). Enactment: Analytic musings on energy, language, and personal growth. *Psychoanalytic Dialogues, 13*, 633–655.

Blechner, M. J. (1992). Working in the countertransference. *Psychoanalytic Dialogues, 2*, 161–179.

Blechner, M. J. (1993). Homophobia in psychoanalytic writing and practice. *Psychoanalytic Dialogues, 3*, 627–637.

Blechner, M. J. (2005a). The gay Harry Stack Sullivan: Interactions between his life, clinical work, and theory. *Contemporary Psychoanalysis, 41*, 1–20.

Blechner, M. J. (2005b). Disgust, desire and fascination. *Studies in Gender and Sexuality, 6*, 33–45.

Boesky, D. (1988). Criteria of evidence for an unconscious fantasy. In H. Baum et al. (Eds.), *Fantasy, myth and reality: Essays in honor of Jacob A. Arlow* (pp. 111–131). Madison, CT: International Universities Press.

Bonovitz, C. (2005). Locating culture in the psychic field: Transference and countertransference as cultural products. *Contemporary Psychoanalysis, 41*, 55–76.

Boulanger, G. (2007). *Wounded by reality: Understanding and treating adult onset trauma*. Hillsdale, NJ: Analytic Press.

Brenner, C. (1995). Some remarks on psychoanalytic technique. *Journal of Clinical Psychoanalysis, 4*, 413–428.

Brisman, J. (2002). Wanting. *Contemporary Psychoanalysis, 38*, 329–343.

Bromberg, P. (1998). *Standing in the spaces*. Hillsdale, NJ: Analytic Press.

Bromberg, P. (2006). *Awakening the dreamer: Clinical journeys*. Hillsdale, NJ: Analytic Press.

Buechler, S. (2002). More simply human than otherwise. *Contemporary Psychoanalysis, 38,* 485–497.

Buechler, S. (2004). *Clinical values: Emotions that guide psychoanalytic treatment.* Hillsdale, NJ: Analytic Press.

Chodorow, N. (1976). *The reproduction of mothering.* Berkeley: University of California Press.

Chodorow, N. (1994). *Femininities, masculinities, sexualities.* London: Free Association.

Coen, S. J. (1992). *The misuse of persons: Analyzing pathological dependency.* Hillsdale, NJ: Analytic Press.

Coen, S. J. (2000). Why we need to write openly. *Journal of the American Psychoanalytic Association, 48,* 449–470.

Coen, S. J. (2002). *Affect intolerance in patient and analyst.* Northvale, NJ: Jason Aronson.

Cohen, E. (2003). *Playing hard at life: A relational approach to treating multiply traumatized adolescents.* Hillsdale, NJ: Analytic Press.

Cole, G. (2002). *Infecting the treatment: Being an HIV-positive analyst.* Hillsdale, NJ: Analytic Press.

Conci, M. (In press). *Sullivan revisited: His relevance for contemporary psychiatry, psychotherapy and psychoanalysis.* New York: Analytic Press.

Cooper, A. (1985). A historical review of psychoanalytic paradigms. In A. Rothstein (Ed.), *Models of the mind* (pp. 5–20). New York: International Universities Press.

Cooper, S. H. (2000a). *Objects of hope: Exploring possibility and limit in psychoanalysis.* Hillsdale, NJ: Analytic Press.

Cooper, S. H. (2000b). Elements of mutual containment in the analytic process. *Psychoanalytic Dialogues, 10,* 169–194.

Crastnopol, M. (1999). The analyst's personality: Winnicott analyzing Guntrip as a case in point. *Contemporary Psychoanalysis, 35,* 271–300.

Crastnopol, M. (2001). Convergence and divergence in the characters of analyst and patient: Fairbairn treating Guntrip. *Psychoanalytic Psychology, 18,* 120–136.

Crastnopol, M. (2002). The dwelling places of self experience. *Psychoanalytic Dialogues, 12,* 259–284.

*The crying game.* (1993). Directed by Neil Jordan. Miramax.

Davies, J. M. (1994). Love in the afternoon: A relational reconsideration of desire and dread in the countertransference. *Psychoanalytic Dialogues, 4,* 153–170.

Davies, J. M. (1998). Multiple perspectives on multiplicity. *Psychoanalytic Dialogues, 8,* 195–206.

Davies, J. M. (2004). Whose bad objects are we anyway? Repetition and our elusive love affair with evil. *Psychoanalytic Dialogues, 14,* 711–732.

Davies, J. M., & Frawley, M. G. (1994). *Treating the adult survivor of childhood sexual abuse: A psychoanalytic perspective*. New York: Basic Books.

D'Ercole, A., & Drescher, J. (2004). *Uncoupling convention: Psychoanalytic approaches to same-sex couples and families*. Hillsdale, NJ: Analytic Press.

Dewald, P. A. (1972). *The psychoanalytic process: A case illustration*. New York: Basic Books.

Dimen, M. (1991). Deconstructing difference: Gender, splitting, and transitional space. *Psychoanalytic Dialogues, 1*, 335–352.

Dimen, M. (2001). Perversion is us? Eight notes. *Psychoanalytic Dialogues, 11*, 825–860.

Dimen, M. (2003). *Sexuality, intimacy, power*. Hillsdale, NJ: Analytic Press.

Dinnerstein, D. (1976). *The mermaid and the minotaur*. New York: Harper & Row.

Drescher, J. (2002). Causes and becauses: On etiological theories of homosexuality. *Annual of Psychoanalysis, 30*, 57–68.

Druck, A. (1989). *Four therapeutic approaches to the borderline patient*. Northvale, NJ: Jason Aronson.

Ehrenberg, D. (1992). *The intimate edge*. New York: Norton.

Eisold, K. (1994). The intolerance of diversity in psychoanalytic institutes. *International Journal of Psychoanalysis, 75*, 785–800.

Eisold, K. (2000). The rediscovery of the unknown: An inquiry into psychoanalytic praxis. *Contemporary Psychoanalysis, 36*, 57–75.

Epstein, L. (1984). An interpersonal-object relations perspective on working with destructive aggression. *Contemporary Psychoanalysis, 20*, 651–662.

Epstein, L. (1999). The analyst's "bad-analyst feelings": A counterpart to the process of resolving implosive defenses. *Contemporary Psychoanalysis, 35*, 311–325.

Epstein, L., & Feiner, A. (Eds.). (1979). *Countertransference*. New York: Jason Aronson.

Fairfield, S. (2001). Analyzing multiplicity. *Psychoanalytic Dialogues, 11*, 221–251.

Farber, L. H. (1966). *The ways of the will: Essays toward a psychology and psychopathology of will*. New York: Basic Books.

Feldman, M. (1997). Projective identification: The analyst's involvement. *International Journal of Psychoanalysis, 78*, 227–241.

Ferenczi, S., & Rank, O. (1924/1956). *The development of psychoanalysis*. New York: Dover.

Fiscalini, J. (1988). Curative experience in the analytic relationship. *Contemporary Psychoanalysis. 24*: 125–141.

Fiscalini, J. (1994). The uniquely interpersonal and the interpersonally unique: On interpersonal psychoanalysis. *Contemporary Psychoanalysis*, *30*, 114–134.

Fiscalini, J. (2004). *Coparticipant psychoanalysis: Toward a new theory of clinical inquiry*. New York: Columbia University Press.

Fiscalini, J., & Grey, A. L. (Eds.). (1993). *Narcissism and the interpersonal self*. New York: Columbia University Press.

Fonagy, P. (1999, April). The process of change and the change of process: What can change in a "good" analysis? Keynote address presented at the Division of Psychoanalysis (39), American Psychological Association Spring Meeting, New York.

Fonagy, P. (2001). *Attachment theory and psychoanalysis*. New York: Other Press.

Fonagy, P. (2003). Genetics, developmental psychopathology, and psychoanalytic theory: The case for ending our (not so) splendid isolation. *Psychoanalytic Inquiry*, *23*, 218–247.

Fosshage, J. L. (2003). Contextualizing self psychology and relational psychoanalysis: Bi-directional influence and proposed syntheses. *Contemporary Psychoanalysis*, *39*, 411–448.

Frank, K. A. (1999). *Psychoanalytic participation: Action, interaction, and integration*. Hillsdale, NJ: Analytic Press.

Frank, K. A. (2005). Toward conceptualizing the personal relationship in therapeutic action: Beyond the "real relationship." *Psychoanalytic Perspectives*, *3*, 15–56.

Frankel, J. (1998). Are interpersonal and relational psychoanalysis the same? *Contemporary Psychoanalysis*, *3*, 485–500.

Frawley-O'Dea, M. G. (1997). Supervision amidst abuse. In M. H. Rock (Ed.), *Psychodynamic supervision: Perspectives of the supervisor and the supervisee* (pp. 315–335). Northvale, NJ: Jason Aronson.

Frawley-O'Dea, M. G., & Goldner, V. (2007). *Abusive priests: Who they were and were not*. Hillsdale, NJ: Analytic Press.

Freud, S. (1905/2000). Three essays on the theory of sexuality. In *The standard edition of the complete psychological works of Sigmund Freud* (24 vols.; vol. 7; James Strachey, ed., pp. 123–243). New York: Norton.

Freud, S. (1912/2000). Papers on technique: The dynamics of transference. In *Standard edition*, *12*, 97–108.

Freud, S. (1915/2000). Papers on technique: Observations on transference-love (Further recommendations on the technique of psycho-analysis, III). In *Standard edition*, *12*, 157–171.

Freud, S. (1920/2000). Beyond the pleasure principle. In *Standard edition*, *18*, 1–63.

Freud, S. (1923/2000). The ego and the id. In *Standard edition*, *19*, 1–66.

Frie, R. (2002). Modernism or postmodernism? Binswanger, Sullivan, and the problem of agency in contemporary psychoanalysis. *Contemporary Psychoanalysis, 38*(4), 635–673.

Friedman, L. (1988). *The anatomy of psychoanalysis*. Hillsdale, NJ: Analytic Press.

Friedman, L. (1999). Why reality is a troubling concept. *Journal of the American Psychoanalytic Association, 47*, 401–425.

Friedman, L. (2006). What is psychoanalysis? *Psychoanalytic Quarterly, 75*, 689–713.

Fromm, E. (1941). *Escape from freedom*. New York: Holt, Rinehart & Winston.

Fromm, E. (1955). *The sane society*. New York: Harper & Row.

Fromm, E. (1964). *The heart of man*. New York: Harper & Row.

Frommer, M. (1994). Homosexuality and psychoanalysis: Technical considerations revisited. *Psychoanalytic Dialogues, 4*, 215–233.

Frommer, M. (2006). On the subjectivity of lustful states of mind. *Psychoanalytic Dialogues, 16*, 639–664.

Fromm-Reichmann, F. (1959). *Psychoanalysis and psychotherapy: Selected papers of Frieda Fromm-Reichmann* (E. V. Weigert, Ed.). Chicago: University of Chicago Press.

Gabbard, G. O. (1995). Countertransference: The emerging common ground. *International Journal of Psychoanalysis, 76*, 475–485.

Gabbard, G. O. (1996). *Love and hate in the analytic setting*. Northvale, NJ: Jason Aronson.

Gabbard, G. O., & Lester, E. P. (1995). *Boundaries and boundary violations in psychoanalysis*. New York: Basic Books.

Gartner, R. (1999). *Betrayed as boys: Psychodynamic treatment of sexually abused men*. New York: Guilford.

Gergen, K. (2001). Psychological science in a post modern context. *American Psychologist, 56*, 803–813.

Gerson, B. (1996). *The therapist as a person: Life crises, life choices, life experiences, and their effects on treatment*. Hillsdale, NJ: Analytic Press.

Gerson, M. (1996). *The embedded self: A psychoanalytic guide to family therapy*. Hillsdale, NJ: Analytic Press.

Gerson, S. (2004). The relational unconscious: A core element of intersubjectivity, thirdness, and clinical process. *Psychoanalytic Quarterly, 73*, 63–98.

Gill, M. (1982). *The analysis of transference* (Vol. 1). New York: International Universities Press.

Gill, M. (1983). The interpersonal paradigm and the degree of the therapist's involvement. *Contemporary Psychoanalysis, 19*, 200–237.

Gill, M. (1984). Psychoanalysis and psychotherapy: A revision. *International Review of Psychoanalysis, 11*, 161–179.

Gill, M. (1994). *Psychoanalysis in transition*. Hillsdale, NJ: Analytic Press.

Gilligan, C. (1982). *In a different voice.* Cambridge, MA: Harvard University Press.

Goldberg, J. (2007). Refinding the good old object: Beyond the good analyst/bad parent. *Contemporary Psychoanalysis, 43,* 261–287.

Goldman, D. (1993). *In search of the real: The origins and originality of D. W. Winnicott.* Northvale, NJ: Jason Aronson.

Goldstein, G. (n.d.). The analyst's resistance to transference. Unpublished manuscript.

Grand, S. (2000). *The reproduction of evil: A clinical and cultural perspective.* Hillsdale, NJ: Analytic Press.

Greenberg, J. (1986). Theoretical models and the analyst's neutrality. *Contemporary Psychoanalysis, 22,* 89–106.

Greenberg, J. (1991). *Oedipus and beyond.* Cambridge, MA: Harvard University Press.

Greenberg, J. (1995). Psychoanalytic technique and the interactive matrix. *Psychoanalytic Quarterly, 64,* 1–22.

Greenberg, J. (2001). The analyst's participation: A new look. *Journal of the American Psychoanalytic Association, 49,* 359–398.

Greenberg, J., & Mitchell, S. (1983). *Object relations in psychoanalytic theory.* Cambridge, MA: Harvard University Press.

Grotstein, J. S. (2000). *Who is the dreamer who dreams the dreams? A study of psychic presences.* Hillsdale, NJ: Analytic Press.

Guarton, G. B. (1999). Beyond the dialectics of love and desire. *Contemporary Psychoanalysis, 35,* 491–505.

Guntrip, H. (1975). My experience in analysis with Fairbairn and Winnicott. *International Review of Psychoanalysis.* 2: 145–156.

Hansell, J. H. (1998). Gender anxiety, gender melancholia, gender perversion. *Psychoanalytic Dialogues, 8,* 337–351.

Harris, A. (1991). Gender as contradiction. *Psychoanalytic Dialogues, 1,* 277–300.

Harris, A. (2005). *Gender as soft assembly.* Hillsdale, NJ: Analytic Press.

Hirsch, I. (1983). Analytic intimacy and the restoration of nurturance. *American Journal of Psychoanalysis, 43,* 325–343.

Hirsch, I. (1984). Toward a more subjective view of analyzability. *American Journal of Psychoanalysis, 44,* 169–182.

Hirsch, I. (1987). Varying modes of analytic participation. *Journal of the American Academy of Psychoanalysis, 15,* 205–222.

Hirsch, I. (1988). Mature love in the countertransference. In J. Lasky and H. Silverman (Eds.), *Love: Psychoanalytic perspectives* (pp. 200–212). New York: New York University Press.

Hirsch, I. (1990). Countertransference and participant-observation. *American Journal of Psychoanalysis, 50,* 275–284.

Hirsch, I. (1992). An interpersonal perspective: The analyst's unwitting participation in the patient's change. *Psychoanalytic Psychology, 9,* 299–312.

Hirsch, I. (1993). Countertransference enactments and some issues related to external factors in the analyst's life. *Psychoanalytic Dialogues, 3,* 343–366.

Hirsch, I. (1994). Countertransfereence love and theoretical model. *Psychoanalytic Dialogues.* 4: 171–192.

Hirsch, I. (1995). Therapeutic uses of countertransference. In M. Lionells, J. Fiscalini, C. H. Mann, & D. B. Stern (Eds.), *Handbook of interpersonal psychoanalysis* (pp. 643–660). Hillsdale, NJ: Analytic Press.

Hirsch, I. (1996). Observing-participation, mutual enactment, and the new classical models. *Contemporary Psychoanalysis, 32,* 359–383.

Hirsch, I. (1998a). The concept of enactment and theoretical convergence. *Psychoanalytic Quarterly, 67,* 78–101.

Hirsch, I. (1998b). Further thoughts about interpersonal and relational perspectives. *Contemporary Psychoanalysis, 34,* 501–538.

Hirsch, I. (1999). Contrasting classic American  film with "The Crying Game." *Journal of the American Academy of Psychoanalysis.* 27: 151–166.

Hirsch, I. (2003a). Psychoanalytic theory as one form of countertransference. *Journal of the American Psychoanalytic Association, 51*(Suppl.), 181–201.

Hirsch, I. (2003b). Reflections on clinical issues in the context of the national trauma of September 11th. *Contemporary Psychoanalysis, 39,* 665–681.

Hirsch, I. (2007). Imperfect love, imperfect lives: Making love, making sex, making moral judgments. *Studies in Gender and Psychoanalysis, 8,* 355–371.

Hirsch, I. & Hirsch, C. (2000). Seinfeld's humor noir: A look on our dark side. *Journal of Popular Film and Television.* 28: 116–123.

Hirsch, I., & Kessel, P. (1988). Reflections on mature love and countertransference. *Free Associations, 12,* 60–83.

Hoffman, I. Z. (1983). The patient as interpreter of the analyst's experience. *Contemporary Psychoanalysis, 19,* 389–422.

Hoffman, I. Z. (1987). The value of uncertainty in psychoanalytic practice. *Contemporary Psychoanalysis, 23,* 205–214.

Hoffman, I. Z. (1991). Discussion: Toward a social-constructivist view of the psychoanalytic situation. *Psychoanalytic Dialogues, 1,* 74–105.

Hoffman, I. Z. (1998). *Ritual and spontaneity in the psychoanalytic process.* Hillsdale, NJ: Analytic Press.

Hoffman, M. (2004). From enemy combatant to strange bedfellow: The role of religious narratives in the work of W. R. D. Fairbairn and D. W. Winnicott. *Psychoanalytic Dialogues, 14,* 769–804.

Hopkins, L. B. (1998). D. W. Winnicott's analysis of Masud Khan: A preliminary study of failures of object usage. *Contemporary Psychoanalysis, 34,* 5–47.

Hopkins, L. B. (2006). *False self: The life of Masud Khan.* New York: Other Press.

Iannuzzi, V. P. (2005). In Levenson's wake: Introduction to an interview with Edgar A. Levenson, M.D. *Contemporary Psychoanalysis, 41,* 581–592.

Imber, R. (2000). The dilemma of relational authority. *Contemporary Psychoanalysis, 36,* 619–638.

Isay, R. (1989). *Being homosexual.* New York: Farrar, Strauss.

Jacobs, T. J. (1986). On countertransference enactments. *Journal of the American Psychoanalytic Association, 34,* 289–307.

Jacobs, T. J. (1991). *The use of the self.* Madison, CT: International Universities Press.

Jacobs, T. J. (2001). On unconscious communications and covert enactments: Some reflections on their role in the analytic situation. *Psychoanalytic Inquiry, 21,* 4–23.

Josephs, L. (1995). *Balancing empathy and interpretation: Relational character analysis.* Northvale, NJ: Jason Aronson.

Josephs, L. (2001). Psychoanalysis as forbidden pleasure. *Contemporary Psychoanalysis, 37,* 265–281.

Josephs, L. (2004). Seduced by affluence: How material envy strains the analytic relationship. *Contemporary Psychoanalysis, 40,* 389–408.

Kaftal, M. (1991). On intimacy between men. *Psychoanalytic Dialogues, 1,* 305–328.

Kantrowitz, J. L. (1992). The analyst's style and its impact on the analytic process: Overcoming a patient–analyst stalemate. *Journal of the American Psychoanalytic Association, 40,* 169–194.

Kantrowitz, J. L. (1993). The uniqueness of the patient–analyst pair: Approaches for elucidating the analyst's role. *International Journal of Psychoanalysis, 74,* 893–904.

Knoblauch, S. H. (2000). *The musical edge of therapeutic dialogue.* Hillsdale, NJ: Analytic Press.

Kohut, H. (1984). *How does analysis cure?* Chicago: University of Chicago Press.

Kuriloff, E. A. (2005). Being flooded with the variety, richness, and unending flux of human experience: Synopsis of commentaries. *Contemporary Psychoanalysis, 41,* 751–763.

Kwawer, J. S. (1998). Fundamentalism reconsidered: Reflections on psychoanalytic technique. *Contemporary Psychoanalysis, 34,* 565–576.

Langan, R. (1999). Coming to be: Change by affiliation. *Contemporary Psychoanalysis, 35,* 67–80.

Lasky, E. (1984). Psychoanalysts' and psychotherapists' conflicts about setting fees. *Psychoanalytic Psychology, 1,* 289–300.

Lasky, R. (1993). *Dynamics of development and the therapeutic process.* Northvale, NJ: Jason Aronson.

Layton, L. (1998). *Who's that girl? Who's that boy? Clinical practice meets postmodern gender theory.* Hillsdale, NJ: Analytic Press.

Layton, L. (2004). Dreams of America/American dreams. *Psychoanalytic Dialogues, 14,* 233–254.

Leary, K. (1997). Race, self-disclosure, and "forbidden talk": Race and ethnicity in contemporary clinical practice. *Psychoanalytic Quarterly, 66,* 163–189.

Levenson, E. A. (1972). *The fallacy of understanding.* New York: Basic.

Levenson, E. A. (1981). Facts or fantasies: The nature of psychoanalytic data. *Contemporary Psychoanalysis, 17,* 486–450.

Levenson, E. A. (1982). Playground or playpen. *Contemporary Psychoanalysis, 18,* 365–372.

Levenson, E. A. (1983). *The ambiguity of change.* Northvale, NJ: Jason Aronson.

Levenson, E. A. (1988). Show and tell: The recursive order of transference. In A. Rothstein (Ed.), *How does treatment help? On the modes of psychoanalytic therapy* (pp. 135–143). Madison, CT: International Universities Press.

Levenson, E. A. (1991). *The purloined self.* New York: Contemporary Psychoanalysis Press.

Levenson, E. A. (1992). Harry Stack Sullivan: From interpersonal psychiatry to interpersonal psychoanalysis. *Contemporary Psychoanalysis, 28,* 450–456.

Levin, A. J. (1957). Oedipus and Samson the rejected hero-child. *International Journal of Psychoanalysis, 38,* 105–116.

Liss-Levinson, N. (1990). Money matters and the woman analyst: In a different voice. *Psychoanalytic Psychology, 7,* 119–130.

Little, M. I. (1990). *Psychotic anxieties and containment: A personal record of an analysis with Winnicott.* Northvale, NJ: Jason Aronson.

Maroda, K. J. (1981). *The power of countertransference.* Chichester, UK: Wiley.

Maroda, K. J. (1999). *Seduction, surrender, and transformation: Emotional engagement in the analytic process.* Hillsdale, NJ: Analytic Press.

Maroda, K. J. (2005). Legitimate gratification of the analyst's needs. *Contemporary Psychoanalysis, 41,* 371–388.

McLaughlin, J. T. (1991). Clinical and theoretical aspects of enactment. *Journal of the American Psychoanalytic Association, 39,* 595–614.

Meltzer, D. (1994). *Sincerity and other works: Collected papers of Donald Meltzer* (A. Hahn, Ed.). London: H. Karnac.

Mendelsohn, E. (2002). The analyst's bad-enough participation. *Psychoanalytic Dialogues, 12,* 331–358.

Mitchell, S. A. (1988). *Relational concepts in psychoanalysis.* Cambridge, MA: Harvard University Press.

Mitchell, S. A. (1993). *Hope and dread in psychoanalysis.* New York: Basic Books.

Mitchell, S. A. (1997). *Influence and autonomy in psychoanalysis.* Hillsdale, NJ: Analytic Press.

Mitchell, S. A. (2000). *Relationality: From Attachment to Intersubjectivity.* Hillsdale, NJ: Analytic Press.

Morrison, A. (1989). *The Underside of Narcissism.* Hillsdale, NJ: Analytic Press.

Moses, I. (unpublished paper). An interpersonal critique of relational psychoanalysis: Inference and technique.

Myers, K. (2008). Show me the money: The therapist's desire, subjectivity and relationship to the fee. *Contemporary Psychoanalysis,* in press.

Nachmani, G. (n.d.). On courage: A character study of people who prevail in adversity. Unpublished manuscript.

Newirth, J. (2003). *Between emotion and cognition: The generative unconscious.* New York: Other Press.

Newman, D. (2006). *Talking with doctors.* Hillsdale, NJ: Analytic Press.

Ogden, T. (1994). *Subjects of analysis.* Northvale, NJ: Jason Aronson.

Pizer, B. (1997). When the analyst is ill: Dimensions of self-disclosure. *Psychoanalytic Quarterly, 66,* 450–469.

Pizer, S. (1998). *Building Bridges: The Negotiation of Paradox in Psychoanalysis.* Hillsdale, NJ: Analytic Press.

Poland, W. S. (1992). Transference: "An original creation." *Psychoanalytic Quarterly, 61,* 185–205.

Prince, R. M. (1985). *The legacy of the Holocaust: Psychohistorical themes in the second generation.* New York: Other Press.

Racker, H. (1968). *Transference and countertransference.* New York: International Universities Press.

Reich, A. (1951). On countertransference. *International Journal of Psychoanalysis, 32,* 25–31.

Renik, O. (1993). Analytic interaction: Conceptualizing technique in the light of the analyst's irreducible subjectivity. *Psychoanalytic Quarterly, 62,* 553–571.

Renik, O. (1995). The ideal of the anonymous analyst and the problem of self disclosure. *Psychoanalytic Quarterly, 64,* 466–495.

Renik, O. (2006). *Practical psychoanalysis for therapists and patients.* New York: Other Press.

Renik, O. (Ed.). (1998). *Knowledge and authority in the psychoanalytic relationship.* Northvale, NJ: Jason Aronson.

Richards, A. D. (1999). A. A. Brill and the politics of exclusion. *Journal of the American Psychoanalytic Association, 47,* 9–26.

Richards, A. D. (2003). Psychoanalytic discourse at the turn of our century: A plea for a measure of humility. *Journal of the American Psychoanalytic Association, 51,* 73–89.

Richards, A. D., & Richards, A. K. (1995). Notes on psychoanalytic theory and its consequences for technique. *Journal of Clinical Psychoanalysis, 4,* 429–456.

Richards, A. K. (1999). A romance with pain: A telephone perversion in a woman? *International Journal of Psychoanalysis, 70,* 153–164.

Richman, S. (2002). *A Wolf in the Attic: The Legacy of a Hidden Child of the Holocaust.* New York: Haworth Press.

Richman, S. (2006). When the analyst writes a memoir: Clinical implications of biographic disclosure. *Contemporary Psychoanalysis, 42,* 367–392.

Rucker, N., & Lombardi, K. (1997). *Subject relations: Unconscious experience and relational psychoanalysis.* London: Routledge.

Safran, J. D. (2003). The relational turn, the therapeutic alliance, and psychotherapy research. *Contemporary Psychoanalysis, 39,* 449–475.

Sandler, J. (1976). Countertransference and role-responsiveness. *International Review of Psychoanalysis, 3,* 43–48.

Sandler, J. (1983). Reflections on some relations between psychoanalytic concepts and psychoanalytic practice. *International Journal of Psychoanalysis, 64,* 35–45.

Satran, G. (1995). The patient's sense of therapeutic action: An introduction. *Contemporary Psychoanalysis, 31,* 124.

Schachtel, E. (1959). *Metamorphosis: On the development of affect, perception, attention, and memory.* New York: Basic Books.

Schafer, R. (1983). *The analytic attitude.* New York: Basic Books.

Schrier, D. (1996). *Sexual harassment in the workplace and academia: Psychiatric issues.* Washington, DC: American Psychiatric Press.

Searles, H. F. (1960). *The nonhuman environment: In normal development and schizophrenia.* New York: International Universities Press.

Searles, H. F. (1965). *Collected papers on schizophrenia and related subjects.* New York: International Universities Press.

Searles, H. F. (1979). *Countertransference and related subjects.* New York: International Universities Press.

Seligman, S. (1999). Integrating Kleinian theory and intersubjective infant research: Observing projective identification. *Psychoanalytic Dialogues, 9,* 121–159.

Seligman, S. (2003). The developmental perspective in relational psychoanalysis. *Contemporary Psychoanalysis, 39,* 477–508.

Shear, J. (1985, March 3). About men: Going bald gracelessly. *New York Times Magazine,* 66.

Singer, E. (1965a). *Key concepts in psychotherapy.* New York: Basic Books.

Singer, E. (1965b). Identity vs. identification: A thorny psychological issue. *Review of Existential Psychology and Psychoanalysis, 2,* 160–175.

Singer, E. (1968). The reluctance to interpret. In E. F. Hammer (Ed.), *Use of interpretation in treatment: Technique and art* (pp. 364–371). New York: Grune & Stratton.

Singer, E. (1971). The patient aids the analyst: Some clinical and theoretical observations. In B. Landis & E. S. Tauber (Eds.), *In the name of life: Essays in honor of Erich Fromm* (pp. 56–68). New York: Holt, Rinehart & Winston.

Singer, E. (1977). The fiction of analytic anonymity. In K. Frank (Ed.), *The human dimension in psychoanalytic practice* (pp. 181–192). New York: Grune & Stratton.

Skolnick, N. J. (2006). What's a good object to do? *Psychoanalytic Dialogues, 16,* 1–27.

Slavin, M. O., & Kriegman, D. (1992). *The adaptive design of the human psyche: Psychoanalysis, evolutionary biology, and the therapeutic process.* New York: Guilford.

Slavin, M. O., & Kriegman, D. (1998). Why the analyst needs to change: Toward a theory of conflict, negotiation, and mutual influence in the therapeutic process. *Psychoanalytic Dialogues, 8,* 247–284.

Slochower, J. A. (1996). *Holding and psychoanalysis: A relational perspective.* Hillsdale, NJ: Analytic Press.

Slochower, J. A. (2003). The analyst's secret delinquencies. *Psychoanalytic Dialogues, 13,* 451–469.

Slochower, J. A. (2006). *Psychoanalytic collisions.* Hillsdale, NJ: Analytic Press.

Smith, H. (2001). Obstacles to integration. *Psychoanalytic Psychology, 18,* 485–514.

Spence, D. (1982). *Narrative truth and historical truth.* New York: Norton.

Stern, D. B. (1987). Unformulated experience and transference. *Contemporary Psychoanalysis, 23,* 484–490.

Stern, D. B. (1990). Courting surprise: Unbidden perceptions in clinical practice. *Contemporary Psychoanalysis, 26,* 452–478.

Stern, D. B. (1996a). The social construction of therapeutic action. *Psychoanalytic Inquiry, 16,* 265–293.

Stern, D. B. (1996b). Dissociation and constructivism: Commentary on papers by Davies and Harris. *Psychoanalytic Dialogues, 6,* 251–266.

Stern, D. B. (1997). *Unformulated experience.* Hillsdale, NJ: Analytic Press.

Stern, D. B. (2003). The fusion of horizons: Dissociation, enactment, and understanding. *Psychoanalytic Dialogues, 13,* 843–873.

Stern, D. B. (2004). The eye sees itself: Dissociation, enactment, and the achievement of conflict. *Contemporary Psychoanalysis, 40,* 197–237.

Stern, D. N. (1985). *The interpersonal world of the infant: A view from psychoanalysis and developmental psychology.* New York: Basic Books.

Stern, D. N., Sander, L. W., Nahum, J. P., Harrison, A. M., Lyons-Ruth, K., Morgan, A. C., et al. (1998). Non-interpretive mechanisms in psychoanalytic therapy: The "something more" than interpretation. *International Journal of Psychoanalysis, 79,* 903–921.

Stoller, R. (1968). *Sex and gender.* New York: Science House.

Stoller, R. (1975). *Perversion: The erotic form of hatred.* New York: Pantheon.

Stoller, R. (1979). *Sexual excitement: Diagnosis of erotic life.* New York: Pantheon.

Sullivan, H. S. (1953). *The interpersonal theory of psychiatry.* New York: Norton.

Sullivan, H. S. (1954). *The psychiatric interview.* New York: Norton.

Sullivan, H. S. (1956). *Clinical studies.* New York: Norton.

Summers, F. (1999). *Transcending the Self: An Object-Relations Model of Psychoanalytic Therapy.* Hillsdale, NJ: Analytic Press.

Szymanski, K. (n.d.). *The power of mutual healing.* Unpublished manuscript.

Tansey, M. & Burke, W. (1989). *Understanding Countertransference.* Hillsdale, NJ: Analytic Press.

Tauber, E. S., & Green, M. R. (1959). *Prelogical experience: An inquiry into dreams and other creative processes.* New York: Basic Books.

Thompson, C. (1950). *Psychoanalysis: Evolution and development.* New York: Hermitage.

Thompson, C. (1952). Countertransference. *Samiksa, 6,* 205–211.

Tuch, R. (2001). Questioning the psychoanalyst's authority. *Journal of the American Psychoanalytic Association, 49,* 491–513.

Varga, M. (2005). Analysis of transference and transformation of enactment. *Psychoanalytic Review, 92,* 559–574.

Wachtel, P. (1980). Transference, schema, and assimilation: The relevance of Piaget to the psychoanalytic theory of transference. *Annual of Psychoanalysis, 8,* 59–76.

Wachtel, P. (1982). Vicious circles: The self and the rhetoric of emerging and unfolding. *Contemporary Psychoanalysis, 18,* 259–273.

Wallerstein, R. (1995). The relation of theory to technique. *Journal of Clinical Psychoanalysis, 4,* 527–542.

White, K. (2002). Surviving hating and being hated: Some personal thoughts about racism from a psychoanalytic perspective. *Contemporary Psychoanalysis.* 38: 401–422.

Whitson, G. (n.d.). Money matters in psychoanalysis: The analyst's co-participation in the matter of money. Unpublished manuscript.

Wilner, W. (2000). A legacy of self: The unique psychoanalytic perspective of Benjamin Wolstein. *Contemporary Psychoanalysis, 36,* 267–279.

Winnicott, D. W. (1949). Hate in the counter-transference. *International Journal of Psychoanalysis, 30,* 69–74.

Winnicott, D. W. (1958). *Collected papers: Through paediatrics to psychoanalysis.* New York: Basic Books.

Wolstein, B. (1954). *Transference.* New York: Grune & Stratton.

Wolstein, B. (1959). *Countertransference.* New York: Grune & Stratton.

Wolstein, B. (1975). Countertransference: The psychoanalyst's shared experience and inquiry with his patient. *Journal of the American Academy of Psychoanalysis, 3,* 77–89.

Wolstein, B. (1977). From mirror to participant-observation to coparticipant inquiry and experience. *Contemporary Psychoanalysis, 13,* 381–386.

Wolstein, B. (1983). The pluralism of perspectives on countertransference. *Contemporary Psychoanalysis, 19,* 506–521.

Wolstein, B. (1997). The first direct analysis of transference and countertransference. *Psychoanalytic Inquiry, 17,* 505–521.

# Index